Ancient History

BLACKWELL INTRODUCTIONS TO THE CLASSICAL WORLD

This series will provide concise introductions to classical culture in the broadest sense. Written by the most distinguished scholars in the field, these books survey key authors, periods, and topics for students and scholars alike.

Ancient History

Monuments and Documents

Charles W. Hedrick, Jr.

Blackwell
Publishing

© 2006 by Charles W. Hedrick, Jr.

BLACKWELL PUBLISHING

350 Main Street, Malden, MA 02148-5020, USA
9600 Garsington Road, Oxford OX4 2DQ, UK
550 Swanston Street, Carlton, Victoria 3053, Australia

The right of Charles W. Hedrick, Jr. to be identified as the Author of this Work has been asserted in accordance with the UK Copyright, Designs, and Patents Act 1988.

First published 2006 by Blackwell Publishing Ltd

1   2006

Library of Congress Cataloging-in-Publication Data

Hedrick, Charles W., 1956–
Ancient history : monuments and documents / Charles W. Hedrick.
p. cm.—(Blackwell introductions to the classical world)
Includes bibliographical references and index.
ISBN-13: 978-1-4051-0657-3 (hard cover : alk. paper)
ISBN-10: 1-4051-0657-3 (hard cover : alk. paper)
ISBN-13: 978-1-4051-0658-0 (pbk. : alk. paper)
ISBN-10: 1-4051-0658-1 (pbk. : alk. paper)
1. History, Ancient—Study and teaching.   2. History, Ancient—
Sources.   3. History, Ancient—Historiography.   I. Title.   II. Series.

D56.H44   2005
930—dc22
2005015010

A catalogue record for this title is available from the British Library.

Set in 10/12.5pt Galliard
by SNP Best-set Typesetter Ltd., Hong Kong
Printed and bound in Great Britain
by TJ International Ltd, Padstow, Cornwall

The publisher's policy is to use permanent paper from mills that operate a sustainable forestry policy, and which has been manufactured from pulp processed using acid-free and elementary chlorine-free practices. Furthermore, the publisher ensures that the text paper and cover board used have met acceptable environmental accreditation standards.

For further information on
Blackwell Publishing, visit our website:
www.blackwellpublishing.com

For My Mother

Contents

Preface

I teach an introductory Survey of Greek History to about 150 students; I cover the late Bronze Age through the Hellenistic period, about 2,000 years, in ten weeks. My Survey of Roman History is comparable in size and scope. In such circumstances it is difficult to give the students more than grand narrative and sweeping generalizations. Yet theory and narrative divorced from an appreciation of evidence are merely indoctrination. Critical understanding requires some interplay between the general and the specific, the narrative and the evidence. For those approaching the sources for ancient history for the first time, obstacles are imposing. The ancient languages themselves are serious impediments for the general reader, and centuries of specialist scholarship in many different languages have erected a barrier between the students and the sources more formidable even than Greek and Latin. Rebarbative though the source material is, students of history need to learn to cope with it, and the earlier the better.

This book is intended as an introduction to the practice of ancient Greco-Roman history. My goals are two-fold. First, I want to provide a general account of the various kinds of evidence available for the study of antiquity and the techniques of interpretation used by scholars. Second, I want to force readers to consider the differences between the modern academic experience of ancient sources – books, inscriptions, coins, and the like – and the use and experience of these same objects within the every-day life of ancient society.

Books such as this one have a history of their own, and not a long one: their production is tied to the institutional pretensions of the academic discipline of history. Such "introductions to history" have typically focused on the nature and interpretation of evidence. One of the earliest of these was published at the end of the nineteenth century by Charles-Victor Langlois and Charles Seignobos, with the title *Introduction aux études historiques* (1898; translated into English in 1909 by G. G. Berry as *Introduction to*

Historical Studies). The centrality of evidence is firmly asserted here: "The historian works with documents. . . . There is no substitute for documents; no documents, no history" (17). At the same time, however, they did not neglect the process of "historical synthesis." The greatest of the introductions to the techniques of historical research was published in 1961 on the eve of the theoretical revolution, Charles Samaran, ed., *L'Histoire et ses méthodes* (*Encyclopédie de la Pléiade*, 11), Paris 1961; though in certain respects dated, it remains unsurpassed. In English there are two comparable books devoted to the nature and study of the evidence for ancient history. Hermann Bengtson, *Introduction to Ancient History*, Berkeley 1970, is essentially a bibliography. The essays collected in Michael Crawford, ed., *Sources for Ancient History*, Cambridge 1983, are of uniformly high quality, even if they share no common vision.

While providing a traditional survey of the evidence for ancient history and its interpretation, I also attempt to provide a critical history of the idea of evidence itself, contrasting especially ancient social with modern academic understanding of historical sources. My argument is historicist: the social, economic, and cultural context of knowledge plays a large part in determining the nature of knowledge itself. Historical understanding needs to be understood historically; and it is not enough to apply this criticism to the past, we must have the courage to apply it to ourselves as well.

The decisive moment in the formation of our contemporary approach to the study of the past comes at the beginning of the nineteenth century, with what we might call the "academicization" of knowledge, that is, the segregation of historical practice from its traditional, informal place in society and its enshrinement in the specialist and professional citadel of the university. The emergence of professional, "scientific" historiography in the nineteenth century, however, has a history, one that goes back the Renaissance, and some may feel that I have given short shrift to this "antiquarian background" to "scientific" historiography. I acknowledge the importance of the antiquarian historians, but insist that the epochal shift occurs with the establishment of history as an academic discipline. As will be seen, scholars of the late nineteenth and early twentieth centuries concur with this assessment: they saw their project as a radical departure from the antiquarians' work.

I expect to be castigated by some of my professional colleagues for my use of personal anecdotes in this book. The complete self-effacement of the author from the writing is the neurotic obsession of the professional academic. For example, one of the most eminent historians of the ancient world today, William V. Harris, has recently remarked that "it is a deplorable habit to pepper works of scholarship with the first-person pronoun. This book is about the Greeks and the Romans, not about me" (*Restraining Rage*, Harvard 2001, x). Being a professional academic I share his discomfort. Yet the inclusion of these anecdotes is not an indulgence or a *captatio benevo-lentiae*, that is, a rhetorical ploy to seize the interest and sympathy of the reading public. I intend them to illustrate the differences between informal, socially embedded knowledge of the past and the academic study of history. Our informal knowledge of the past is personal and idiosyncratic, bristling with local associations and allusions, in constant flux. By contrast academic history aspires to produce an account of the past that is impersonal, universal, fixed once and for all. More generally, modern academic historians need to recognize that when they write, even about people as distant as the Greeks and Romans, they always inevitably also write about themselves – and nothing is more revealing about modern academics than their mania for concealing their own role in the writing of the history.

The organization of this book recapitulates contemporary disciplinary distinctions and will for that reason displease some readers. I begin by considering the conceptions of time and space, chronology and geography, that underpin modern historicist interpretation. I then proceed to deal with various categories of evidence and their contemporary specialist fields of study. Other organizations were possible. I might for example have organized the book as a narrative of the emergence of the various subfields, beginning with numismatics and epigraphy, proceeding through chronography and ending with papyrology. But the contemporary ancillary disciplines have by virtue of their institutionalization an intellectual and even social force that in my view justifies the organization I have adopted. It would be silly to attempt to study inscriptions without reference to the scholarly apparatus that has built up through the modern discipline of epigraphy.

I have appended a concise bibliographical essay to the end of each chapter. Here I refer to general introductions, indices, research tools, and perhaps a few exemplary interpretations. My goal in these bibliographical appendices is to convey the minimum of information necessary to read and understand a professional academic article. My European friends will notice that the bibliographies are almost completely restricted to works written in English. I regret this, but do not apologize. The book is written for a beginning-level, English-speaking audience. On the other hand, I do not regret, but should apologize for, my occasional citation of scholarly works in languages other than English: in such cases either I have been unable to locate some comparable essay in English, or the work is of such importance that even those who cannot read it should know about it. I have tried to refer in the text to works cited in the bibliographic essays. Other perplexing abbreviations can be resolved by consulting the index. I have supplemented the printed works cited in the bibliography with references to a number of reputable websites. I do this with some hesitation, for I worry that the addresses will not prove stable in the long term, and the useful resources on the web are far outnumbered by the disreputable and unreliable. Even so, the benefits of electronic resources far outweigh such trivial risks, particularly for students and scholars who do not have the good fortune to live within driving distance of a major research library. Students will be amused to see that professional scholars have as much trouble with the consistent spelling of Greek names as they do. In cases where names are commonly used in English I have used the familiar forms: so Ephesus (as opposed to Ephesos); in cases where names are not in common use I have tried to preserve a more faithful transliteration: so Oxyrhynchos.

It will be noted that there are no illustrations in this book. I would have liked to have included some, but on consideration I decided it was not necessary. Pictures of objects I discuss here are widely available both in books and on the web – I chose them with this accessibility in mind. Trees need not be harvested so that they can be illustrated yet again.

Various scholars have greatly obliged me by reading chapters of this book and commenting on them. I have always considered their suggestions carefully, though I have not always followed them. I acknowledge my debt to them here, and I will be disappointed if readers reward their kindness by holding them responsible for any persistent mistakes of mine. My thanks to Paul Cartledge, Mark Golden, Ann Hanson, Joe Manning, Jim O'Donnell, Robin Osborne, Peter Rhodes, Richard Talbert, Tom Walsh, and Jim Zetzel. Other friends have, wittingly or unwittingly, contributed ideas or information or reassurance in conversation and correspondence: my gratitude to Bob Babcock, Björn Ewald, David Hoy, Jenny Lynn, Ian Morris, Josh Ober, Bill Metcalf, Peter van Minnen, and Hayden White. I am always grateful for corrections and criticism from benevolent readers.

I was fortunate to be able to do some of the research for this book at the superb facilities of the Beinecke Library in New Haven, Connecticut. The writing of this book was subsidized in part by grants from the Academic Senate at the University of California at Santa Cruz and the Solmsen Fellowship at the Institute for Research in the Humanities at the University of Wisconsin at Madison.

I take pleasure in dedicating this book to my mother, who has asked me for many years now why I do not write something that the general public will find interesting. It seems to me that the question is ambiguous, Mom. Your obvious meaning is that I should go off and write something that will sell a lot of copies. You could however also be asking that I explain to you why it is that what I write has only limited appeal. I doubt that this book will make the New York Times bestseller list; but if you will read it, you will find an explanation.

Charles W. Hedrick, Jr.
hedrick@ucsc.edu
Santa Cruz, California

1

Monuments and Documents

Introduction

When Odysseus went to consult the dead, he slit the throats of black cattle and let their blood drain into a trench he had cut into the earth. Then crowds of parched shades swarmed around, but he parried them away from the blood until the man he wanted approached, the blind seer Tiresias, to drink and prophesy. Ghosts cannot speak until they have drunk blood; consequently mediums must lure the thirsty dead to their séances "by the pricking of their thumbs."

As the first surviving Greek historian, Herodotus, says in the first line of his history, human accomplishments fade with time; and deeds, even the great and remarkable, will lose their renown. The present fades away to join the past and bequeaths nothing to the future but scraps and wreckage, mute and mutilated relics that of themselves tell nothing. Only with the imaginative and reasoned engagement of the living can blood be wrung from stony ruins. The dead can never be resurrected, though they may enjoy a parasitical half-life, on the condition that we invest them with something of ourselves.

History is a story the present tells itself about the past, and its meaning lies in the interaction of the two. To understand history it is not enough to know the past; it is also necessary to come to terms with the nature of the present desire for the past. Historians typically give far more attention to the past than they do to the present; yet the problem must haunt anyone who encounters history. Students, set to memorizing lists of events and tables of dates, bewail the triviality and irrelevance of their task. For the generations of academics who have spilled their hearts' blood on dusty pages to express some small truth, the question is inevitably far more urgent and insistent. What is this ghoulish pact we have struck with the dead? And more pointedly, what has our contract to do with the living?

Pre-modern and non-western histories, by which I mean histories free of the influence of nineteenth-century German historicism, were written out of a cognizance of the implication of the past and present, with a lively sense of the historian's agency in the present. History was regarded as an ally of present social memory, integrated with society, the codification of a communally held knowledge of the past. With the modern world a different vision of the relation of past and present emerges. This knowledge no longer springs from informal popular tradition, or "memory," but is imposed on it. Professional history is not written to supplement the community's memory, but to supplant it. Intrusion of present concerns in the writing of history comes to be regarded as a corruption of the integrity of the past and is castigated as "anachronism." If the past is to be known as itself, for what it is, it must be allowed to "be itself," to speak on its own terms without its deformation by the concerns of the present. This ideal is achieved in two ways: by sequestering the past, then by insisting on systematic interpretation of it.

The antagonism of modern professional history to informal social memory develops for complex yet coherent reasons: changes in the institutional environment of the practice of history; its co-optation by insurgent nationalism; the rise of new methods of source criticism; and a shift in the conception of the nature of language and its proper deployment in realistic description. At the root of these changes lies a new attitude toward the proper relationship of present and past. Truth should not depend on the various and changeable attitudes of the present. "The truth is one" and it must be the same for all and always; otherwise it is not truth. Modern historical knowledge is imagined as objective, in the sense that it is ideally to be disengaged from the present circumstances of its making.

Even in the heyday of nineteenth-century historicism, many scholars realized at some level that the "noble dream" of objectivity was a delusion. The story of the past can only be written in the present, "after the fact." Modern professional history in particular is written with the benefit of an excruciatingly considered hindsight; it is a fundamentally and irremediably anachronistic enterprise. Yet many historians continued to insist that present and past must be kept apart. We may understand that the dead submit to our interrogation only because we infuse them with something of ourselves; yet we know too that what we give them is a contamination: our blood taints them. For historians since the nineteenth century we the living are the phantoms, and truth is obtained on the condition that we exorcize ourselves from history.

It would be perverse to refuse to recognize the gains that have accrued from the methods of modern historiography. Modern historians can in all humility boast that they know more about the human past than any society has ever known, more about the history of Greece and Rome in certain respects than the Greeks or Romans themselves knew. But these gains have come at a cost. Professional historical knowledge, after all, is predicated on the segregation of present and past, and as a consequence, even as the past has come to be better known its relevance to the present has been undermined. As historians cultivate "knowledge for its own sake," the very proliferation of information drowns out what is meaningful in history. The more we know, the less it matters.

This book is among other things an introduction to the historical methods of the contemporary study of the Greco-Roman past; and for students of the ancient world, as for all historians, the principal methodological problem is the interpretation of evidence. History too often is taught as a collection of stories and dates to be memorized. It is easy to make students parrot the details of "true stories." Conveying the intricacies and ambiguities and uncertainties involved in reading evidence, however, poses a dreadful challenge. Yet, if students are to "do" history and not be passive consumers of tales, they must learn how to engage with the sources. The problem is of special significance because the methods of source-criticism employed by historians of antiquity in the nineteenth century subsequently came to dominate the academy: the techniques of modern historiography were invented by theologians and students of Greco-Roman history, and this is the legacy of the nineteenth century to the contemporary profession, both a blessing and a curse.

Method cannot be understood in isolation from other aspects of historical practice. History, like other human activities, cannot be treated as a purely intellectual pursuit; it is also a social practice and a literary product. Practices of knowledge are broadly based in culture. In this chapter I will attempt to contextualize historical method in the general "practice" of ancient history. I begin with a brief account of the emergence of the characteristic attitudes of modern history-writing. I follow this with a discussion of three aspects of professional historical practice: writing, social circumstances, and method, that is, the practices surrounding the interpretation of evidence.

The Development of Modern History-Writing

The modern academic pursuit of history is, from an historical perspective, an aberration, unparalleled in the history of the world. The decisive moment in the formation of modern western historiography occurred at the beginning of the nineteenth century in Germany, with the formation of the institutions that house professional academic historians, and the spread of the relativism characteristic of historicism. But every moment has its own history, and the roots of the characteristic methods and attitudes of nineteenth-century German historicism should be traced as far back as the Renaissance.

Machiavelli's revolutionary essay, "The Prince" contains already the seed of the essential notion of historicism, which is the credo of modern professional historiography. To appreciate Machiavelli's originality, it must be understood that he was working within a genre; political precepts addressed to rulers had been written since the antiquity. In the Middle Ages these precepts typically embodied statements of Christian principle. One of the most famous had been written by Thomas Aquinas, "On the Training of Princes" (*De regimine principum*). Machiavelli in his essay, however, notoriously rejected principle in favor of pragmatism: rulers should suit their actions to their circumstances. To his contemporaries and to many subsequent generations, the argument seemed like an abdication of morality.

Machiavelli has long lost his capacity to shock. To contemporary students his arguments seem obvious, even banal. Their indifference is as much evidence of their lack of sympathetic access to the notion of universal human values as it is of the triumph of Machiavellian relativism. The lesson that everything must be judged "according to context" has been so completely assimilated by the modern world that Machiavelli himself has come to seem a bit tedious. His idea is everywhere in the modern academy; any form of "systems analysis" is Machiavellian at its core. Applied to historians' investigations of the past, it is the basis of nineteenth-century historicism, and it remains the essential presumption of modern academic historical writing. Historians should not look to the past for eternal truths or transcendental lessons; instead they should judge historical events and actors in the light of their context. Such judgment allows the past to be understood "on its own terms," rather than by the anachronistic standards of the present, and it opens the way to an understanding of the forces that shape both past and present. Modern professional historians are not concerned to learn from some supposedly transcendent examples of history, but to contextualize the past and use this knowledge to expose the processes that made the past and lead from it down to the present and into the future.

Machiavelli's contextual pragmatism did not triumph immediately. For centuries moral principle and exemplarity remained dominant, and Machiavelli remained controversial – read and condemned – to the point that his name became synonymous with cynical realism and pragmatic, relativist amorality. At certain points, however, the Machiavellian tension between principle and relativism, exemplarity and context, bubbles up into open debate.

One of the most crucial of these was the "Battle of the Books," that is, the "conflict between the ancients and the moderns" in the late seventeenth century, especially in France and England. The basic issue in this conflict had to do with the relationship between the Greek and Roman classics and contemporary learning. Had the Greeks and Romans established the models of learning for all time, or was it possible for moderns in some respects to surpass them? The debate's premise seems preposterous from the perspective of the twenty-first century. Yet at that time the literature of antiquity had an uncontested prestige in education, and ancient scientific texts – Euclid in mathematics, Galen in medicine, and Aristotle in practically everything – were the foundation of knowledge. Yet recent achievements in science, particularly, were undermining this prestige. Astronomers had overthrown the dominant ancient vision of the universe as centered on the world, and added daily to the store of knowledge about the heavens. Work in mathematics and anatomy improved on the knowledge of the ancients.

So it became increasingly apparent to some that improvement on the ancients was not only possible, but was also a good thing. Yet the prestige of the ancients was difficult to shake off. The resolution of the dispute involved the introduction of a distinction about the nature of knowledge. In what we today call the arts, that is the arena of mimesis, the perfection of the ancients was everywhere conceded. The greatest epics were those of Homer and Vergil. The best of the moderns, such as Pope, might conceivably approach their standard, though they would never equal or surpass it. In areas where knowledge accumulated, however, such as astronomy or physics, it had to be admitted that the moderns could improve on the ancients. Even here, though, the general superiority of the ancients continued to be admitted. Moderns might surpass Aristotle, but only by building on his achievement, which was greater than any that followed might attain. This is the point of Newton's often quoted remark that if moderns could see farther than the ancients, it was only because they stood on the shoulders of giants. Nevertheless, in this admission we see the thin end of the wedge that leads to the modern notion of progress.

In the context of this debate history occupied a pivotal position. On the one hand at this time it continued to be regarded as an essentially literary undertaking. On the other hand, a century of labor by antiquarians had shown that it was possible to increase the fund of information at the disposal of historians. So history was simultaneously a mimetic and a cumulative enterprise. At this time we see a split between the practices of the two. Men of politics continued to compose literary memoirs and histories, and to castigate the triviality of antiquarians who foraged in rubbish heaps to acquire new facts to improve their own understanding and that of their peers. Antiquarians responded by dismissing the literary histories as inaccurate and thoughtless.

In this controversy we see the dichotomy between a traditional under-standing of history through examples and a modern understanding of history as a process. Does history provide a store of transcendental examples of good and bad behavior? Or is it a process leading through the present and into the future? In the former case, we need only look to notable instances of good and bad, success and failure, and model our own behavior accordingly. In the latter, it is necessary to get some sense of the forces driving change; in this way we can understand our own position and make informed plans for the future.

The controversy continues today in the split between "popular" and "academic" history. Politicians, for example, remain strong advocates for the exemplary usefulness of history. Thus William Bennett could compile a collection of anecdotes, historical and otherwise, that he felt had instruc-tional value: his much publicized *Book of Virtues: a Treasury of Great Moral Stories* (New York 1993). It also remains true, I think, that American conservatives today tend to justify actions by appeal to precedent, while liberals are more likely to jettison precedent in favor of cold reason; the essence of the difference between the two is contained in their attitudes toward tradition. For most academics, however, the issue was decided at the beginning of the nineteenth century, in Germany. Since the rise of historicism, the traditional, exemplary understanding of the past has not been academically respectable.

Another of the intellectual impulses that led to the historicist revolution of the nineteenth century was Biblical exegesis, that is, "hermeneutics." Traditional patristic interpretation explained the Bible in light of doctrinal truth, that is, by appeal to the present authority of the church. Scholars approached the sacred text with a preordained notion of its correct interpretation. Passages of the Bible that conflicted with this understanding (and given the heterodox character of the various Biblical texts and the long history of church doctrine, examples of internal incoherence and apparent conflicts with doctrine are legion) had somehow to be forced into conformity. So, for example, many passages were understood allegorically, as meaning something other than what they transparently said. Such interpretative method created problems not only for scholars, but also for the church itself, because allegorical understanding is difficult to control. In the event of a conflict of interpretation between Protestants and Catholics, what criterion, aside from assertion of sheer doctrinal force, determined correctness?

Religious conflict fueled the development of principles of hermeneutic interpretation. In the battles of the Reformation Luther, attempting to combat the authority of the Catholic Church, insisted that the text must be understood without appeal to present doctrine, but in light only of its text, *scriptura sola*. Admittedly, Protestants did not at this time develop coherent principles of interpretation; the first significant philosophical effort in this direction is usually credited to the Jewish Dutch philosopher, Spinoza, in his *Theologico-Political Treatise* (1670). The influential theoretical exposition of principles of hermeneutics, however, comes only at the end of the eighteenth century, with the "father of Protestant Theology," Friedrich Schleiermacher (1768–1834). The development of these critical techniques brought systematic, comparative methods to the Bible; even sacred texts could not be interpreted on the basis of received truth or enlightenment; they had to be understood in relation to their own specific situation and usage. Here again understanding based on a priori principle is replaced with understanding based on context. Symbol and allegory are replaced by system.

Biblical hermeneutics were the seedbed of modern literary and historical interpretation. Application of the techniques of hermeneutics to the words of the Bible and the profane works of antiquity gave rise to the characteristic method of modern classical scholarship, philology. The words philologist and philology, though the latter survives in the name of the professional association of North American Classicists (The American Philological Association), have something of an archaic ring. Dictionaries and encyclopedias will tell you that it has ceded its province to linguistics. The earliest "modern philologists" like Friedrich August Wolf (1759–1824) date to about the same time as Schleiermacher himself, and for the nineteenth and the first part of the twentieth centuries, philology was the dominant model of interpretation of texts, with only a few nay-sayers, such as Friedrich Nietzsche (cf. his 1875 essay "Wir Philologen," "We Philologists"). Nevertheless, the techniques of philology are fundamentally historical, and today pass almost for commonsense, they have been so widely accepted. Again, the heart of the method is the evaluation of usage in context, rather than according to contemporary usage or cognates, or an intuitive sense of what a term must mean.

The relevance of such movements to the origins of nineteenth-century historicism are obvious. Spinoza himself had emphasized the connection between hermeneutic interpretation and history. Nevertheless the elaboration of a historicist philosophy and the rigorous application of historicist principles to the interpretation of evidence had to wait until the nineteenth century, not least because history becomes an academic discipline only at this time. The great philosopher of historicist method was Wilhelm Dilthey (1833–1911), who wrote among other works a life of Schleiermacher. His own statements of historicist method date to the 1880s, but he was theorizing long after the fact. The revolution in historical practice in Germany had begun at the beginning of the nineteenth century.

Historical Writing

Students typically get their first taste of history not by participating in the guild-activities of professional historians or by analyzing sources, but from their textbooks. For many the finished, written history will remain their only access to the past. Writing, however, is only the final act of the process of "doing" history; it puts the seal on the interminable process of research and produces material, lasting evidence of the historian's labor. At the same time, though, as an accomplished historical narrative seamlessly evokes a vanished world, it hangs a discreet veil between readers and the process of making the history. This is one of the chief functions of writing: to replace the uncertainty and stuttering starts and stops of research with the stability, if only provisional, of the conclusion.

The association of history and writing is sanctified by immemorial tradition. History begins when the past is written down. Traditionally the association has been justified with reference to the permanence of writing. Fixed and permanent, writing can serve as a check and replacement for malleable and evanescent social memory and popular tradition; through it the past can be preserved unchanging. So at the beginning of his history, the first surviving Greek historian, Herodotus, claims that it will act as a preservative, "so that the deeds of men should not fail of their fame and become evanescent" (proem). His great successor, Thucydides, will emphasize that his own history is preeminently a written product (in Greek, a *xungraphe*, 1.1).

In the twentieth century contemporary technologies made available to history an array of new forms. The potential of film as a medium for history was recognized from the very beginning: critics already described D. W. Griffith's 1915 epic about the origins of the Ku Klux Klan, *Birth of a Nation*, as "history written with lightning." Historical comic books have long been produced, but Art Spiegelman's *Maus* proved to many academics that the comic book could be an effective vehicle for representing serious historical issues. But why bother creating a static representation of the past at all? Why not instead know the past through creative reenactments of it? Or by using computers to create "models" of the past in which historical ideas can be tested "experimentally," so to speak? Nevertheless, for many it remains commonplace to maintain that history is by definition a written form. Even so, considering alternatives to writing has the salutary effect of forcing some consideration of the function of writing history. What are we trying to accomplish by writing? Why do we write as we do? Why do we write at all?

Modern academic writing is, with some notable exceptions, colorless, uninspiring stuff. As students often remark, it suffers by comparison with the ancient historians. To put down Herodotus or Livy and pick up, say, the

Cambridge Ancient History (CAH), is like shunning a dinner with Rex Reed at a five-star restaurant in favor of an evening at home in front of the television with a bowl of cold oatmeal – though a volume of the *CAH* is admittedly somewhat thicker than a bowl of cold oatmeal. The differences between the two reflect different aims.

Traditionally, history was regarded as high literature, and historians were expected to spend as much time honing their prose as they did on their research. Cicero remarked that history ideally should be written by a person with the gifts and training of the orator (*De Oratore* 51–64). Of course everyone knows that the first job of the historian is to tell the whole truth. And if history is to instruct, its claims must be persuasive. But it is not enough to be convincing. To instruct, history needs to engage the reader. So an historical narrative must also be entertaining, inducing surprise and suspense in its readers, and representing unexpected outcomes, conflicting emotions, grief, anger, fear, delight, and passion.

By contrast most academic historians are more concerned with content than style, clarity than elegance. For example, Mark Gilderhus, in his recent student handbook, *History and Historians*, advises that "the writing calls for an ability to communicate clearly, in the case of history, in plain, jargon-free prose" (6). "Important hallmarks of effective historical writing consist of clarity, precision, and accessibility. In most cases, historians seek to write their narratives in plain English and to convey their thoughts exactly enough so that all interested readers can obtain the means of entry" (95).

Before the rise of historicism, writing was evaluated in terms of the effect it produced on the reader. The first excellence of modern academic writing is characteristically considered to be its accuracy. We might say that the distinctiveness of modern historical writing consists in its content, whereas in earlier eras the affective form mattered much more. Admittedly modern historians aspire to write well, and some do, but elegance of expression is subsidiary to clarity and accuracy. To say something true is always preferable to saying something well. For ancient historians truth matters, but that truth cannot be divorced from the form of its expression. This difference between ancient and modern historical writing is to be explained in part by the perceived goals of historical writing, and in part by ideas about the nature of language itself.

Until relatively recently history was not regarded so much as a "science" or "discipline" as a literary undertaking. In the ancient world historical writing was intended to have an ethical and instructive impact on the reader, and to this end it was thought necessary to excite the admiration or repugnance of readers by touching their emotions. Thus for Greek and Roman historians the goal of writing history was in the first place to put a vivid and engaging picture of the past before readers; they did not so much attempt to represent the past as to bring it alive. The aims of Greco-Roman history were mimetic – which is not to say that ancient historians did not also aspire to tell the truth. By contrast, modern academic historians attempt not so much to excite emotion as to establish the truth of the past "as it actually happened." All that is true is *ipso facto* worth knowing. Every access of knowledge is a contribution to the corpus of knowledge about the past. Thus the content of language is emphasized over its affect: affective rhetoric is specific to the particular history, while the content can be reproduced and verified, and thus can contribute to the growth of knowledge. Here history is conceived in terms of its place in a cumulative enterprise.

The new idea of history required a new idea of writing. As professional academic work presupposes a cumulative idea of knowledge and a culture of debate, it also presupposes a new ideal of language. Traditionally language had been understood as rhetorical, that is, as a thing with its own weight and force. Every act of writing or enunciating had to be understood not only in terms of its content, but also in terms of its affect. If the cumulative scientific endeavor was to be possible, however, it had to be possible to quarantine the content of language from its rhetorical affect. In the context of the production of "objective" knowledge, rhetoric and elegance of presentation are irrelevant. All that matters is content, because only content is susceptible to citation, verification, or falsification. Referential statements live on in the cumulative academic project; style abides with the historian. So it was necessary for historians to imagine language as a kind of tool or instrument that they could cleanly use, rather than as a medium within which they and their statements were contained.

The modern academic project requires some neutral medium of representation; it must somehow be possible to use language in a strictly utilitarian way, as if it were a thing that had no mass of its own, but merely referred, transparently and without rhetorical distortion. And if, as a practical matter, it is impossible to write in this way, it must be at least possible to discriminate sharply between what is rhetorical and what is referential. Such a shift did occur, and is manifested by the end of the eighteenth century by the beginnings of a discursive tradition about language: the rise of philology, which in turn gave birth to the modern discipline of linguistics. Classical rhetoric was replaced by the science of language.

Philology, like historicism, emerged in connection with the hermeneutic tradition in Biblical exegesis. With its insistence on treating language within an historical "horizon of expectations" rather than more or less as an "aesthetic object" with obvious contemporary relevance, philology contributed to the conceptualization of language in terms of an alienated and stable content rather than a present circumstantial affect. At an even more abstract level, language itself becomes an object of study rather than the practical medium within which people work and write. The essential problem of this alienated conception of language is no longer its affective relationship to speaker and audience, but the nature of reference. Thus it was axiomatic for Ferdinand de Saussure (1857–1913) in his foundational work on linguistics that words did not have meaning because of the intentions of the speaker, but because of their place in the system of language. Language speaks through people, not people through language. Classical rhetoric, by contrast, had been devoted to the practical problem of producing affect in the audience and so influencing their reactions.

Academic professionals continue to work within the framework of modern scholarship – they draw salaries from universities, referee tenure cases, publish in professional journals and so on. They are participants in the cumulative project. And as they participate, they must, willy-nilly, subscribe to some such model of referential representation. Without some such conception of representation, scholarly debate and the communal project of progressive knowledge break down.

Social Context of History-Writing

Ideals of writing must be considered in relation to the social situation of historical practice. The most obvious social quality of modern professional historiography is that it is written and read within an academic context. Professional historians are employees of colleges and universities and think tanks. They are paid to write works that are refereed, read, and reviewed by other professional historians. Contemporary historical practice, in other words, must be viewed in the context of higher education. Different nations have different traditions. Here I will focus on the history of American higher education, in part because it is heavily influenced by two of the more important European traditions, in part because I am American and am most familiar with it, and in part because I believe that it is now the dominant ideal of education in the world, and is rapidly being exported and adopted throughout the world.

Broadly speaking, the history of the American colleges and universities can be divided into three periods. The first is the period of the liberal arts college, which runs from the colonial period to about 1870. The second is the period of the research university, running from 1870 to 1945. Finally there is the contemporary period, which began in 1945.

Had you attended school in America in the eighteenth century, you would have found yourself in a predominantly male, religious environment. The liberal arts colleges of the colonial period and early nineteenth century derived from English models, which in turn derived from Renaissance and, at a step further removed, from medieval institutions. These American colleges were small, usually with only a handful of faculty and students. Most were religious foundations, with additional support from local groups – states, municipalities, and the like. There were no specialized departments and instructors were generalists. They regarded themselves as gentlemen-amateurs, and gave their energies chiefly to teaching, not to research. Instruction centered on the classical languages – Greek, Latin, and Hebrew – theology, medicine, and arithmetic. University graduates mostly went on to careers in law, politics, the church, and medicine. The ideals of the traditional liberal arts college continued to be espoused by conservative educators in the nineteenth century. The great manifesto of liberal education is owed to John, Cardinal Newman (1801–90); Newman deprecated the practical or vocational education, in favor of an ideal of "knowledge as its own end" (*Idea of a University*, discourse 7). The purpose of college education was to instill mental and moral discipline. The object of education was ethical. One of the chief duties of the faculty was to stand, in all ways, *in loco parentis* to the young men of the college.

The Morill Act, signed by Abraham Lincoln in 1862, initiated the era of the Land Grant University and revolutionized higher education in America. Under the terms of this legislation, the Federal Government gave aid to states that supported universities that offered agricultural and technical instruction. At a stroke a university education was made available to a much larger number of students and instruction became more practical and vocational. At about the same time American universities began self-consciously to follow the model of German universities. Berlin is generally regarded as the first modern research university, founded by Wilhelm von Humboldt (1767–1835) in 1810. Johns Hopkins is generally regarded as the first modern research university in America, founded in 1876 and modeled on Berlin. The land grant movement was democratizing: egalitarian and popularist. The ideal of the German research university was elitist: professional and specialized. These conflicting ideals have had an abiding impact on higher education in America down to the present day.

In the latter half of the nineteenth century, education changed profoundly. Students were allowed to take electives, which meant that the curriculum was not governed by a unified educational policy. Courses proliferated and became increasingly specialized. Faculty subdivided into departments and a standard, professional career path for faculty developed. The first professional societies, such as the American Philological Association and the American Historical Association, were founded. Faculty became more mobile, seeing themselves increasingly as citizens of their disciplines rather than of their university. The ideal of scientific objectivity came into being, and penetrated the practices of philology and history. And of course, the sciences supplanted the humanities as the dominant influence on the policies of the university. Increasingly a university education was regarded as serving the ends of utility and practicality. Many of the land grant institutions founded in the period had mottoes like "education for efficiency" (Montana State University), and the ideal even infiltrated the older private institutions, such as Harvard.

Now the age of the "multiversity" (otherwise described as "the federal grants university") is upon us. There was a profound shift in the history of American education after World War II. With the passage of the G.I. Bill (or Servicemen's Readjustment Act of 1944), unparalleled numbers of students, including more mature students, descended on the universities. To this time, only a small percentage of the population had attended college. The federal government became involved in higher education through the Defense Department and the National Science Foundation, which channeled billions of dollars into science research in the decades following World War II. The turn from moral instruction to practical instruction, from instruction to research, continued. The economic impact of universities came increasingly to be recognized, and they have more and more formed cooperative partnerships with industry. For example, the vocational extension ("night school") program of the University of California is larger than the traditional academic side. Faculty members are no longer only regarded strictly as teachers and researchers, but as entrepreneurial consultants as well. The size, variety, and scope of undertakings within the university have increased vastly. Not the least of these increases has been in the administration, which now deals with far more than just academic affairs. Whereas the older term "university" carried with it the notion of a single community and a unified sense of purpose, the present day "multiversity" is composed of many communities and has no integrated sense of purpose.

These periods are not absolutely discriminable from one another. Universities are like the Roman state: they cannot bear to discard obsolete practices; so history accumulates, and old ideals endure even while new situations are superimposed on them. And of course different institutions of higher education have different histories. For example, many private colleges originally had religious affiliations, while public institutions were founded by the government. Furthermore, as the late Clark Kerr pointed out, the ideals of the liberal arts, the research university, and the entrepreneurial "multiversity" coexist to a greater or lesser extent in all American research universities. It is even possible to categorize groups within the university roughly according to their allegiance to the ideals of one or the other of these periods. Humanists and generalists and undergraduates subscribe to the college model, which has its antecedents in English higher education. Scientists and specialists and graduate students support the ideals of the German "research university."

Administrators and members of the professional schools are "practitioners" of the "multiversity."

This is a brief overview of the general institutional background against which we must evaluate modern historical practice. At the most basic level, the characteristic practice of the university involves the "setting aside" of the operations of knowledge: the sequestration of intellectuals in the "ivory tower." Thus knowledge of the past is isolated or "abstracted" from society and made the province of specialists, who know it from a cultivated posture of detachment. Historical sources are separated off in museums and archives; the scholars themselves are consigned to the groves (or ghettos) of academe. On the one hand, this isolation allows the modern historian to make the claim of political neutrality and intellectual objectivity; on the other hand, it removes the past and its traces from interaction with society. "History" is created and set in an antagonistic opposition to the collective and culturally meaningful "memory" of society.

Until the nineteenth century, history was an amateur's game and the antiquarian's preserve; and in this character it was consistent with the social circumstances of other "non-modern" and "non-western" historical forms. With the professionalization of the educational institutions that fostered the production of knowledge the ideal of scientific "objectivity" becomes prominent. The idea of a knowledge that is "objective," that is observably, verifiably, self-evidently true, independent of present biases and interpretation, could only have been possible in the context of a group with narrow, closely defined and agreed standards – a group like a self-policing academic community. These standards limit the possibilities of knowledge to an acceptably close range of interpretations. At the same time they work reflexively to define and consolidate the group. Knowledge of the past becomes a specialist project, defined and policed by historical practitioners.

Professional historiography is nationalist in origins and practice. Historians were to produce a knowledge that could be used for nation-building, the unification of population. Professional scholarship was to promote nationalism by replacing informal local knowledges – memory – with a licensed professional truth. Nationalist "objectivity" trumps regional bias and so consolidates multiform local interests by creating a uniform tradition. The eminent German historian Leopold von Ranke (1795–1886), for example, intended that his students would leave his seminar to go teach at local universities and gymnasia, where they would provide a standard truth that would replace the various communal, local knowledges that divided Germany into discrete regions. At one level, then, objectivity may be defined as the word for a politically determined and enforced truth. The political character of this knowledge reflects the nature of community. Nationalism is a top-down knowledge, which works to eradicate local divisions and consensually produced communities and replace them with an "imagined community," which is produced by a central apparatus.

In the ancient world, as in most non-western or pre-modern societies, history-writing was not a career but a vocation. No institutions like modern "research universities" or "think tanks" existed. Certainly there were schools, but these were not the corporate bodies familiar to modern students. Those who taught were generally paid directly by their students for instruction, not for their research and writing. Nor could ancient historians make a living by the income from sales of their work, as do modern freelance writers. The printing press, publishing houses, and protections of copyright law did not exist.

Writers in antiquity did in fact support themselves in a variety of ways. Some taught, parlaying their literary fame into an income by taking on wealthy students; these were chiefly specialists in the useful arts, such as philosophy and rhetoric. Others were supported by wealthy patrons: the famous examples are poets, like Horace and Vergil. In imperial times some distinguished grammarians and orators received payment from the government. Still writers derived income from delivering readings of their works – whether such compensation was conceived as a "fee" or a "gift." And many – including most ancient historians – were simply wealthy enough that they could write without hope or expectation of compensation. In fact, the independence from the constraints of poverty or the influence of patrons and others was one of the conditions for the practice of reputable history. History was a pursuit for those who could freely speak their minds.

The modern social environment of academic history is homogeneous from place to place and time to time – this is one of the hallmarks of modern professional historiography. By contrast, non-western and pre-modern historiography displays an immense variety in its social circumstances. Chinese historiography of the classical period was tied to preparation for a civil-service examination. The historians of the Japanese Mito "School" of the nineteenth century were composed of Samurai, who were each assigned a fiefdom complete with serfs to support them. Just so the social circumstances of the practice of Greco-Roman history vary according to the political context. We hear that Herodotus, who emerges from the poetic culture of archaic Greece, gave recitations – as did poets such as Pindar – and that he was rewarded when his audiences were pleased. Thucydides writes as a disgruntled citizen of a relatively egalitarian Greek city-state, evidently for a small elite. Courtiers wrote histories of Alexander and later Hellenistic monarchs. Senators of the Roman Republic such as Cato wrote among other things the history of their own times. With the empire senators ceased to be political luminaries or even to write – this is one of the chief themes of Sallust and Tacitus – and imperial functionaries like Suetonius begin to compose accounts of the past.

With the establishment of a Christian empire in the fourth century AD, and a sharing of political power between the state and the church, clerics began to write histories of the church, while imperial functionaries continued to write political history.

The complexity of the political situation may be glimpsed by taking a single example. Roman historical writing emerges under the influence of Greek historians in the second century BC. Initially it was monopolized by the senatorial class. This social circumstance was reinforced by the attitude that history was simply an extension of political activity; and since political activity was the prerogative of the senatorial class, so too must be history-writing. It is not that the Romans did not differentiate between political deeds and historical writing: the former were more important than the latter, but not different in kind. Cato the elder, writing at the foundation of Latin historiography, makes the point clearly. He justifies his history by observing that political figures "must give an account no less of their leisure than of their accomplishments" (frag. 2 Peter). The historian Sallust, writing in the altered political circumstances of the mid-first century BC, apologetically notes that some will criticize him for withdrawing from politics and devoting himself to the writing of history. Yet, he claims, the country will reap greater benefit from the leisure he devotes to the writing of history than it will from the political pursuits of others (*Jugurtha* 4). Of course, some non-senators tried their hands at the writing of history. The first certain example of such a one, the historian Livy, deprecates his own lack of social stature. He remarks at the beginning of the proem to his history that he has made a small contribution even if his own light pales beside the luminous genius of the great men who have preceded him (proem). As the power of the senate fails in the early empire, so too does the commitment to the writing of history. At the end of the senatorial historiographic tradition, Tacitus takes this point as the central theme of his historical writing. "The glories and disasters of the Roman Republic have been chronicled by famous pens, and intellects of distinction were not lacking to tell the tale of the Augustan age, until the rising tide of sycophancy deterred them" (*Annals* 1.1). For these senatorial historians, there was no question of accepting "patronage" or "pay" for the writing of history. To the contrary: senators should be independent of such obligations; only so could it be guaranteed that they could speak their minds frankly, without fear of reprisal or hope of compensation, whether in a political meeting or in the writing of history. If senators received a reward for writing history, it was in prestige, not money – though it must be granted that prestige may produce political clout and monetary rewards.

All of this variety can be boiled down to a single point: the nature of history in antiquity is directly tied to the prevailing economic, social and political environment within which it is practiced. Whereas contemporary professional history has been isolated from contemporary politics, ancient historiography was an extension of political behavior, and it was habitually written by political practitioners. If you seek a modern parallel for ancient historiography you will not find it in the academy. Professional historiography shapes all knowledge of the past today. The closest parallel I can offer to ancient practice are the partisan memoirs written by political figures in exile or retirement, and sometimes before. Just so Newt Gingrich or Bill Clinton write after retirement – though no ancient historian ever received a seven-figure publishing contract. Just so Paul O'Neill wrote a scathing account of his time in the Bush White House (*The Price of Loyalty*) and, when asked whether he worried about reprisals, blithely said, "I'm an old guy, and I'm rich. And there's nothing they can do to hurt me." A Roman senatorial historian would have perfect understanding of this attitude.

The writing of history by Romans – and for that matter, by Greeks – was an extension of political activity, and in that sense it is by its nature engaged and activist. If you can understand why someone like Thucydides would devote the heart of his life to writing the history of the Peloponnesian War without hope of monetary profit, or why someone like Tacitus would abandon political life to chronicle the death of the senatorial order and the end of the kind of history-writing he practiced, then you will have understood something fundamental about the centrality of politics in the ancient Mediterranean world and the nature of ancient historiography.

Sources and History-Writing

When affecting a scientific posture, historians like to refer to their sources as "data," that is, as authoritative information that is "given" to them. Societies produce all sorts of artifacts for all sorts of reasons, but few to serve as evidence for the convenience of future generations of historians. True, in the modern world some objects, such as forgeries, are produced for use as historical sources. Yet it is an important part of the modern idea of the source that it was originally produced for some non-historiographic purpose – political, cultural, social – for which it can subsequently serve as evidence. If it is produced for posterity, its motivation is suspect. I take as examples some objects that are typically exploited as sources by ancient historians. Inscriptions were originally displayed to honor patrons or cement alliances, perhaps sometimes even to communicate information; literary texts were read for edification or pleasure, or set out on the ancient equivalent of coffee tables to impress guests; records were generated for bureaucratic convenience, coins for publicity and exchange; houses were built for shelter, walls for defense. Gravestones and memorials may be set up to honor individuals or glorify events to the city. My list of functions is intended to be exemplary, not exhaustive. In all cases, the significance of the text or object is tied up with the present life of the community: its political institutions, its social hierarchy, its collective memory. Their functions are not static but change with time. A historian can use any of these things – and others besides – as evidence, to reconstruct the events of the past, but only by segregating an "original meaning" from the later accretions and uses they acquire in the life of the community. To put the point succinctly, historians convert cultural utensils into historical evidence. That oxymoronic phrase used by the statistically oriented, "control of the data," is revealing. Evidence is not "given" to historians; they manufacture it themselves as part of the process of "doing" history. Consequently the idea of evidence has a history, one contingent on the circumstances of the historical practice that produces it.

Although the transformation of an object from social implement to historical source may have a number of consequences, in general the treatment of a thing as evidence draws a line between the community and its past – or more accurately, it effaces the investment of the present from history and de-politicizes the role of the past in the contemporary community. Let me try to generalize this point by drawing a distinction, which I will continue to observe throughout this book, between the "monument" and the "document." By "monument" I mean a trace of the past that is integrated in the present life and traditions of the community; it is the source allied with a bottom-up knowledge, the communal memory of society. By the word "document" on the other hand, I mean institutionalized evidence, a source that has been abstracted from social interaction. The knowledge derived from "documents" is authoritative, "top-down."

The word "monument" derives from a Latin root meaning "to remember": it comes immediately from the verb *moneo*, meaning "to remind," hence "to warn" or "to advise." Etymologically, a monument is "a reminder." Reminders do not of themselves signify, but take their meaning from interaction with those who already know. The word "document" on the other hand derives from the Latin word signifying "to instruct." By contrast the document is a lesson, new information imparted to those who do not know. In the case of the monument, knowledge and its object are integrated; in the case of the document, they are detached.

The history of the usage of these terms reflects the same dichotomy. Greek and Roman historians had no generally accepted, specialized term for "historical evidence." Certainly they interpreted certain objects as evidence. Thucydides for example occasionally justifies himself saying that an object or phenomenon serves as a *tekmerion* or *semeion*, a sign or indication, of the truth of an assertion. Other ancient historians make comparable statements, which reflect their use of evidence. Such terms however are not standard from author to author, and they should in any event be understood as alluding to the historian's process of interpretation rather than to a category of objects.

The word *monumentum* was used by Romans to designate material objects, including written texts, which recall the past, but it would not have been employed to describe an oral source. Thus Cicero, in his essay *On Old Age*, has the speaker, Cato, declare that in writing his own historical work, the *Origines*, he has "collected all the monuments (*monumenta*) of antiquity" (38). At the end of antiquity and in the early Middle Ages popular usage becomes more restricted, normally taking in only gravestones and other architectural objects. The word *documentum* is not uncommon in classical Latin, but not in the sense of historical source. Rather it meant something closer to its etymological root: "instruction" or "lesson" or even an "example." Thus for instance Tacitus says at the beginning of his biography of his father-in-law, the *Agricola*, that he and his contemporaries have furnished future generations with a great lesson (or example, *documentum*) in suffering" (2).

The word "document" is in common use today as a generic term for "historical source," almost exclusively written sources. Used of material objects the word would be understood metaphorically. This usage, including the restriction to written sources, can be traced only to the middle of the nineteenth century, and it does not become normal until the end of the century. Before this, in early modern times, the word was used in its traditional sense of "proof," hence notably to describe a text introduced as legal evidence. The common term for "historical source," including both written texts and material objects such as coins, was "monument," a word applied even to archival texts. Thus, as late as the 1820s, the great collection of historical texts from various archives in Germany was inaugurated with the title *Monumenta Germaniae Historica* (Munich 1819–1969).

The point so far is merely philological; the shift in word-usage, however, reflects a larger change in the way that historical evidence is conceived and treated within society. The document is conceived to stand outside of the present and to be independent of the historian's work; its meaning is authoritative, not a reflection of communal knowledge. Consequently the introduction of the idea of the document contributed to the ideal of historical objectivity. If one only has the self-discipline to approach the document without preconceived notions, it will speak and tell things unknown.

Behind the development of the concept of the document looms the institutional edifice of modern professional scholarship. Modern study of sources is characterized by a concern with standardization (through publication of corpora) and the establishment of an agreed scholarly method of interpretation. Standardization allows for common citation of a conventional repertoire of sources, agreed method forges communal consensus. The end goal was the establishment and enforcement of a political – as opposed to an intellectual – "truth." The characteristic modern institutions of knowledge – museums, libraries, archives, universities – made possible the establishment of academic consensus in two ways: by segregating and systematizing.

The essential gesture involved in the transformation of a monument to a document is its isolation from the community. Inscriptions, sculptures, pots, and so on are lodged in museums. Manuscripts are deposited in libraries or archives. "Ruins" are rechristened "sites" and actually fenced off from the community. Information is then reproduced and distributed through the publication of collections, corpora, which provide widespread and systematic scholarly access to a common body of documentary materials. The great, cumulative historical project inaugurated in the nineteenth century would not have been possible without this basic "source-work." To put the point brutally and concisely, there is no such thing as a "document" in the ancient world; the earliest origins of the notion date to the time of the Renaissance, and the idea is not fully elaborated until the nineteenth century.

The commitment to a systematic approach to the sources is perhaps the defining methodological commitment of nineteenth-century historicism. Scholars of the nineteenth century had a keen sense that their work was distinct from all that had gone before. The uniqueness of their approach, they believed, was manifested most significantly in their practices of source-criticism. Here is Ulrich von Wilamowitz-Moellendorff (1848–1931), who may be regarded as one of the eminences of the nineteenth-century tradition of classical scholarship, discussing in 1908 the greatest ancient historian of the eighteenth century, Edward Gibbon (1737–94), the author of *The Decline and Fall of the Roman Empire* (1776–88):

> Of course his work is admirable. Of course no Greek produced anything like it. And yet, if we apply to it the canon of historical research which the nineteenth century brought into vogue, it can only be called a work of research in the same qualified sense as the works of the ancients. Gibbon was no researcher in the strict sense. He made no inquiry into sources; he arrived at no new fact or datum. Despite all the labour he spent in reading his original authorities, despite all the freedom of his judgement, he walked in a prescribed path and he accepted a tradition. ("On Greek Historical Writing," 3; spellings *sic*)

Evidence cannot be understood in isolation, simply in light of the critical judgment brought to it by the historian of the present day. It must be placed in a context, and interpreted in light of other comparable evidence. Thus the most striking feature of nineteenth-century source criticism is the obsession with taxonomy: how best to order and arrange sources in relation to one another. And this interest led in turn to an insistence on a systematic approach to evidence. Those who wish to understand an inscription or a coin or a pot must first look at hundreds of inscriptions or coins or pots. Only when the source is placed in its context and read against other comparable objects can it "speak for itself" and yield up its secrets. Those who attempt to interpret a piece of evidence in isolation are doomed merely to project their own preconceived ideas onto the past.

How, though, should scholars define context? The context of the source was defined by two fields, temporal and geographic, and these remain the essential unities of history down to the present. The basic methodological problem is defining the arbitrary boundaries of the context of the source: in temporal terms, its "period," in geographic terms, its "region." The pioneers of historicism were aware that the creation of period and region were arbitrary acts of interpretation, bound up with global historical interpretation. Inevitably, perhaps, over time the regions and periods of history became reified, as though they had some real existence outside of interpretation. As people increasingly recognize today, stimulated by such movements as World History, meaningful alternatives to the traditional periods and regions can be created. It is an enlightening historical game, for example, to play with accepted periodizations: when, for example, does the Roman Republic end? When does the Roman Empire begin? 65 BC? 44? 23? AD 14? 69? When did the Peloponnesian War begin? Even Thucydides wavered.

The institutionalization of the historical source, its conversion from "monument" to "document," is complicit with the professionalization of history in the nineteenth century and with the new ideals of representation that were promoted at that time. The isolation of the document protects historical sources from the anachronistic contaminations, or even from material damage, but it also "abstracts" them from meaningful interaction with society.

Since the nineteenth century, professional historians have worked from texts already disengaged from society, institutionalized, and thus pre-constituted as documents. As a result, the monumental qualities of evidence, its connections with contemporary life in all its variety, are routinely ignored. One effect of the nineteenth-century historical project was the wholesale conversion of the monumental capital of society into documents reserved for the study of professionals. Of course, contemporary historians can make use of "un-institutionalized" sources, if they wish; this has been the point of the "Oral History" and "Public History" movements. But even in such cases, there seems to be an irresistible urge to "archive" the sources as quickly as possible, "for the use of future generations" of professional historians: witness the collections of the Holocaust museums, or the archive of Yugoslavian epic at Harvard. Thus even here cultural monuments are inexorably converted to academic documents.

By contrast, traditional historians, in Greece and Rome and elsewhere, began their work from the monument. They were not concerned to isolate and preserve their sources so that future generations of historians should be able to replicate their research. They had no sense of history as a cumulative group project. Of course they read one another's work and might agree or disagree with each other, as Herodotus took Hecataeus to task, or Livy dismissed Valerius Antias. We know that historians often took up the historical tale at the point where a predecessor left off, as Xenophon began his *Hellenica* at the point where the history of Thucydides left off. But there was no traffic in debate about the establishment of evidence and its significance, as we find among modern historians. The print apparatus that subsidizes such ongoing debate was wholly lacking before the fifteenth century; and in any event, in antiquity historians did not concentrate on the production of collections of evidence to be put at the disposal of their fellows. For them, the initial problem of source-work was to transform the monument to a document, to recover the "documentary" significance of the evidence from the tissue of political and social relationships that enshroud the traces of the past. True, some collections of "primary source material" were made, such as Krateros' compendium of Greek inscriptions (see below, chapter 6); but these were not academic subsidia. Krateros' collection was not made for the same reasons, nor did it have the same functions, as a modern epigraphical corpus. The research of the pre-modern historian always sprang out of an appreciation of the engagement of the source with the political and social activities of the present.

Bibliographical Essay

General reference works

The first resort for questions about all aspects of the ancient world should be Simon Hornblower and Antony Spawforth, eds., *The Oxford Classical Dictionary*, 3rd edn., Oxford, 1996 (reprinted with trivial revisions 2003), abbreviated here and elsewhere *OCD*[3]; commonly used abbreviations (e.g. authors' names, journal titles, reference works) are explained there at xxix–liv). A more recent and expansive resource is the German encyclopedia edited by Hubert Cancik and Helmuth Schneider, *Der neue Pauly: Enzyklopädie der Antike*, Stuttgart 1996–2003. The first 12 volumes deal with the ancient world; volumes 13–15 treat the history of scholarship; volume 16 contains indices; supplementary volumes began to appear in 2004. The entire work is currently being translated into English: *Brill's New Pauly: Encyclopedia of the Ancient World*, Leiden 2002–; four volumes have so far appeared. The word "Pauly" in the title alludes to the monumental and irreplaceable German classical encyclopedia of the nineteenth and twentieth centuries, inaugurated by August von Pauly and revised and continued by Georg Wissowa et al., *Pauly's Realenzyklopädie der classischen*

Altertumswissenschaft, 68 vols. and 15 vols. of supplements, Stuttgart 1893–1978 (abbreviated Pauly-Wissowa or *RE*). For classical antiquities (implements, material object, customs, and daily life) the best available reference work remains Charles Daremberg and Edmond Saglio, *Dictionaire des antiquités grècques et romaines*, Paris 1877–1919; in English William Smith, ed., *A Dictionary of Greek and Roman Antiquities*, 2 vols., New York 1854–7, continues to be useful. The standard annual bibliography for scholarship on the ancient world is *L'Année Philologique*, which can be searched in part via the web: www.annee-philologique.com/aph. In English two general "introductions to ancient history" can be consulted: the first, Hermann Bengtson, *Introduction to Ancient History*, Berkeley 1970, has good bibliographies as of 1970, but is otherwise so antiquated as to be useless; the second may be highly recommended: M. Crawford, ed., *Sources for Ancient History*, Cambridge 1983.

On the history of scholarship, in addition to the *New Pauly*, John Edwin Sandys, *A History of Classical Scholarship*, Cambridge 1903–8; sections of the work have been updated by Rudolph Pfeiffer, *History of Classical Scholarship from the Beginnings to the End of the Hellenistic Age*, Oxford 1968, and *History of Classical Scholarship from 1300 to 1850*, Oxford 1976.

The past decade has seen a substantial quantity of reputable scholarship made available on the World Wide Web, along with much else. The most elaborate internet resource for classical antiquity now available is the *Perseus* website, based at Tufts University (www.perseus.tufts.edu). A fine search engine for recent bibliography is the *Bryn Mawr Classical Review* (ccat.sas.upenn.edu/bmcr/). A stable gateway to academic resources for the study of classics on the web is maintained by the editor of the *Thesaurus Linguae Graecae* at the University of California, Irvine, Maria Pantelia (www.tlg.uci.edu/index/resources.html). "The Stoa" (www.stoa.org) includes useful information of all kinds, including notably "Diotima," a collection devoted to the study of women in classical antiquity. For Roman material, William Thayer's *Lacus Curtius* (penelope.uchicago.edu/Thayer/E/Roman/home.html). The introduction to classical bibliography by Jacques Poucet and Jean-Marie Hannick, *Bibliotheca Classica Selecta* (bcs.fltr.ucl.ac.be/default.htm), will repay examination, even for those who do not read French.

Introduction

For the metaphor of history-writing as the invocation of ghosts, see U. von Wilamowitz-Moellendorff, *Greek Historical Writing, and Apollo: Two Lectures Delivered Before the University of Oxford June 3 and 4, 1908*, 25–6, who uses it to make a point entirely opposed to the one I make here:

> The tradition yields us only ruins. The more closely we test and examine them, the more clearly we see how ruinous they are; and out of ruins no whole can be built. The tradition is dead; our task is to revivify life that has passed away. We know that ghosts cannot speak until they have drunk blood; and the spirits which we evoke demand the blood of our hearts. We give it to them gladly; but if they then abide our question, something of us has entered into them, something alien, that must be cast out, cast out in the name of truth.

For a survey of some of the ideas informing various nineteenth-century historical work, see H. White, *Metahistory*, Baltimore 1973; on the ideal of historical objectivity see P. Novick, *That Noble Dream: the "Objectivity Question" and the American Historical Profession*, Cambridge 1988; for a concise introduction to historicism, see Paul Hamilton, *Historicism*, 2nd edn., London 2002. The organization of my discussion of historiography is informed by M. de Certeau, "The Historiographical Operation," in *The Writing of History*, New York 1988, 54–113.

The development of modern history-writing

On Machiavelli, see e.g. Leo Strauss, *Thoughts on Machiavelli*, Glenco 1958, and Sheldon Wolin, *Politics and Vision: Continuity and Innovation in Western Political Thought*, expanded edn., Princeton 1960, 2004, chapter 7. The conservative, exemplary attitude of Machiavelli's *Discourses* should be noted. For an assessment of Strauss's criticisms of Machiavelli's role in originating "modernism," see Harvey Mansfield, *Machiavelli's Virtue*, Chicago 1996, chapter 9. For the crucial role of the "Battle of the Books" in defining modern ideas about the past, Joseph Levine, *The Battle of the Books: History and Literature in the Augustan Age*, Ithaca 1991; Daniel Woolf, *The Social Circulation of the Past: English Historical Culture 1500–1730*, Oxford 2003. On the tension between "exemplary" and "processual" visions of the past, Reinhard Koselleck, "Modernity and the Planes of Historicity" and "Historia Magistra Vitae: the Dissolution of the Topos into the Perspective of a Modernized Historical Process," both reprinted in his *Futures Past: On the Semantics of Historical Time*, Cambridge, Mass. 1985. For the historical relationship between biblical hermeneutics, historicism, and philology see Tzvetan Todorov, *Symbolism and Interpretation*, Ithaca 1982.

Historical writing

On the implications of writing for historiography, see for example the various essays of Eric Havelock, including *Preface to Plato*, New York 1967, and *The Literate Revolution in Greece and its Cultural Consequences*, Princeton 1982; more recently see François Hartog, *The Mirror of Herodotus: The Representation of the Other in the Writing of History*, Berkeley 1988, 260–309. On history and film see the various essays of Robert Rosenstone, particularly his *Visions of the Past: the Challenge of Film to Our Idea of History*, Harvard 1995; Robert Darnton, "Television: an Open Letter to a TV Producer," in *The Kiss of Lamourette: Reflections in Cultural History*, New York 1990, 53–9. On history and "comix," Joseph Witek, *Comic Books as History: the Narrative Art of Jack Jackson, Art Spiegelman and Harvey Pekar*, Mississippi 1989. For Cicero's ideas about history and rhetoric, A. J. Woodman, *Rhetoric in Classical Historiography: Four Studies*, London 1988, 70–116. I cheerfully concede that some ancient historical writing is dull while some modern writing is vivid. Few contemporary historians can touch the Victorians: see for example anything by A. E. Housman or T. Rice Holmes. More recently see Ronald Syme, whose pungent, almost perverse style was self-consciously modeled on Tacitus. For the implications of the difference between mimetic and cumulative ideals of historiography see again Joseph Levine, *The Battle of the Books: History and Literature in the Augustan Age*, Ithaca 1991, in particular chapter 9. For traditional and modern ideals of language, cf. chapters 2–4 and 7–8 of M. Foucault, *The Order of Things: an Archaeology of the Human Sciences*, New York 1970; R. Barthes, "The Old Rhetoric: an Aide-Mémoire," reprinted e.g. in *The Semiotic Challenge*, New York 1988, 11–94. Saussure's classic work is his posthumous *Course in General Linguistics* (1915).

Social context of history-writing

Regarding the periods of education in America, for the liberal arts college see John, Cardinal Newman's book, inspired by the English Oxbridge system, *The Idea of the University* (1852); for the research university, Abraham Flexner, *Universities: American English German* (1930); on the "multiversity," Clark Kerr (emeritus chancellor of my own university), *Uses of the University* (1963, now in its 4th edn., 1995). Among general surveys I recommend John Brubacher and Willis Rudy, *Higher Education in Transition: a History of American Colleges and Universities*, New Brunswick 1997; Laurence Veysey, *The Emergence of the American University*, Chicago 1970. Something of the administrative reality of the American classics and ancient history establishment seeps to the surface of the website of the *American Philological Association* (www.apaclassics.org). Some highly regarded works on the relationship between academic history and popular memory are Jacques LeGoff, *History and Memory*, New York 1992, and Pierre Nora, *Les lieux de mémoire*, Paris 1984–; for ancient history and (scholarly) cultural memory, Jan Assmann, *Moses the Egyptian: the Memory of Egypt in Western Monotheism*, Harvard 1997. For the relationship between knowledge and nationalism, Ernst Gellner, *Nations and Nationalism*, Oxford 1983; on history and nationalism, Peter Novick, *That Noble Dream: the "Objectivity Question" and the American Historical Profession*, Cambridge 1988; for German education and nationalism, Georg Iggers, *The German Conception of History: the National Tradition of Historical Thought from Herder to the Present*, Middletown 1968; Fritz Ringer, *The Decline of the German Mandarins: the German Academic Community, 1890–1933*, Cambridge, Mass. 1969. On Ranke, see Georg Iggers and James Powell, eds., *Leopold von Ranke and the Shaping of the Historical Discipline*, Syracuse 1990. For the impact of printing on the practice of history, Elizabeth Eisenstein, "Clio and Chronos: an Essay on the Making and Breaking of History-Book Time," *History and Theory*, Beiheft 6 ("History and the Theory of Time"), 1966; more generally see her *The Printing Revolution in Early Modern Europe*, Cambridge 1983; various essays collected in Robert Darnton, *The Kiss of Lamourette: Reflections in Cultural History*, New York 1990, 107–90. For literary patronage in the ancient world see Barbara Gold, *Literary Patronage in Greece and Rome*, Chapel Hill 1987; and Peter White, *Promised Verse: Poets in the Society of Augustan Rome*, Cambridge, Mass. 1993. The ideal independence of the historian was a trope in ancient historiography: James Luce, "Ancient Views on the Cause of Bias in Historical Writing," *CP* 84 (1989), 16–31. On historiography and the civil service in China see e.g. Benjamin Elman, *A Cultural History of the Civil Examinations in Late*

Imperial China, Berkeley 2000. Margaret Mehl, *History and the State in 19ʰ Century Japan*, New York 1998, provides a wonderfully stimulating account of Japanese historiography; for the Mito School, Victor Koschmann, *The Mito Ideology: Discourse, Reform, and Insurrection in Late Tokugawa Japan, 1790–1864*, Berkeley 1987. Generally on the republican senatorial "annalistic" tradition of historiography, E. Badian, "The Early Historians," in T. A. Dorey, ed., *The Latin Historians*, London 1966, and the introduction to S. P. Oakley, *A Commentary on Livy, Books VI–X*, Oxford 1997; for Livy's attitude about social status and history-writing, the book by my colleague Gary Miles, *Livy: Reconstructing Early Rome*, 47–54; for Tacitus, Ronald Syme, *Tacitus*, Oxford 1958.

Sources and history-writing

On the distinction between monument and document, see Jacques LeGoff, "Documento/Monumento," in the *Enciclopedia Einaudi*, vol. 5, Turin 1978, 38–48. For an appreciation of the argument in English, see Armando Petrucci, *Writing the Dead: Death and Writing Strategies in the Western Tradition*, Stanford 1998, 54–60; cf. more generally the introduction to Michel Foucault, *The Archaeology of Knowledge*, repr. New York 1972. For a recent attempt to define the document from an analytic (rather than an historical) perspective, see Mogens Hansen, "What is a Document?: An Ill-Defined Type of Source," *Classica et Mediaevalia* 52 (2001), 317–43.

Scholars of the nineteenth century already recognized that techniques of scholarship prefigured academic thought. Hegel for example argued in his *Phenomenology of Mind* (1807) that whereas philosophy used to work from life to abstraction, in his day scholars approached problems with their abstractions ready-made: cf. Leo Strauss, "Political Philosophy and History," in *What is Political Philosophy?* New York 1959, 74–5.

2

Geography

Introduction

A little while after I left Los Angeles for Philadelphia and graduate school, some classicists invited me to a dinner party at Bryn Mawr College. Early in the evening the conversation turned to Los Angeles and the left coast; I kept my mouth shut and my head down. My hostess, a New Yorker, was of the opinion that Californians were incapable of learning Latin: mastery of an inflected language requires discipline and precision; confronted with a periodic sentence, young Californians, their brains spotted with the melanoma of precocious senility brought on by years of walking in the sun without their hats, lack the attention span necessary to make sense of it; by the end of the sentence they have forgotten the beginning and so cannot grasp it whole.

In the popular cultural geography of the United States, California and New York City are two opposed poles, its Athens and Jerusalem (I'll leave the reader to decide which is which). In the characters of the two, many of the perceived virtues and vices of present America are distilled; and the characters of the people are thought to rely on the climate and geography of the place. California's population sprawls over a coastal plain. The climate is perennially warm and sunny, the scenery dramatic. The suburban life-style, the weather, and the natural beauty induce a drowsy lassitude, a mental addiction to free-association, and glassy-eyed awe of every banal truism. The population of New York City, by contrast, has been pressed into the confines of a few small islands. They live one on top of the other without hope of escape. The weather is changeable and extreme: biting winters, torrid summers, and oppressive gloom for much of spring and fall. The crowding, inescapable clutter, and weather make New Yorkers as twitchy and hyperactive as gerbils. If Californians are slack-jawed, slavering golden retrievers, New Yorkers are yappy, aggressive Pomeranians.

A less innocuous instance of the same reasoning is notably to be found in nineteenth-century imperial thinking. Since the nineteenth century, Europeans have asked themselves why they are so special. Why does Europe rule the world? Perhaps, they thought, it was Europe's temperate climate that led to its distinction: not too hot nor too cold, but just right. By contrast, the heat of equatorial regions corrupts those who live there. No work ethic can take root among those reared in such oppressive weather; afternoon comes and everyone quits working and takes a lazy siesta. So Noel Coward wrote that colonial populations were bemused by their encounters with Europeans: "only mad dogs and Englishmen" were crazy enough to "go out in the midday sun." For this reason, among others, civilized life could not grow from seed in such places; it had to be transplanted. Comparable reasoning has been used to explain the intellectual accomplishments of various peoples. The luminous, stony landscape of Greece produced luminous, stony thinkers. As M. Cary notes in his 1949 book on *The Geographic Background of Greek and Roman History* (Oxford 1949)

> If, following the practice of the ancient Greeks, we consider the influence of the world's climates upon the health and temperament of its peoples, we shall find that the Greek climate is by no means of the restful "Riviera" type. For persons of a nervous disposition it is over-stimulating, and herein we may discover part cause of that contentiousness of disposition which has always been the besetting fault of the Greek people. But for those of normal constitution it is a tonic that tautens the fibres of body and mind. . . . Greece therefore is a natural home of artists and thinkers who do not shut their eyes to the world. (39) The quickening and energizing properties of the Greek weather are nowhere more apparent than in Attica. Its crisp and buoyant air, and its translucent sky, against which the Attic landscape stands out clear-cut as in a cameo, combine to nurture keen wits and perceptive minds. (79)

People who live in hard, clear climates tend to have hard, clear thoughts and make hard, clear art; it would follow that people who inhabit lands with foggy, soft climates must have foggy, soft thoughts, and make foggy, soft art. The cultural geography epitomized in these remarks presumes that environment plays a determinative role in forging human character. The idea is of hoary antiquity and remains persistent today, both in popular thought and to some extent in academic thought – perhaps deservedly so. There is obviously some truth to the notion that people are prey to their surroundings: modern research shows, for example, that months of overcast weather may lead to depression, for example – come February we are ready for spring and sunshine. The name for the symptomatic depression, SAD (an acronym for "Seasonal Affective Disorder"), was coined in the 1980s.

At the same time, there is an obvious desire to make sense of the world and cultural difference by schematizing and rationalizing relationships.

Cultural geography is tied to cosmology. The point is most clearly illustrated by maps, which represent the order in pictorial form.

Nature and Culture

Climate and geography appear to be historical constants. For this reason they are regarded as crucial historical sources. By looking at a place and its climate it is possible to throw light on the events of the past that occurred in the same place. Examination of a battlefield may confirm or falsify or explain a literary account of an engagement that occurred there a thousand years before. Knowledge of contemporary climate helps us to understand the nature of agriculture, knowledge of geography helps explain patterns of interstate relations and trade. By the same token, however, the present accessibility of geography and climate and its usefulness in understanding the past suggests that nature is something transcendental. Changeless, inexorably demanding, the environment appears to provide an absolute check on human behavior, without regard for historical change. Admittedly some changes can be documented: sea levels may rise and fall, there may be variations in climate – generation-long droughts, increases or declines in average temperatures – but over the long term the shape of space and climate remain relatively constant. For this reason, geographic considerations are almost always at the heart of attempts to provide absolute laws on human history – so Marxist and "Annales" interpretations and more recently neo-Darwinist interpretations of history have been founded ultimately on environmental imperatives. The rallying cry of historicism however, is that "man does not have a nature, he has a history." Environmental concerns stubbornly resist the claim, retorting that man does have a nature, and that nature can be seen in the life-or-death struggle with the environment.

The traditional view of cultural geography, which sees environment as determinative of human character, is absolutist in its approach to history and to humanity, and is consequently sympathetic with the pre-modern, non-historicist vision of the past. For example, if we allow the strict principle that environment determines character, then the Mycenaeans of the thirteenth century BC and the Athenians of the fifth century BC, Byzantine Greeks of the ninth century AD and the Greeks of the twentieth century AD must all share some bedrock of nature. Consequently the events of history can serve as a general model for present behavior.

As we have seen, modern writers of history – that is, of historicizing history – insist on the primacy of context in historical interpretation, and for historicists the two chief determinants of context are time and place. To think of an historical event contextually, it is first necessary to articulate time and

place into meaningful unities, fields of common historical play, in relation to
which an event can be understood. In terms of time, this means the establishment of periods. A region is to geography what a period is to time: the
articulation of a space of comparability, within which there may be some
general equivalence among historical phenomena. On close examination
such divisions prove to be arbitrary, in the sense that they are tied to the
interpretation deployed: a period or region that makes sense in a political
interpretation may not make sense in view of an economic explanation or a
cultural explanation. Nevertheless, for historicist interpretation to be possible, a preliminary move must be the establishment of the field of the context.
The traditional view of cultural geography, then, poses a problem for historicism, as historicism does for traditional cultural geography. Is the environment "outside of history," that is, is human cultural geography natural
or historical?

The history of western thought about the relationship between culture
and geography has been dominated by three ideas. The first, which emerges
from religious beliefs, explains that the world is static, the product of
rational design, created for the benefit of humanity: human prosperity or
suffering depends on harmonious interaction with an eternal nature; nature
exists for the purpose of satisfying human needs. The second develops from
speculation about illness and its remedies: geography and climate influence
the characters and physical qualities of people. The third, which is tied to
human technological activity, emphasizes the role of humans as environmental agents: people, by their efforts can change nature itself. These ideas need
not conflict with one another; they may, and do, coexist. What they have in
common, in their traditional formulations, is the notion that people are part
of nature and live in harmony with it. Man may be supreme and exceptional
among the creatures of the world, but he still belongs to the natural order.
Even when people modify the environment, they do so within the limits of
what nature – the divine design or their own innate characters – allows.

The socialization of geography is as old and universal as ethnocentrism,
and it certainly permeated Greek and Roman thought. The impulse to associate human characteristics with the physical and climatological qualities of
the world is irresistible. Paleolithic hunter-gatherers doubtless sat around
their campfires and discussed how the climate or water made the people in
the next tribe over lowbrow or egg-headed. The three traditional ideas about
the connection are amply illustrated in ancient authors.

The idea that the world exists in accordance with some divine plan and
is at the disposition of humankind, if they know how to take advantage of
it, can be traced in Greece at least to the pre-Socratic philosophers, and it
finds its full expression by the fourth century, notably in the *Memorabilia* of
Xenophon (4.3), where Socrates is made to describe the ways in which the

Gods have made nature for the benefit of humanity. The ancient tradition of thought in this vein was summarized by Cicero, in an essay that had an enormous impact on later European thought, *On the Nature of the Gods*, the *De Natura Deorum*. The discussion stretches in particular through the second book: "The world and all the things in it were made for the sake of Gods and men" (2.53, 133).

The notion that the environment has a determinative influence on human nature is notoriously attested in an emblematic fifth century BC medical essay entitled *Airs, Waters and Places*, which is attributed to the semi-legendary founding hero of Greek medicine, Hippocrates. The text was perhaps intended to acquaint a medical practitioner, arriving in a new place, with the local information required to treat people. The treatise recognizes two explanations for cultural diversity: custom (*nomos*) and nature (*physis*). For example, a northern people known as "the longheads" (*makrokephaloi*) shape their children's heads from birth; thus local custom (and inheritance of the acquired characteristics) shapes their personal appearance. Contact with other peoples weakens the custom and so reduces the incidence of "long-headedness" (14). At the same time climate, food supply, and geography also determine physical and mental qualities of people. The text emphasizes this point throughout. In one particularly dense section (24), the author contrasts various cultures of Europeans: people living in temperate mountainous regions will tend to be large, persistent, and courageous; those living in hot meadows will not have this persistence and courage, though these qualities can be produced by the force of law (or custom, *nomos*); those inhabiting temperate but infertile lands will usually be stubborn and independent; those who dwell in fertile and temperate regions will tend to be "fleshy, ill-articulated, moist, lazy, and generally cowardly in character. Slackness and sleepiness can be observed in them, and as far as the arts are concerned they are thick-witted, and neither subtle nor sharp." Although the stated impulse for this essay is medical, the idea itself is probably more traditional.

The notion of a determinative cultural geography looms large in ancient historiography and ethnographic writing. The idea is already central in Herodotus, the first preserved Greek historian. It occurs most interestingly in his ethnographic treatments of the peoples of the far north and those of the far south: they are opposed and balanced with one another. Thus people of the far south, pygmies, tend to be burnt black by the sun, and are very small. People of the far north, Scythians, are tall and very fair. Scythians have hard heads, Egyptians have heads as delicate as eggshells. In the north, women urinate sitting down (as do the Greeks); in the south they urinate standing up, while men urinate sitting down. An emphatic statement of the principle comes at the very end of the history, where the historian relates an anecdote about the Persian king, Cyrus. There the king tells his countrymen that they are better off remaining in their own rocky country than migrating to the fertile valleys of their subjects: "from soft lands come soft men."

The idea is to be found in philosophic authors too, perhaps most famously Aristotle (*Politics* 4.7, 1327b), who contrasts cold and hot climates and their effect on character. Peoples of the north are brave, but without skill or intelligence; they keep themselves free, but cannot govern themselves or others. Peoples who live in warm climates are the opposite. Intelligent and skillful, they are cowardly and so are subject to others. The Greeks, on the other hand, inhabit an intermediate, temperate region, and consequently have the best qualities of both.

The correlation between cultural variation and geographic variation is one of the most persistent themes of ancient historiography. The second century BC historian Polybius in a famous digression noted that the harsh circumstances of Arcadia produced harsh people, and suggested that culture had a mitigating effect on them (4.20). The later Hellenistic historian, Posidonius, had an enormous influence on the Roman tradition; his work survives chiefly in citations from Roman authors. He put forward an elaborate theory of various geographic zones, and their impact on the natures of the peoples who dwelt in them. His influence is subsequently to be found on Roman authors of all kinds, historians and poets, philosophers (Cicero *De Re Publica* 2.4–6) and architects (Vitruvius 1.4).

Not all ancient thinking is thrall to simple environmental determinism; critics are also to be found. The Roman geographer, Strabo, bridling at the simplifications of Posidonius, agreed that climate had its influence on peoples, but insisted that culture mattered as much and more.

> It is not due to the nature of the country, but rather to their education, that the Athenians cultivate eloquence, while the Lacedaemonians do not, nor do the Thebans, who live even closer. Nor are the Babylonians and Egyptians philosophers by nature, but by reason of their institutions and education. Likewise the excellence of horses, oxen and other animals results not only from the places where they live, but also from their breeding. Posidonius mixes up all these distinctions. (2.3.7)

Some historians too can be critical, or at least think in different ways, about the relationship between culture and environment. Less essential, more circumstantial arguments are to be found. All ancients were aware as a practical matter that geographic and environmental factors mattered, and could use them in making specific decisions, whether military or economic. Thucydides, for example, can make an argument that seems very modern in its character: at the beginning of his work he suggests that in early Greece migrations were common, prompting overpopulation. These migrations particularly affected the fertile areas of Greece; Attica with its poor soil was desired by none, and so was relatively stable in this period (1.1–2). The *Athenian Constitution* that has been preserved among the writings of Xenophon shows similar sensitivity to the strategic value of the sea, and its usefulness in gaining access to the resources of other peoples' lands (2.2–8, 11–16).

Another major strand of ancient thought deals with the ability of people to master their environment through technology. The idea is expressed particularly frequently in connection with agriculture. Perhaps the most famous statement is to be found in one of the choruses of Sophocles' drama, the *Antigone*. Man's art, the ability to grow crops, navigate the seas, hunt, and build have raised him above creation: "there are many awesome things, but none more than man" (332–75). Comparable ideas can be found associated with the notion of *homo faber*, man the builder: it is through technology that man opposes nature. Strabo provides another Roman instance of the thought. Commenting on Egypt, he observes that engineering rectified the problems of the periodic inundations of the river, through irrigation. The Egyptians gave such care to the management of the river that in this case it might be said that "industry had triumphed over nature" (17.3).

These traditional conceptions of people as environmental agents are only apparently opposed to the notions of divine providence in nature and environmental determinism. In all cases nature is imagined as being outside of human control. We may attempt to channel nature, but in the end we are still subject to it and must live in harmony with it: see for example the myth of Prometheus as told in Plato's *Protagoras* (320d–322d).

Modern historicist views of the relationship between nature and culture have affinities with the third of these ideas. The notion of man as an environmental agent who is capable of modifying nature itself is probably universal. In the modern conception, however, human culture is imagined as existing in opposition to the environment. People have it in their power to change and even destroy the natural world – indeed they have always done so, by domesticating plants and animals in the Neolithic, for example.

Modern thought about man and the environment begins with the eighteenth century, when the focus of interpretation shifts from nature to the human; both came to be regarded as subject to change and history. The interpretation is characterized by an increasing acknowledgment that human activity has shaped the geography and climate of the world as much as natural events, such as floods and ice ages. The relationship between people and environment is not to be conceived as unilateral. Certainly the environment influences people – but people make their environment as well, through agriculture, engineering, and more generally through technology. Thus cultural geography is produced through a negotiation between people and nature, and the effect of environment on history is "denaturalized." The environment itself is a cultural artifact, and needs to be considered not as permanent and timeless, but as subject to the same processes that shape human society. With the eighteenth century nature itself is integrated into history. It becomes possible to think of both environment and culture developmentally, that is, as a part of history, and the path to contemporary "environmental history" is laid open.

The move from a model in which a static nature has a determinative role to a conception in which humankind lives with nature in a mutable and developing symbiosis brings with it a change of emphasis. Instead of focusing on the impact of environment on character, historians concentrate instead on the medium of interaction between people and nature, that is, on technology, and more abstractly, on economics. It would be a mistake to imagine that the traditional determinative, characterological idea has vanished; the ideas persist, and continue to pop up in the most sophisticated analyses. But professional historiography for most of the nineteenth and twentieth centuries seldom concerned itself with the problem springing from environmental determinism, that is, fundamental human nature, but with historical attempts of humankind to master nature itself: the history of technology and economy comes to the fore.

This historicist vision of cultural geography was, unsurprisingly, devised at the end of the eighteenth century. The chrysalis of the idea is to be seen in the writings of Johann Gottfried von Herder (1744–1803), notably in his *Outlines of a Philosophy of the History of Man* (*Ideen zur Philosophie der Geschichte der Menschheit*, 1784–91), or in Montesquieu's *Letters* (1721). The arguments, however, are set forth most unequivocally and their implications drawn most uncompromisingly by Buffon (Georges Louis Leclerc, Comte de Buffon, 1707–88), in various essays that he published during the second half of the eighteenth century, which were drawn together with the general title, *Natural History* (*Histoire naturelle*, 1749–1804). So in the introduction of his work "On the Periods of Nature" ("Des epochs de la nature") he can say that "the entire face of the earth bears today the stamp of the power of man, which although subordinate to nature, often has done more than she, or at least has so marvelously aided her, that it is with the help of our hand that she has developed to her full extent and that she has gradually arrived at the point of perfection and magnificence in which we see her today." The environment has its history too, and that history is part of human history; as he remarks elsewhere in the same introduction, "the state in which we see nature today is as much our work as it is hers. We have learned to temper her, to modify her, to fit her to our needs and our desires.

We have made, cultivated, fertilized the earth; its appearance, as we see it today, is thus quite different than it was in the times prior to the invention of the arts." Of course there is such a thing as "primeval" nature, a nature untouched by man. But this we seldom meet, for the history of man has been in large part the history of creating a new nature, distinct from this primeval nature. Primeval nature at no time controlled man; at most it imposed limits. The world is, so to speak, a blank canvas. We must paint on the canvas, but we can use whatever colors we have available to us on our palette. The process of making a new nature began with sedentary life, if not before – even using the most primitive tools, people have always been able to modify the landscape. Geography is changed through engineering, animals by breeding, the climate itself by deforestation. The environment has been constantly remade by man, and the changes are not recent; they are as old as humanity itself.

The relationship of this idea to the old notion of man as an historical agent is obvious. But traditional thought emphasized the connections of technology with culture and society. It was quite another matter to see this agency, as does Buffon, from the perspective of changes made to the earth itself. From the traditional perspective such changes are part of the history of culture, which is opposed to a constant nature. With Buffon the difference between culture and nature itself begins to collapse, and nature itself may be said to be integrated into history.

Buffon's ideas were further developed in the nineteenth century in the work of two of the acknowledged founders of modern geography, Alexander von Humboldt (1769–1859) and Carl Ritter (1779–1859). Nevertheless, intellectual changes take hold gradually, and it may fairly be said that the implications of these ideas do not become widely known and accepted until the end of the nineteenth century, under the influence of thinkers like Darwin and Marx. For a thorough-going and pessimistic elaboration of these ideas about the human impact on the environment, the world had to wait for George Marsh's *Man and Nature; or Physical Geography as Modified by Human Action* (1863), which drew an apocalyptic picture of a nature shaped and destabilized by human activity – the ultimate consequences of which could not be forecast. Nevertheless, the timing of the eighteenth-century development of these ideas is significant, and needs to be considered in relation to the development of other ideas about the human past; that is, historicism.

Traditionally the historical past had been regarded as structurally constant; events occurred, the actors changed, but the structure of life and society remained constant. *Homo sum, humanum nil alienum a me puto*, said Terence (*Heauton Timoroumenos 77*); "I am a man, and I regard nothing human as foreign to me." The essential experience of life was regarded as constant, and consequently the lessons to be learned from the past were generally applicable to the present. One guarantee of this constancy was the stability of nature itself.

The causes for this shift in the ideas about the nature of the relationship between man and nature were manifold. No small part was doubtless the increasing power of people to remake the landscape in the nineteenth century. A contributing cause, however, was the more general rethinking of the nature of the past at this time: historicism. These shifts are consonant with the ideas of historicism. Historicism changes the idea by insisting on the historicity of the human: customs and events, even thought itself, must be understood in context, not as something timeless. People do not have a nature, they have a history. Thus the change in thought about the environment can be seen as complicit with the change in other attitudes about the past. Everything changes and nothing stays the same. The environment does not provide an eternal and timeless backdrop to an exemplary past. It, like the nature of humanity itself, changes. The environment is not a guarantee of past meaning, but is subject to the same processes as human history.

The most influential attitude toward the question of the relationship between history and geography in the twentieth century is owed to the French "Annales" school. In Fernand Braudel's memorable formulation, what matters in history is not politics or events, but enduring factors, such as climate and geography, which determine such events. Political history, he says, is like froth dancing on an ocean wave. Understanding requires engagement with the deeper currents driving the swell. Despite the primacy they gave to environmental factors, however, the Annalistes remained true to the historicist ideals forged in the nineteenth century. The environment may permit or restrict certain possibilities, but it does not constrain the essential nature of people.

Inscribing Order: Mapmaking

Such ideas about the relationship between history and geography can be clearly seen in the history of mapmaking. A map is an attempt to reduce space and organize it according to reason. On the one hand maps describe the physical world in a way that allows readers to orient themselves within it. It is understood that there is some general correlation, whether structural or conventional, between the physical world and the drawing. We might say at some level that a map aspires to be a "realistic representation" of the world, and succeeds to the extent that people can verify its content against the physical world in which they live. In the modern world the pretensions of maps to realism are founded on measurement, system, and standardization.

At the same time, maps are ultimately rationalizations of space. Jorge Borges famously imagined a map that had a 1:1 correspondence with the territory of a state, so when it was unrolled, it simply covered what it represented. Outside of such fantasies, however, no map can actually coincide with what it represents. To begin with, maps work by reducing space. Consequently all maps inscribe parochial human knowledge: the structure of the depicted world works to define and support social rules and values. These two functions of the map can exist in harmony or conflict; we might characterize them as realist versus constructivist or objectivist versus subjectivist.

Cartography was dominated increasingly from the Renaissance on by a consensually-approved ideal of standardized and objective representation of the real world. The ideal triumphs throughout Europe no later than the seventeenth century, and has remained dominant ever since. This development continues to underpin modern mapmaking practices. Nevertheless, modern mapmaking begins with the eighteenth century. The development that marks the onset of cartographic modernity is the nationalization of the process of mapmaking. To that time, maps had been made by individual scholars. With the eighteenth century nascent nations became occupied with the surveying and mapping of their territories, for various political reasons: military security; establishment and policing of borders; control of population. One effect of the mapping was to create a representation of the state that all could know, and which could thus serve as an underpinning of national identity. One thing national maps represent is the sovereignty of the state. The resources that nations put into the collection of survey data beggared the information at the disposal of private individuals. Maps became considerably more detailed, and, because they were made and disseminated by a central authority, more standardized. The ideals of mapmaking altered substantially as well. The object of mapmaking was explicitly to produce a detailed and correct relational representation of terrain. In this way the distance between a philosophic, abstracted depiction of the world and the practical representation of orientations and directions – objects on the ground – was dissolved. The cartographic truth can be independently verified by observation on the ground. It is not that earlier civilizations lacked the method for measuring territory. The Romans, for example, had knowledge of elaborate surveying techniques. These were not, however, put at the service of mapmakers. So modern cartographers criticized earlier maps on grounds of inaccuracy, schematism, idealization: that is, subjectivity. A good map, it came to be thought, should be independent of the cartographer and his ideals. A map is a relational model of the world, and the guarantee of the map's quality lies in the system by which it is made. System thus replaces subjectivity – which is the essence of the nineteenth-century historicist revolution. Investigators should not attempt to understand things individually: this only leads to subjective understanding. An objective under-standing, an understanding that controls subjectivity, is systematic; only by viewing things in a context can one understand them in themselves.

The system of the modern map is the grid marked out by the lines of longitude and latitude. The view of the world depicted corresponds to nothing that could ever be seen in reality, because there is no perspective: each place is drawn as though seen from above; the point of perspective of the subject is dissolved into innumerable vantage points. Thus the organiz-ing point of reference on a map is no particular subject's viewpoint, but the system of the grid itself.

It must be said that the grid system of longitude and latitude is consider-ably older than the eighteenth century. The system was developed from the third century BC on, but received its full elaboration in antiquity by the second century AD Alexandrian, Ptolemy, in his *Geographia*. Despite various inaccuracies Ptolemy established the general principles of the geographic grid, dividing the spherical world by latitudinal lines into regions he called *klimata* – districts marked by positions and times of the "setting" of the sun – whence our English word "climate."

Ptolemy's reputation perished in western Europe with the end of antiq-uity, though his writing had an abiding impact on Arab world. When map-makers of the Renaissance learned of Ptolemy once more via the Arabs, the impact was revolutionary: western maps came to be organized according to astronomically determined lines of longitude and latitude, and western maps ever since have been Ptolemaic in this basic organizational principle.

Despite having the idea of a map as a representation of the world accord-ing to a grid system, mapmakers of the Renaissance did not have the resources to do extensive surveying. Thus their maps were necessarily idealized to a great extent. Empirical mapping had to wait for the growth of national survey projects in the eighteenth century. Thus what distinguishes modern maps from the map of Ptolemy and from Renaissance maps is not the orga-nizational principle, but the empirical survey and measurement that lies behind it. Ptolemy's map was abstract and philosophical. The innovation of the eighteenth century lies in the merging of the philosophical with the empirical.

Ancient Maps

In antiquity maps even such as Ptolemy's were at heart cosmological con-structs: expressions of an understanding of a universal order, an attempt to render an abstract vision of the world according to reason rather than on the basis of numerous empirical measurements and positions. To the extent that we know the practical maps in use in antiquity, they were not made in conformity with these ideas; that is, they were not drawn with reference to some schema such as the grid of longitude and latitude.

The tension between philosophically motivated representations of the world and the practical knowledge of it exists in Greek thought as far back as it can be traced. Thus Herodotus describes the earliest maps of the classical Greek tradition with amusement: "The ancients drew the earth as a disk, and in its center, Delphi; for Delphi has the navel of the world." "It makes me laugh to see how many people have produced maps of the world and no one has completed the task intelligently; they all represent Ocean flowing round the earth and the earth itself perfectly round as though finished on a lathe" (4.36 and 5.49).

This criticism of the schematism of early maps should not be taken to mean that Herodotus aspired to an "objective" understanding of the physical character of the world. His own conceptions of geography were perhaps not so geometrical as those of earlier philosophers; still they were typical of the beliefs of the day, and served, as we might have expected, to reinforce social practices and beliefs of the Greeks. Thus in a perennially common ethnocentric move, a place in Greece – Delphi – was regarded as the center of the world, "for it has the navel of the world." The "equatorial" dividing line between north and south was marked by the "Royal Road" of a neighboring super-power, the Persian Empire. East and west were discriminated by two rivers, the Nile and the Danube, which were regarded as running north–south, on a line with one another. Such beliefs of course have nothing to do with any geographic realities; but organizational principles are necessary to any map, and these served the Greeks.

A more practical and influential matter is the ancient theory of the continents, which has continued to have a considerable influence down to the present day. According to Herodotus, again, the early Greeks divided the world into three continents: " I am amazed that people ever divided Libya, Asia, and Europe as they have, for they are utterly unequal. Europe extends the entire length of the other two, and its breadth, in my opinion, cannot even be compared to them" (4.42). He follows this remark with a discussion of the sizes of the three continents as they were known in his time. Again, as an empirical matter, his conception is as false as the one he criticizes. Europe and Asia form a single land mass. A geographical distinction between the two can only be justified if your attention is centered on the Mediterranean, as the Greeks' was, and you do not allow your eye to stray to the north of the Black Sea.

We have many verbal descriptions of the physical world from antiquity, but few actual maps. There is no doubt that the ancients made use of maps from early times; according to Herodotus (5.49), at the end of sixth century the tyrant of Miletus, Aristagoras, could use "a bronze tablet on which was engraved the whole circuit of the world with all its seas and rivers" to help him persuade the Spartans to lend him military aid: bemused by the minia-turization, the Spartans ironically decided not to help. Augustus' lieutenant (and later son-in-law), Agrippa, was detailed to make a general map of the Roman roads. The project took 20 years to complete, and resulted in a circular map of the world, which was displayed in Rome. But these maps have not survived to us.

The most famous surviving instance of a map from antiquity is the so-called "Peutinger map." This map was preserved in medieval copy that eventually came into the hands of a collector named Konrad Peutinger. It is, by scholarly consensus, a more or less faithful copy of a late antique Roman map. The map is a parchment strip, more than seven yards long and about a foot and a half tall. Roads are drawn in straight lines, with distances between significant points noted. Towns and villas are drawn in perspective. Distortions can be conveniently evaluated by examining its representation of the Mediterranean. Given the shape of the map, it obviously can have little relationship to the reality of the Mediterranean; as has been frequently noted, the sea in this case seems to be portrayed more as a river. Furthermore, this map makes no use of Ptolemy's astronomical conventions: it is intended for practical travel, not to illustrate general principles. Practical maps and philo-sophic maps were made for different purposes. Thus in the Peutinger map one of the most basic rules of modern mapmaking is ignored: there is no consistent scale. The conventions of representation and the absence of scale self-evidently did not make it impossible to use the map to orient oneself. Certain maps in the modern world, such as subway diagrams, are schematic and drawn to no consistent scale. Effective use requires only understanding of convention.

As Herodotus noted, early maps are schematic. It is easy and pleasant to laugh at the naiveté of earlier writers, but there is a hard kernel of truth to Herodotus' criticism. The point applies to all maps, including those Herodotus espoused, and even to our own. Any map is a simplification and a rationalization of space: it is an attempt to make order out the physical world. Organization must be to some extent arbitrary, and to understand what it represents, one must attempt to understand the principles of orga-nization and their links to cultural values. To understand, one must look to the principles of organization.

The standard example of ideology in the modern world map is the widely used map based on the "Mercator projection." The world, as many of us have come to believe, and as some also did in antiquity, is spherical, and for it to be represented on a map it must somehow be "projected" onto a flat surface. Various methods of projection are possible; all will necessarily involve some degree of distortion. One of the most common was designed by the sixteenth-century geographer Gerardus Mercator for the use of sailors. His projection has the effect of exaggerating the size of the space in the northern hemisphere – including, notably, Europe. Further north the exaggeration becomes increasingly noticeable: thus Greenland on this map appears to be roughly the size of South America. As is often pointed out, the distortions of the "Mercator projection" have the same effect as traditional ethnocentric "centering" of one's own nation on the map. Yet, for all its limitations, the "Mercator projection" does serve as a standard – which antiquity never developed.

As in the study of other sources, modern understanding of geography has been predicated on an attempt to "de-socialize" it, to remove it from its relation to society and treat it as distanced, objective. Points in space, like sources of other kinds, need to be understood in terms of their relations to one another rather than as a projection of human society. Modern maps may be said to emerge with the notion of scale – that is, with the idea that socially "empty" space needs to be treated equally with the socialized and "full" and occupied space of civilization. The dissolution of perspective in favor of the grid rigidifies this move from socially embedded space to systematic and objective space.

Geography and Ancient History

When historians today discuss the relationship between geography and ancient history, it is in modern terms. We are all "environmental possibilists" today. Thus the relationships between the ancients and their environment is not usually understood as a form of environmental determinism, but rather as a history of simultaneous adaptation and modification. The history of technology, for example, is often understood as the story of how people adapt to and modify the natural world around them.

Consult any modern map of the ancient Mediterranean. Certain features typically provoke comment from modern historians. The qualities of ocean and land and their relation to the early development of political systems and economy are frequently emphasized. The ocean is both a divider and a unifier: a divider because it separates land masses; a unifier because ocean facilitated trade. Bulk trade – grain shipments and the like – in particular, was always cheaper and faster by boat. Greece and Rome developed on peninsulas that have from the Stone Age been used as "bridges" running from north to south by mariners who liked to hug the coast. The closely-packed islands of the Aegean served as "stepping stones" for mariners since at least the Neolithic.

The land, by contrast, is almost universally seen as divisive. The Balkan and Italian peninsulas are mountainous, and politically they were fragmented. The vast number of Greek city-states can be explained in terms of the geographic fragmentation of the peninsula. But though the land is fragmented, the sea unites. Greece has a longer coastline than any other state on the Mediterranean.

The geographic position of states is often tied to their political histories. Athens extended her fortification walls to the Piraeus to take advantage of her proximity to the ocean. She is clearly marked for distinction in trade; the large territory she possessed made it possible to sustain a relatively large population. She was also blessed with remarkable mineral resources: notably the silver deposits of the Laurion district in southeastern Attica. Like most of the Greek mainland, Athens faced to the east. Athenians could sail securely by using the Cycladic islands as stepping-stones, and much of the history of Athens down to the present has been played out in interactions to the east.

By contrast Rome did not seem geographically marked out for greatness. The Italian peninsula was divided along a north–south axis by the Apennines and the bulk of the arable land lay to the west of the mountains. The city of Rome grew up inland, at a frequented ford of the Tiber river. In early times she was notoriously un-nautical. Geographically, then, Rome does not seem to have been marked for distinction. Contrast her great rival, Carthage, which was situated on a great natural harbor at a strategic point in the Mediterranean, where north–south traffic made land in Africa, and where the sea narrowed to channel east–west traffic. Whereas Greece looked east, Rome looked west. The Apennine mountains run down the spine of Italy on the east. Most flat land and manageable harbors on the peninsula look to the west. It is no accident that the early development of Rome's empire took place chiefly to the west.

The available natural resources also play a part in historical reasoning; they are in particular frequently tied to explanation of economic and political eminence. Surpluses present an opportunity for export, lacks an impetus for import. At all times the raw materials for tools were in high demand. In the Stone Age obsidian was imported to the Greek mainland. Later, the raw materials for bronze, copper, and tin supplied substantial incentive for trade – in the case of tin, the trade was likely very far flung, extending perhaps to the Caucasus or even to England. Later iron became the material of preference for tools, and areas with substantial easily accessible deposits, such as Laconia and Etruria, prospered. Precious metals, such as gold and silver, were available only in select locations, and when they were mined they quickly circulated through trade.

The territories of Greece and Italy were rocky and did not possess large open plains for the growing of food. Only about 25 percent of the total acreage of Greece, for example, is cultivable, and what land is available is rocky and not very productive. The main crops, the so-called Mediterranean triad, furnished the basis of the ancient diet. Two of these, vine and olive, were quite suitable to the land. The third, grain, could not be grown in the abundance we today associate with the vast fields of the American Midwest; as population grew, grain was imported from the "breadbaskets" of the Mediterranean world, Egypt and the Black Sea, North Africa and Sicily. As early as the Bronze Age, surplus population was sustained by importing food. Timber was another necessity for the seagoing civilizations of the Mediterranean, and the search for large supplies of ship-building timber took them far afield.

What the ancients did possess in abundance they put to good use. Marble served as a luxury building material for the Greeks, and the Romans later made their buildings of concrete and faced them with marble. Potters' clay was abundant and furnished antiquity with its most ubiquitous legacy to the present.

Greece and Rome enjoy a "Mediterranean climate," that is, weather something like that of southern California. Rainfall is not plentiful by northern standards. Annual rainfall might run to 30 or 40 inches, with two thirds of that coming in the winter. The dryness of the climate leads, some argue, to the early formation of states. Since water is not everywhere available, groups of people congregate around the available supply – perennial springs and rivers. This concentration leads to the necessity of social compacts, and encourages sedentary occupation.

Winter days were relatively warm: average temperatures in Athens and Rome run to about 50 degrees. Temperatures in the summer can be brutally hot, topping 90 or even a hundred degrees. The historical implications of weather are debatable. It has often been held that the weather in Greece and Rome led to "outdoor" politics: people could meet in large open places to hear and debate matters of public policy. By contrast, a wintry or rainy place encourages more restricted political activity with smaller numbers meeting indoors.

Conclusion: Antiquity and the West

Certain traditional notions about geography and climate have lingered on, and exercise an unflagging influence on the thoughts of contemporary scholars. Classical antiquity has traditionally been the study of Greece and Rome. Why is classical antiquity not extended to take in North Africa, the Near East, Egypt? To some extent, particularly among archaeologists, this tight focus has been overthrown; nevertheless it remains very much alive. The basic constitution of the field is owed to a longstanding, traditional line of thought about the organization of the world, which is cosmological in origin. The focus on Greece and Rome depends on a distinction, both geographical and social, between east and west. The two traditional ancient civilizations are imagined as the foundational civilizations of the west – that is, of modern Europe and America.

Even though modern thinking about the environment is not determinist, we continue to think of space in social terms – and vice versa. The very foundational definitions of the field are complicit with fundamental geographical notions. Why does ancient history traditionally include only Greece and Rome, and not the Near East and Egypt? Ancient history is based on a geographical idea, that of the West. The idea of the West and the place of Greece and Rome in this story has been criticized frequently in recent years. Doubtless the most influential attack was framed in Edward Said's book, *Orientalism* (New York 1978) which traced the history of the idea of the East, chiefly in the early modern period. Later Martin Bernal, in his *Black Athena: the Afroasiatic Roots of Classical Civilization* (London 1987–) concentrated on the place of Africa in European thought, chiefly again in the early modern period. The point of each was comparable: the Orient and Africa were defined in relation to the virtues of the West – they were "others," used by the West to define itself.

The origins of the concept of "the West" can be traced back to the Greeks. The fact that the term defines community according to place, or even direction, rather than by some other criterion, such as ethnicity or language (e.g. "whites" or "Indo-Aryan speakers"), is unusual. The distinction between East and West, slave and free, appears as early as the opening chapters of the first surviving Greek historian, Herodotus. The dividing line between the two was traced between Greece and Asia Minor. Although the Greeks were certainly aware that folk existed at least as far east as India, for them "the East" coincided with the territory of their great imperial enemy, the Persian Empire. For a very long time, Europeans thought of "the Orient" in these very restricted terms. The Greeks' West by contrast extended no further than the Greek-speaking lands of the Mediterranean littoral. This geographic conception of the West was later elaborated to take in first the Roman Empire, and later still all of "Christendom."

The basic geographic dichotomy that we find in Herodotus has continued to suffuse western thought ever since. Its most famous and influential modern exponent must surely be Hegel. I certainly do not mean to suggest, however, that Herodotus' concept of "the West" is identical with later European notions. The rise of Christianity, for example, leads to the geographic extension of the idea of the West to take in northern Europe and the assimilation of a religious polarity: Christians versus pagans or infidels. Increasing familiarity with India and China led to second thoughts about the usefulness of the distinction, and then to the extension of the notion of the East from the Persian Empire further east. The European discovery of the New World unbalanced the polarity further, by introducing them to people that fit usefully into neither side of the dichotomy. With the scientific revolution of the Enlightenment, reason and superstition were grafted onto the dichotomy.

The geographic idea of the West explains the constitution of ancient history. Egypt and the Near East and countless other ancient civilizations do not figure in classical ancient history because they are not western. Greco-Roman civilization is the heart of the tale because Greece and Rome are the "cradles of Western civilization." In the idea of the West we can also discern various notions about geography. The West originated in a habit of thinking that was strongly inflected by environmental determinism, and it has survived the historicist notion of humankind as environmental agents.

Bibliographical Essay

The gold standard among atlases of the classical world is now Richard J. A. Talbert et al., *Barrington Atlas of the Greek and Roman World*, Princeton 2000. Hermann Bengtson and Vladimir Miojcic, eds., *Grosser historischer Weltatlas, vol. 1: Vorgeschichte und Altertum*, 6th edn., Munich 1978, includes maps illustrating ancient history beyond the Greco-Roman. Other worthwhile atlases include Nicholas G. L. Hammond, *Atlas of the Greek and Roman World in Antiquity*, New Jersey 1981; Richard J. A. Talbert, *Atlas of Classical History*, London 1985. For a review of modern atlases of the ancient world see Richard J. A. Talbert, "Mapping the Classical World: Major Atlases and Map Series 1872–1990," *JRA* 5 (1990) 5–38. The most affordable atlases now available have been provided by Penguin: these include Bill Manley, *The Penguin Historical Atlas of Ancient Egypt* (1996); Robert Morkot, *The Penguin Historical Atlas of Ancient Greece* (1996); Chris Scarre, *The Penguin Historical Atlas of Ancient Rome* (1995).

On the web, William Thayer's *Lacus Curtius* site (above, bibliographical essay to chapter 1) includes an impressive geographic gazetteer of the Roman world. Useful maps are also provided on the *Interactive Ancient Mediterranean*, a site hosted by the University of North Carolina, Chapel Hill (iam.classics.unc.edu/index.html).

For the roles of climate and geography in ancient history see now Peregrine Horden and Nicholas Purcell, *The Corrupting Sea: a Study of Mediterranean History*, Blackwell 2000; M. Cary, *The Geographic Background of Greek and Roman History*, Oxford 1949, was long a standard.

Introduction

On the question of a geographic basis for European sovereignty, see Jared Diamond's bestselling *Guns, Germs and Steel: the Fates of Human Societies*, New York 1996. The song "Mad Dogs and Englishmen," was included in Coward's 1924 musical, "The Third Little Show," and has much in common with the attitudes expressed in literature and political speeches of the great age of the British Empire. For a contrast between the climates of Greece and China and the cultural significance of the difference, see John Linton Myres, *Geographical History of Greek Lands*, Oxford 1953.

Nature and culture

For the history of thought about the relationship between culture and nature see the classic book by Clarence Glacken, *Traces on the Rhodian Shore: Nature & Culture in Western Thought from Ancient Times to the End of the Eighteenth Century*, Berkeley 1976, and the more succinct essay by the same author, "Environment and Culture," in Philip Wiener, ed., *Dictionary of the History of Ideas: Studies of Selected Pivotal Ideas*, New York 1973, vol. 2, 127–34; similar ideas are developed more recently by Max Oelschlager, *The Idea of Wilderness: from Prehistory to the Age of Ecology*, New Haven 1991. For the ancient world see Christian Jacob, *Géographie et ethnographie en Grèce ancienne*, Paris 1991. For the attitudes of the Annales school toward geography see Lucien Febvre, *Geographical Introduction to History* (1925). The famous applications of the attitude to history are owed to Fernand Braudel: see e.g. *The Mediterranean and the Mediterranean World in the Age of Philip II* (1966); *Civilization and Capitalism, vol. 1: the Structures of Everyday Life* (1979). Recent work on "landscape archaeology" is also relevant: I single out the various writings of Susan E. Alcock, for example, *Archaeologies of the Greek Past: Landscape, Monuments and Memories*, Cambridge 2002.

Inscribing order: mapmaking

Borges' cartographic fantasy is to be found in a story he authored with Adolfo Casares, "On Exactitude in Science," reprinted for example in his *A Universal History of Infamy*, Penguin 1975. For the history of mapmaking see John Wilford Noble, *The Mapmakers*, rev. ed., New York 2000; for a critical perspective on modern scientific mapmaking see various essays by J. B. Harley, e.g. *The New Nature of Maps: Essays in the History of Cartography*, Baltimore 2001, or Christian Jacob, *The Sovereign Map: Theoretical Approaches to Cartography Through History* (a translation of his *L'empire des cartes*, forthcoming). For a contrast of ancient and modern ideals of mapmaking, see the review article by Kai Brodersen, "Mapping in the Ancient World," *JRS* 94 (2004), 183–90.

Ancient maps

Generally on ancient maps, see Oswald A. W. Dilke, *Greek and Roman Maps* (Aspects of Greek and Roman Life), London 1985; J. B. Harley and D. Woodward, eds., *The History of Cartography, vol. I, Cartography in Prehistoric, Ancient, and Medieval Europe and the Mediterranean*, Chicago 1987; C. Adams and R. Laurence, eds., *Travel and Geography in the Roman Empire*, New York 2001; Richard Talbert and

Kai Brodersen, eds., *Space in the Roman World: Its Perception and Presentation*, Münster 2004. The Peutinger map has been recently considered, with useful review and criticism of modern scholarship, by Richard Talbert, "Cartography and Taste in Peutinger's Roman Map," in the same volume, 113–41; it is fully reproduced by E. Weber, *Tabula Peutingeriana, Codex Vindobonensis 324: Vollständige Faksimile-Ausgabe im Originalformat*, Graz 1976. Among the many essays on the "Mercator projection," I recommend Marshall Hodgson, "In the Center of the Map: Nations See Themselves as the Hub of History," in his *Rethinking World History: Essays on Europe, Islam and World History*, edited by Edmund Burke III, Cambridge 1993.

Conclusion: antiquity and the West

In addition to the books of Said and Bernal, Antony Pagden has given critical attention to the idea of the West in recent years: *The Idea of Europe: from Antiquity to the European Union*, Cambridge 2002. For the ideology of the division of continents, see Martin Lewis and Karen Wigen, *The Myth of Continents: a Critique of Metageography*, Berkeley 1997. For America's status as a civilization, see the stunning book by Max Lerner, *America as Civilization*, New York 1957. The idea that Americans come from Mars, Europeans from Venus, we owe to Robert Kagan, *Of Paradise and Power: America and Europe in the New World Order*, New York 2003.

3

Chronology

Introduction

"I love my mother; I have lived my life by her example." The view of the past as a repertory of salubrious examples, a stockpile of experience and knowledge for the present to learn from and exploit, is traditional and remains yet potent. The sentiment is imprinted on us from childhood. We all learn at the outset by imitating our parents and other elders; the force of the idea is strengthened by the relationships of love or hate, respect or rebellion, that we cultivate with them.

For the past to have an exemplary force it must be regarded as forming a continuum with the present, homogenous in the essentials. My mother can serve as a model of good or bad behavior for me to the extent that I share her circumstances. When our situations become incomparable her example becomes irrelevant. So if I say that there are limits to my imitation of my mother, that "in certain respects she is the child of another generation," I am turning away from the exemplary view of the past in favor of a historicizing view. I can no longer measure my life against my mother's; I must rather try to understand her. The historicist vision of the past presumes a new conception of time. Whereas exemplary time unites present and past, historicism must articulate time, partition it, in order to differentiate contexts: historical periods emerge. As a result, the thread of common experience that has traditionally united the generations is severed. Once contextualized, the exemplary authority of the past unravels; in the name of understanding, the present abdicates its ethical prerogative to praise and condemn.

The historicist vision of time is complicit with the modern emphasis on universal, absolute chronology. One of the more onerous chores involved in studying history is the memorization of dates. Students are routinely expected to be able to assign years to more important events. Given the difficulty and apparent pointlessness of the undertaking, they may well wonder why such dates matter at all. Granted that historians should care about cause and effect, they must master relative chronology, that is, the sequence of events. But why go to the bother of memorizing absolute dates like 490 BC or AD 14? Would it not be enough to know that Darius' invasion of Greece occurred after the Ionian Revolt, or that Tiberius succeeded Augustus?

Absolute chronology provides a universal measure by which to gauge the relationships of past events with one another – and with the present. The modern, numerical system of dating has the advantage of spelling out the relationship, as other systems, such as those that assign names of magistrates to particular years, do not. Americans, asked to characterize the relationship between John Quincy Adams and George W. Bush, might seize on some perceived similarity: "sons of presidents who themselves became president." The relationship between the battle of Fort Sumter and the Moon Landing is more puzzling; but all things can be related in terms of dates, and the two are 108 years apart.

Chronology, then, provides a capacious framework that can accommodate any and all things. At the same time, because modern historians all subscribe to the same system, it provides the basis for a cumulative, universal history. There may be no logical connection between the outbreak of the Peloponnesian War in 431 BC and the protests of Tiananmen Square in 1989, but because the two are dated according to the same system, a temporal relationship is established between them; contemporary China and ancient Greece are woven into the same "big story." At the same time our chronology subtly undermines other meanings of history, because it creates an intellectually vacuous yet ostensible relationship where none exists. In modern history-writing any two events can and will be related temporally, whether or not they have any meaningful coherence.

For such reasons, absolute chronology matters to modern historians. But what is the relationship between this intellectual system and social conceptions of time? Certainly the cycle of days and months and seasons has mattered in most societies; traditionally people have lived according to the rhythms of the agricultural year. But why do societies care about the chronology of years? Social concern for keeping track of annual chronology is of relatively recent vintage. Peasants in the Middle Ages, for example, tracked the calendar of the year carefully, in order to properly observe important church festivals; they were largely indifferent to annual chronology. If they needed to refer to an event of a year in the past they appealed to local, idiosyncratic, relative chronology: "I was born in the year after the plague," or "my son died four years ago," and so on. Of course such a system of year-reckoning will have a more direct significance for locals, keyed as it is to significant events in the life of the individual and community, instead of to a generally accepted numerical sequence of years.

In the contemporary world we have many reasons to remember the years according to our abstract numerical dating system. Most of these are associated with the political order; we know our dates as part of our subordination to the state. We can drive at 16, serve in the army at 18, and drink at 21. We are eligible for senior citizens' discounts at 55. To track such dates (and many others) over a population that numbers in the hundreds of millions, a numerical chronological system is an enormous convenience.

Ancient historians, like modern historians, were concerned with relative dating and took care in their writings to provide an internally coherent chronology, but they did not all use same chronological system. The interest in providing a unified and universal chronological system that applied from historian to historian only developed in the Hellenistic period, and even then when, say, a Roman read Thucydides, he may have known that the events described had occurred approximately four or five hundred years before his time; but in terms of absolute chronology the dates mentioned in the history will have meant almost as little to him as they do to modern readers. The story floated free (in chronological terms), without any obvious relation to Roman time. The imprecision was tolerable because the value of the past resided not in its place in a generalized temporal process, or progress, but in its value as a set of timeless examples of behavior. To the extent that human nature was constant, to the extent that Thucydides' history was a "possession for ever," the exact dates of the Peloponnesian War are trivial. With the development of an overarching chronographic system, however, significance is tied to mere sequence, rather than logical coherence. History becomes "one damn thing after another."

At the time of my last revision of this sentence, it is – or now was – 4:19 p.m., June 15, AD 2005. The system exemplified in this date derives from Roman and Christian tradition, and has been in use, in one form or another in the west for the past 1,500 years. At present it is the dominant dating system in the world: other systems survive, for instance in the Arab world, but the western dating system is accepted as the international standard. We imagine that this is an "absolute" system of dating, and convert all historical dates to our system, which produces the historical unity required for the "grand narrative" of modern academic history. Yet even our modern system is only as durable as our society. If modern civilization should fail, as did those of antiquity, and at some point in the future someone wished to decipher the dates in our history books, they would be almost as impenetrable as the dates used by Greek city-states in the fifth century BC. The possibility was envisioned by the architects of the Hoover Dam, who dated the dedication of the facility not only in terms of our calendar, but also with reference to a "celestial clock," a paving mosaic showing the positions of the planets and stars at the time of the dedication.

In antiquity there was no single, universally accepted dating system. Some ancient historians attempted to reconcile the dates found in these various systems, but none succeeded entirely, nor ever inspired universal imitation. When reading ancient historians and other sources modern scholars encounter a bewildering variety of dating systems. The conversion of such dates to our modern dating system has been one of the major projects of modern historiography.

Calendrical Time

Every society keeps track of the cycle of days, months, and seasons. The impulse arises in large part from the need to keep track of the times of year suitable for planting, harvesting, and trading. All pre-modern societies live in intimacy with the cycles of agriculture, and so the recurring events of the farmer's year assume a great importance.

Certain units of time are susceptible of observation: the recurring pattern of night and day, the phases of the moon, the cycle of the seasons. It should not be imagined that, because I use the word "natural," the perception of units of time is universally uniform. For example, in the modern world the smallest units of time in common use are seconds, minutes, and hours. These are not "natural" units, but are measurable only with mechanical clocks, which only come into use in medieval times. Nevertheless, moderns tend to regard such units as uniform and unchanging. The ancient Greeks and Romans also divided the day into hours, which they were able to measure very precisely using sundials and water-clocks, but because the length of the day varied according to season, so too did the length of their hours. Or again, we commonly regard a day as beginning at midnight, or perhaps, informally, at sunrise. Jews and Catholics preserve a more ancient tradition and for religious purposes begin their days at sundown. In this they are consistent with ancient Greco-Roman ideas. The modern idea of the seven-day "week" and the planetary names of the seven days are not ancient; they begin with the medieval period.

The history of the calendar is largely the story of the reconciliation of the three naturally recurring units of time; the day, the lunar month, and the solar year. Everyone takes the day as the basic unit of time, for obvious reasons: of the observable units of time it is shortest and most intrusive. The lunar month is also relatively brief and readily calculable. The phases of the moon require almost exactly twenty-nine and one-half days to complete their cycle. So the lunar month can be reconciled with the pattern of days merely by alternating the length of the month between 29 and 30 days.

The serious difficulties arise with the attempt to reconcile the lunar month with the solar year. The length of the year is not easily determinable; the ancients probably calculated it either by observing the recurring revolutions of the night sky, or by plotting the point of the rising of the sun as it moved from north to south with the seasons. By the beginning of the second millennium BC the Babylonians knew the length of the solar year very precisely; the Greeks and Romans knew its length to within hours. The solar year lasts almost 365.25 days. This period cannot be satisfactorily divided into lunar months. If we allow for 12 months (as do most societies) we will have only 354 days. If we insert a thirteenth month we will have far too many days; 383 and a half. Traditional societies typically esteem the lunar cycle and are unwilling to abandon it. As a result ancient calendrical notations were frequently out of sync with the solar year. The ancients were aware of the problem and dealt with it by occasionally inserting extra, "intercalary" months to bring the calendar back into correspondence with the seasons. Nevertheless, even when we are furnished with a precise date by an ancient source, it may for this reason be impossible to convert it to our own notation: no matter how well we know a given calendar, we can seldom be certain in what relation a date stands to the cycle of seasons. All Greek calendars frequently fell out of step with the solar year. So Thucydides, for example, dismisses all ancient dating systems as too unreliable for use in his history (cf. 5.20), and records events in his history with reference to seasons or agricultural events ("the ripening of the grain").

In addition to this basic problem of the meaning of calendrical notation, there is the issue of variety. Every Greek state that had pretensions to autonomy used its own local system of dating. Over 1,000 examples of local Greek calendars are known. There is a fair degree of homogeneity in the names given to months – states that shared the Ionian dialect or Dorian dialect, for example, also shared certain institutions and observances, and these are reflected in many month names. But there is no necessary correlation among any of these calendars as to the beginning of the year, or what time a month began. Later, the Romans, through their empire, successfully imposed their system of time reckoning on many, but even so the Roman calendar was most uniformly adopted in the western part of the empire, where there was no long tradition of urban life. States in the east, where political institutions were deeply rooted, clung to their traditional dating schemes. So even in the period of Roman domination, many Greek states preserved their traditional calendars, as did Egypt.

The Roman calendar is one of the enduring legacies of antiquity to the modern world. We take the names of our months, for example, directly from it. Here too, however, as in other traditional states, lunar months and solar years cohabitated uncomfortably. For example, in 214 BC, because of the disarray caused by Hannibal's invasion of Italy, the calendar had been allowed to go 117 days in advance of the solar year. The Romans traditionally dealt with such problems as did the Greeks, by inserting an intercalary month after the last month of the year (which for them was February). Finally in 46 BC Julius Caesar adopted a radical solution to the problem by abandoning lunar months altogether. Henceforth there would be no correlation between the month and the phases of the moon; length of months would vary between 28 and 31 days. Every four years an additional day would be added to make up for the additional quarter day of the solar year. It is the Julian Calendar, with some minor modifications, that we have inherited.

Chronology

The practical social and technological incentives that encourage the reckoning of the calendar year are lacking when it comes to tallying the years themselves. Knowledge of chronology is not useful for the community in the same ways as the knowledge of the calendar. Calendars are attested almost as early as writing is in Greece and Rome – Hesiod's *Works and Days*, for example, is cast in part as a "farmer's almanac" – and they doubtless antedate writing. Annual chronologies by contrast are attested only late, and their applications are chiefly associated with the imperatives of political organizations and the handmaiden of politics, history.

Our system of dating originates in Christian scholarship, as the abbreviations A(nno) D(omini), the year of the Lord, and B(efore) C(hrist) indicate. The date of the birth of Christ was calculated (wrongly) by a monk named Dionysius Exiguus, "Small Dennis," in the sixth century AD, who thought it appropriate to date religious events in terms of a Christian era. The principle of "era" dating was not new or original with this system. There are examples of comparable dating systems in antiquity, and it is likely that Dionysius proposes his system in reaction to another Christian dating system, which took the beginning of its era from the persecutions of Diocletian at the end of the third century AD – a system which continues in use among Egyptian Copts today. Jewish era dates, which are regularly inscribed on the cornerstones of synagogues, begin from Abraham. And within a hundred years of Dionysius another great religious era was inaugurated with the flight of Muhammad from Mecca to Medina. Dates in the Muslim world continue to be calculated from this event.

The Christian Era system of dating was initially used for scholarly purposes. Before, and for long after, his work political communities continued to date events with reference to various local chronologies, in the west typically regnal years of popes or local rulers. Some medieval historians, notably Cassiodorus and Bede, made use of the Christian chronological system, but most continued to date events in terms of local political chronology. The use of Christian era dates does not become widespread in Europe for 800 years after Dionysius calculated it, and even then it was only used for events "after Christ." The incorporation of pre-Christian events into this chronology, with the designation "B(efore) C(hrist)" does not begin until the seventeenth century AD. The Christian Era chronology remains in common use today. The alternative designations, C(ommon) E(ra) and B(efore) the C(ommon) E(ra), have been in use since the end of the nineteenth century; they do not, however, supplant the calculation of the Christian Era, only rechristen it.

Ancient Greek chronologies, though they record dates and events going back to the eighth century BC, are not attested before the end of the fifth century BC. So the Athenian archon list is first attested by a fragmentary inscription of the late fifth century (*IG* I^3 1031 = ML 6); the list itself we know from various sources included names of office-holders going back to 683 BC. We hear that a philosopher of the late fifth century renowned for his memory, Hippias of Elis, composed a list of Olympic victors, which presumably went back to the traditional foundation date of the festival in 776 BC (Plutarch *Numa* 1; Plato, *Hippias Maior* 285 E); and there are other instances as well.

The question of sources for the archaic period is one of the major problems in all of Greek history: the Greeks of the fifth century BC thought that they knew their chronologies and histories for at least three centuries before, yet we know almost nothing of their sources. Various solutions have been proposed: some believe that chronological lists must have been kept from the eighth century BC on, but that no evidence for them earlier than the fifth century has survived. Others believe that the traditions for the archaic period must stem from unattested written sources, such as archives. Others argue for oral tradition, or even simple fabrication. Or again the lists may have been composed on the basis of the evidence to hand, which would have included some written texts, oral tradition, and other kinds of evidence such as monumental dedications.

One political aspect of these early chronological lists is often overlooked: their original purpose is in large part honorific, and this element never recedes far from view. It was a great honor to give your name to a year, and at all times politicians sought this honor. The first inscriptional chronologies were displayed probably to honor office-holders and to give an incentive to others to seek like honors.

Traces of on the order of 200 chronological systems have survived from ancient Greece; most independent states developed their own systems for dating years. Typically these were based on sequences of local significance:

names of priests or priestesses, magistrates, victors in games, and the like. The position for which the year is named is described as "eponymous." So each year received its own name: for instance, "the archonship of Eukleides." In the modern Christian Era system of dating, years are numbered. So sequence and relation to other years are obvious from the notation itself. Thus the Athenian year named by "the archonship of Eukleides" corresponds to 404/3 BC in our dating system. In most ancient chronological systems years receive idiosyncratic names, which have no intrinsic relationship to each other. To put years in relation to one another, and to the present, one must know the list of magistrates by heart. It would be as though we dated events by regnal years of American presidents. The nature of the relationship between "the first year of Warren G. Harding's presidency" and "the first year of George W. Bush the younger's second term as president" is not obvious; and how long ago, precisely, was the first year of Garfield's presidency? By contrast, the chronological relationship between 1881 and 2001 is patent, even if the numerical system lacks the richness of connotation of the named sequence.

Even if an ancient Greek cared about the precise chronology of the distant past (and there is no reason to think that many of them had reason to do so), the information was not easily accessible. The nature of a chronological list of names discouraged numerical precision, as the welter of competing chronological schemes discouraged absolute dating and integrated universal history. Of course many ancients cared about tradition; but ancient history for many was a set of stories floating relatively free in a vague and imprecise time. The meaninglessness of chronology to many did not impugn the moral force of history. To some extent it may have contributed to the exemplary power of the past, by taking them out of time and idealizing them as eternal examples to be imitated. "Anachronism" is a vice only to modern historians, with our concern for precise dating and contextualization. Ancient historians no more worried about clothing Trojan heroes in the customs of their own time than ancient painters of pottery worried about dressing them in the armor of hoplites.

Ancient historians did worry about precise, integrated chronology, and their uniqueness in this respect is proven by the mere fact of their struggles to provide precision in the absence of satisfactory political chronology. So by the end of the fifth century BC when Thucydides came to write his history of the Peloponnesian war, he dated its outbreak in three ways: by the chief magistrates of the two major contenders, that is Athenian Archon and Spartan Ephor, and with reference to Priestess of Hera at Argos (2.2). Another historian, Hellanikos, had recently written a book on these priestesses, so presumably the chronology would have been more or less accessible to Thucydides' readers. Having established the beginning point he dates other events with reference to it: "sixteen years before the outbreak of the war," or "in the first year of the war," and so on. The system devised by Thucydides' great predecessor, Herodotus, to date events as far back as the mythical hero Herakles, is far more complex and impressive.

From the later fourth century BC on, increasing interest in providing a general chronological framework into which all of the past can be dissolved is apparent. Various "chronicles," or sequential lists of events were composed, and there were notable attempts to devise universal chronologies. The most important and famous of these was developed by an historian from Sicily, Timaeus of Tauromenium. In his work *Olympic Victors* (*Olympionikai*), Timaeus produced synchronized lists of victors in the Olympic footrace, Athenian archons, Spartan Kings and Ephors, and Priestesses of Hera at Argos. Henceforth some historians routinely dated events with reference to the Olympic competitions, which were held, in antiquity as now, every four years. Whatever the importance of this development for the practice of history, it had no importance for politics and society; Olympic chronology did not displace the various local chronologies of Greece for use in day-to-day transactions.

The Romans kept a chronological list of magistrates going back to the foundation of the Republic, in 509 BC, and even back through the regal period to the foundation of the city, in 753 BC (other dates are attested). Their eponymous officials were the two chief officers of the state, the consuls. As in the Greek case, the evidence for these lists is much later. The first Roman historians wrote in the second century BC; the first surviving chronologies date to the first century BC. Unlike the Greeks, however, the Romans of the Late Republic provide an account of their sources. The most important and controversial of these are the records produced by the board of state priests, the pontifices.

The pontifices were traditionally associated with the oldest methods of time-reckoning in the Roman state. We hear that the chief of the board, the Pontifex Maximus, kept a rudimentary chronology by driving a nail each year into the temple of Jupiter Optimus Maximus, on the citadel of Rome, the Capitoline hill. More importantly the board kept a list of magistrates, along with a list of notable religious occurrences of the year, and displayed it each year on wooden boards, outside the ceremonial residence of the Pontifex. These lists were compiled at the end of the second century BC, when they filled 80 books, called the *Annales Maximi*. Early Roman historians claim to have consulted these books, sometimes to their annoyance. The elder Cato criticized their lack of narrative coherence and the tedious lists of grain shortages and eclipses (*Origines*, frag. 77 Peter). The reliability of the earlier parts of the list is controversial, though the Romans regarded it as accurate. Be that as it may, a virtually complete list of consuls from 509 BC to AD 541 can be reconstructed. By the second century BC, though, there are contemporary literary and documentary sources, and in the first century BC we see the first epigraphically preserved consular chronologies, called *fasti*.

Alongside the official, politically-sanctioned dating system of consular years, was another system of dating, known as dating "from the foundation of the city," *ab urbe condita*, commonly abbreviated *AUC*. Livy most famously makes use of this system – in fact his history is commonly called the *Ab Urbe Condita*. The system was evidently devised by Livy's older contemporary, the polymath M. Terentius Varro (116–29 BC), doubtless under the influence of Greek chronological systems such as the Olympiads.

Roman chronology, like the Roman calendar, spread throughout the empire. Again, like the calendar, it was more uniformly used in the western, Latin-speaking half of the empire than in the east, and for the same reason: centralized political culture was more deeply entrenched in the east than in the west. So a whole variety of competing chronological systems continued to flourish through the years of Roman control.

Here again, as in the Greek case, there are three environments for chronology. There is the general social context: annual chronology probably mattered little to the bulk of the population of the Roman world. There is the political environment: for limited administrative purposes – enforcement of contracts, terms of office, penalties, and the like – it was necessary to keep track of the count of years, but only for the recent past. As in the Greek case, there was an honorific aspect to Roman chronology: to give one's name to the year conferred a certain kind of immortality, and senators in the Republic and Empire sought the honor vigorously. And finally there is the historiographic context.

Modern Dates for Ancient Events

Julius Caesar was killed in the year when Caesar was consul for the fifth time, and Antonius for the first time. The conversion of this date to the modern notation of "44 BC" is the result of centuries of work.

The first step in determining modern dates for ancient events was to reconstruct the various chronologies of the ancient world. From various sources sequential lists of Athenian archons or Roman consuls were reconstituted. Some lists are better known than others. The Athenian archon list, for example, is poorly attested in the sixth, but well attested in the fifth and fourth centuries BC. In the third century BC there are serious problems with the reconstruction; the state of the list improves again in the second century

BC. The list of Roman consuls is, with only a few problematic spots, solid from beginning to end.

Once the chronological lists have been reconstructed, they are correlated. For instance, if an historian mentions that an individual was archon in Athens in the same year that another was consul in Rome, the two lists can be drawn together at that point. The most important ancient chronologies are: the Egyptian Pharaoh Lists, which are particularly important for events from the Bronze Age through the archaic period; the list of Olympic victors and the Athenian Archon list, which are important for Greek antiquity; and the list of Roman consuls and *AUC* era dates, which provide the foundation for the chronology of the Hellenistic and Roman periods. Synchronisms among these lists (and others) are attested in thousands of instances, and thus a general chronology of the ancient world can be worked out.

But this chronology remains relative. To move from these various ancient dating systems to our modern notation it is necessary to "peg down" these systems with some absolute dates. Astronomy provides the key. The ancients compulsively noted celestial aberrations such as comets, regarding them as of fundamental importance. The most important of these, for the purposes of chronology, are solar and lunar eclipses, for astronomers can date these with precision. So, for instance, when Thucydides mentions an eclipse (and he mentions several in the course of his history, see e.g. the famously disastrous eclipse at 7.50), these provide us with absolute dates, which can in turn be used to fix absolutely his chronology of the war.

The chronology of the ancient world now found in books and laboriously memorized by students was determined over the course of several centuries. Much of the basic groundwork was accomplished from the sixteenth through the eighteenth centuries. The project was the collaborative labor of physicists and philologists, who compiled tables of hundreds of citations from the ancient texts, correlating these with astronomical tables of eclipses. One of the greatest of these "chronologers" was Joseph Scaliger (1540–1609), but many other famous intellectuals worked on the system as well. The physicist Isaac Newton (1643–1727), for example, not only wrote on problems of ancient chronology, but composed historical essays as well – in addition to his ground breaking work on problems such as gravity and optics.

Chronological work was considered important in the early modern period for a number of reasons. To begin with, chronology was the place where the natural and eternal time of God and the stars intersected with the evanescent "sublunary" doings of human kind. In a very real sense, what mattered to early chronologers was not so much the dating of events as the chronological system itself, because in the order of time God's providence was revealed. Thus some chronological work was turned to religious purposes – the famous calculations of the date of the creation by Bishop James Ussher (1581–1656), or attempts to predict the second coming and the end of the world. Some early chronologers deprecated such religious ends, but nevertheless insisted on the salutary moral and intellectual effects of the discipline required for the labor.

Periodization

Tables

Greek

Bronze Age (3000–1200)
Dark Ages (1200–800)
Archaic (800–480)
Classical (480–323)
Hellenistic (323–31)

Roman

Regal period 753–510
Early Republic 510–214
Middle Republic 214–133
Late Republic 133–31
Principate 31–96
High Empire 96–284
Late Empire 284–476

Periodization, the articulation of past time, is one of the most rudimentary forms of modern historical interpretation, and one of the first tasks for beginning students is to memorize the names and dates of the periods. Because periods are so basic to the practice of modern history, there is always the danger of treating them as though they were an objective reality. It is all the more important to realize that the currently accepted periodic organization of ancient history is an interpretation – as any periodic organization necessarily is. Periods do not exist in history; they are made by historians, and are always arbitrary: different interpretations of the past will require different periodizations: an economic history of Rome, for example, may be articulated differently than a political interpretation. For historical actors time may be broken up according to idiosyncratic personal experience: the eighteenth birthday or departure for college, for example, may retrospectively mark an "epoch" in a person's life.

For historical actors as they live in the moment, however, time is experienced as a continuum. Yet modern historians find periods essential for their work, and so use them anyway, because they are "good to think with." The constitution of a period is a simplification. Though there may be differences from one period to the next, there are also always similarities, continuities. What needs to be understood is the motivation for marking a break at a particular point: What story is implied by the particular periodization?

The impulse to periodize is one of definition and differentiation. Periods are defined by certain qualities that distinguish them from what goes before and what comes after. In the first place, though, periods are used to distinguish past from present: they mark out something distinctive from the point of view of the historian. Consequently periodization is bound up with some of the leading modern historical notions: for example, anachronism or progress, depending on whether the period is conceived as similar or different from the present.

The very idea of Greco-Roman antiquity must be understood not as a reality, but as a periodization – that is, as the creation of historians. In one of the most notable developments of western historiography, scholars of the Renaissance attempted to distance themselves from their immediate past, which they characterized as a degenerate interruption: thus they name it Medieval. Petrarch (1304–74) is usually considered the first to have dismissed the thousand years between the end of Rome and his own time as an age of darkness, the "Middle Ages." His own time he and his contemporaries imagined as a "rebirth," or "reflowering" (the word "Renaissance" is somewhat later than Petrarch) of the ideals of antiquity. Here then is created a grand tripartite division of time: Antiquity, Middle Ages and Modernity. By the seventeenth century the familiar dichotomy of ancient vs. modern will have emerged from this initial discrimination. This fifteenth-century periodization continues to resound in contemporary scholarship.

The Renaissance periodization of history was not the first attempt to articulate the past. From the beginning Christians had a lively sense that the coming of Christ had inaugurated a new era in human affairs. The Church father Augustine proposed to divide all of human history into four kingdoms. There are some indications that Greek and Roman historians as well had a rudimentary sense of historical periods. Homer, for example, can observe that his heroes can heft stones or cups that "many men today could not budge." Hesiod notoriously proposed a vision of the past divided into periods distinguished by typologies of metal – though his "ages" seem too schematic and typologized to correspond to our modern ideas of historical periods. Romans of the Republic had a lively sense of their own degeneracy, and spent much time arguing about when the decline had set in. And so on.

Nevertheless, the sense of periodization in antiquity is by and large very weak; dimly realized, it never achieved the reification of periods in the modern world. Nor are these internally consistent, which is the heart of the modern idea of the period: that is, ancients did not think of periods as historical fields, which delimit a context of interpretation for events within them. Homer does not attempt to delineate a historically contextual account of the Trojan War consistent with the putative uniqueness of the heroic age. This is chiefly because ancients, unlike moderns, had a strong sense of continuity with their past. Thus too, they had very little sense of "anachronism." Periodization is about the recognition of discontinuity, not continuity. For Athenians of the fifth century, the heroes who fought at Troy were essentially like them; just so the Romans imitated ancestors who might have been better, but were not fundamentally different. Periodization and a sense of the historical world are bound up with each other. Division of the present from the past and the past into various periods is a denial of the importance of tradition; periodization emphasizes the difference of the past from the present world, as the idea of the historicity of past events is conducive to dividing the past into periods.

As Joseph Scaliger pointed the way to the modern chronology of the ancient world, he was among the first to attempt to divide human history into reasoned and coherent fields. The specific periods now in use in Greek and Roman history, however, need be traced back no further than the eighteenth century. The origins of the present scheme of Greek history are due chiefly to the influence of an art historian, Johann Winckelmann (1717–68). When thinking about culture, Winckelmann used the analogy of a living organism: plants and animals grow, mature, and decay. This paradigm is not original with him; the Italian Humanists of the fourteenth and fifteenth centuries also typically broke history in three periods, beginning from a central period, defining what preceded it as "development," and what followed as "decline." The influence of the idea continues to be felt; the triplets into which ancient history is repeatedly broken should be understood to reflect an implicit biological metaphor.

The core periods of Greek history stem from Winckelmann's typology of Greek sculpture. Winckelmann distinguished four periods: a "severe style" (through 460); a "high" style (460–400); a "beautiful" style (400–320); and the "decline of art" after the conquests of Alexander the Great. The Archaic, Classical, and Hellenistic periods can be recognized in this typology. The standard historical names for the periods gradually became standardized. "Archaic" came into common use in the course of the nineteenth century, and traditionally describes the developments leading into the Classical. "Classical" was a loan word from Latin and was applied generally to the "best" periods of ancient art and literature (as it continues to be) from

the eighteenth century on. The designation "Hellenistic," for the period
after the conquest of Alexander, was coined by the German historian Johann
Gustav Droysen (1808–84) in 1833. This was regarded as a period of deca-
dence, a falling away from the standards of the Classical, due in some part
to the miscegenation of the Greeks with various barbarian peoples. The
scheme has survived for three hundred years, though not without some
elaboration. Archaeological research in the late nineteenth and twentieth
centuries opened up Greek pre-history. The Bronze Age was identified with
the period of the Homeric heroes; the "Dark Ages" with a period of poverty
and ignorance (somewhat like the Renaissance vision of the Middle Ages),
about which little could be known.

The association of the Bronze Age with Homeric heroes was an attempt
to reconcile this new archaeological evidence with the traditional periodic
organization of Greek history; the dismissal of the "Dark Ages" is part of
this effort. The classical Greeks are the inheritors of Homer, not of impov-
erished savages. Yet the subsistence of this gap remains troubling, and has
had a destabilizing effect on the general picture. As more becomes known
of the "Dark Ages," as the nature of the Homeric poetry is elucidated, the
general background of the classical world becomes more suspect. The Dark
Ages are not an interruption, but the origin of classical civilization. The
Homeric Bronze Age is a pipe dream, a fiction.

The present periodization of Roman history has not got the straightfor-
ward pedigree of the Greek, nor is there the uniformity of designation;
different national traditions, for example, divide the Republic and Empire in
different ways. The periodization of Roman history is the result of a more
complex development, emerging in part from attempts to organize the
history of literature, in part from typologies of art or sequences of
archaeology, and in part from divisions that go back all the way to proposals
of the Romans themselves. For example, the basic discrimination between
Republic and Empire was one that some Romans seem to have insisted on,
and has ever since been observed. The subordinate divisions of the Republic
and Empire are far less reified and regular than the divisions of Greek
history. The threefold division of the Republic into early, preliterate times
(509 until roughly 250), middle, down to the time of the Gracchi, and late,
the age of Cicero and Caesar, develops out of a literary typology, first
proposed by Friedrich von Schlegel (1772–1829) at the beginning of the
nineteenth century. So too does the division of the Empire into three
periods, including Principate (to 96), "high" empire, the period already said
by Gibbon at the end of the eighteenth century to be the happiest in
the history of the human race (96–193). Late Antiquity emerged from
typologies of art history, and was traditionally considered a period of deca-
dence (beginning variously with the end of the Antonine dynasty (193), the

end of the Severan dynasty and the beginning of the crisis of the third century (231), the accession of Diocletian (287), or even with Constantine (306). The first to use the name was the Swiss historian Jacob Burckhardt (1818–97), at the end of the nineteenth century. Since the beginning of the twentieth century there have been attempts to discard the vision of Late Antiquity as one of decline, in favor of seeing it as a period of birth, birth of the "middle ages," or better, as a culture of its own, not defined as "pre-" or "post" anything else.

Again, recent discoveries have led to challenges and compromises with traditional periodizations. Archaeological investigations of prehistoric periods have been most unsettling. For example, in archaeological publications on the early history of Rome, one can see disturbing pressures brought to bear on schemes derived from literary sources – for example, the periodization of the regal period and the foundation of the Republic, or the relationship between Latium and Etruria; at the same time, interestingly enough, it is clear that archaeologists are often predisposed to reconcile their new discoveries with traditional narratives.

Conclusion

Toward the beginning of the eighteenth century John Potter published a well regarded account of "Greek antiquities" (*Archaeologiae Graecae*, 2 vols., London 1698–9). Writing in the wake of the "Battle of the Books," Potter was sensitive to the differences between his own world and the world of the Greeks and Romans. Nevertheless, when he turned to the ancient world, he did not attempt to deal with sources according to their periods, but cited from authors indiscriminately: so, for example, in treating the literary evidence for ancient shields he discusses citations from Homer, Vergil, and Martial side-by-side. It is not that he regards the history of antiquity as a chaotic, senseless jumble. To the contrary, for Potter – as for most historians from the Renaissance down to the nineteenth century – the ancient world formed a seamless, exemplary whole that could be exploited without regard to historical differences within it. The lessons of virtue taught by Greeks and Romans were universal, and hence entirely coherent and comparable.

The historicist conception of time only replaces the exemplary notion gradually, and it never entirely supplants it. The tension between exemplarity and historicism remains very much alive – as it should, for the two complement one another. Contextual interpretation produces nuanced understanding; but the past only matters if we are willing to grant it a place in the present. Homer and Thucydides, Vergil and Tacitus, can be treated as "children of their own generation." As such they become mere historical curiosities. Such authors have survived and continue to be read, however, because many have felt that what they have to say in some respects transcends their bounded circumstance. The vindication of the past from forgetfulness and irrelevance depends on the willingness of the living to identify with it. Most of our dead fade into the documentary oblivion of archives and photograph albums and family Bibles, as though they had possessed no name or reputation in life. To the extent anything or anyone lives on it is through identification, in the hearts and characters of the living (cf. Tacitus, *Agricola* 46).

Bibliographical Essay

On the chronology of the ancient world see in the first instance Elias J. Bickerman, *Chronology of the Ancient World* (*Aspects of Greek and Roman Life*), London 1980; Alan E. Samuel, *Greek and Roman Chronology: Calendars and Years in Classical Antiquity* (*Handbuch der Altertumswissenschaft*, 1, 7), Munich 1972. The most famous and best attested Greek calendar is the Athenian: compare the general account of Benjamin D. Meritt, *The Athenian Year* (*Sather Classical Lectures*, 32), Berkeley 1961, and W. K. Pritchett's more technical comments, most recently in *Athenian Calendars and Ekklesias* (*Archaia Hellas*, 6), Amsterdam 2001. On the Roman Republican calendar start with Agnes Michels, *The Calendar of the Roman Republic*, Princeton 1967. For a readable general history of the western calendar, see David E. Duncan, *The Calendar: the 5000-Year Struggle to Align the Clock and the Heavens, and What Happened to the Missing Ten Days*, London 1998.

Introduction

For the predominance of exemplary thinking in ancient historiography see Jane D. Chaplin's nuanced book on *Livy's Exemplary History*, Oxford 2000; more generally see Reinhard Koselleck, "Modernity and the Planes of Historicity," and "Historia Magistra Vitae: the Dissolution of the Topos into the Perspective of a Modernized Historical Process," both reprinted in his *Futures Past: on the Semantics of Historical Time*, Cambridge, Mass. 1985, 3–38. For the time-reckoning of medieval peasants see Emmanuel Le Roy Ladurie, *Montaillou: Cathars and Catholics in a French Village, 1294–1324*, London 1978.

Chronology

On the origins of Greek chronography, Charles W. Hedrick, Jr., "The Prehistory of Greek Chronography," in V. Gorman and E. Robinson, eds., *Oikistes: Studies in Constitutions, Colonies and Military Power in the Ancient World, Offered in Honor of A. J. Graham* (*Mnemosyne* supp. 233), Brill 2002, 13–32; for early Roman chronography see Gregory S. Bucher, "The *Annales Maximi* in the Light of Roman Methods of Keeping Records," *AJAH* 12 (1995), 2–61.

Modern dates for ancient events

For a table of synchronisms between the ancient chronologies and astronomical events, see the appendix to Elias J. Bickerman, *Chronology of the Ancient World* (*Aspects of Greek and Roman Life*), London 1980. On the work of chronographers from the sixteenth to eighteenth centuries see James Johnson, "Chronological Writing: its Concepts and Development," *History and Theory* 2 (1962), 124–45; Anthony Grafton, "Joseph Scaliger and Historical Chronology," *History and Theory* 14 (1975), 156–85. For a medieval example of the ideological importance of the chronology in and of itself, see Hayden White, "The Value of Narrativity in the Representation of History," reprinted in his *The Content of Form: Narrative Discourse and Historical Representation*, Baltimore 1987, 1–25.

Periodization

The bibliography on ancient periodization is almost entirely in German: begin with the soon-to-be translated article "Epochenbegriffe" in the *Neue Pauly* 13; in English one may consult the more general essay by René Wellek on "Periodization in History" in Philip Wiener, ed., *Dictionary of the History of Ideas: Studies of Selected Pivotal Ideas*, New York 1973, vol. 3, 476–86. On the work of Joseph Scaliger and much else, see Anthony Grafton, *Joseph Scaliger, A Study in the History of Classical Scholarship*, 2 vols., Oxford 1983–93, especially the second volume, on historical chronology. For the history of the Greek period of "the Dark Ages," see Ian Morris, "Periodization and the Heroes: Inventing a Dark Age," in M. Golden and P. Toohey, eds., *Inventing Ancient Culture: Historicism, Periodization, and the Ancient World*, Routledge 1997, 96–131; on the status of "Late Antiquity" as an integral period, see the introduction to Glen W. Bowersock, Peter Brown, and Oleg Grabar, *Late Antiquity: a Guide to the Post Classical World*, Cambridge, Mass. 1999. On John Potter and the nature of his writing on Greek antiquities, see Joseph Levine, *The Battle of the Books: History and Literature in the Augustan Age*, Ithaca 1991, 165–7.

4

Literary Texts

Penguin Evidence

I owe my first experience of a "primary source" for Greco–Roman history to a Penguin paperback, Robert Graves' venerable translation of Suetonius' spicy *Lives of the Twelve Caesars* (first published the year after I was born, 1957). Such literary accounts are certainly the most extensive, accessible, and palatable sources for ancient history available to undergraduates. Professionals too have traditionally used them as their primary guides to antiquity. Modern narratives of the Peloponnesian War or the early Roman Principate are frequently little more than respectful rehashes of Thucydides or Tacitus, supplemented where possible by archaeology or epigraphy.

Any literary account is a retrospective, self-conscious interpretation of historical events, far removed from "primary evidence" – that is, evidence that attests by the very fact of its existence an historical event. Suetonius, for example, writes a century after the events that he recounts, never at less than three degrees of separation from "primary evidence:" his tale is based on earlier literary sources, which are in turn based on "primary evidence," or on yet other literary accounts. His writing *is* "primary evidence" for the literary pretensions of imperial courtiers in the second century AD; it is *not* "primary evidence" for the life of Julius Caesar. In certain cases, literary texts may have a closer relationship to events. Thucydides, for example, was an eyewitness of the Peloponnesian War; he says that he kept an account of the war "as it happened." Yet his history is not primary evidence, except insofar as it is regarded as a reflexive product of its times; it is an exquisitely considered interpretation, written with the full benefit of hindsight.

This general problem besets the use of any literary text, ancient or modern, as evidence. Even so, historians can with due caution reasonably use the accounts of literary authors as sources; when they do so, however, another more specific set of issues arises. Ancient texts were not written, circulated, or read in the same ways as modern mass-produced texts. The contemporary experience of reading a text like that of the Penguin paperback of Suetonius is a deformation, the more insidious for its subtlety, of the ancient experience of reading a manuscript. Modern appreciation of the historical significance of ancient literary texts has been complicated by changes in the nature of books themselves, and these differences reinforce the modern idea of the document.

Most students will never read an ancient author except through the intermediary of a modern text. The same is true of most professionals. Of course, a competent Greek or Roman historian can read Polybius or Cato in the original Greek or Latin; few, however, will have any experience of these authors except through modern critical editions. They do not approach the authors through the manuscripts, which provide, after all, the only evidence for the texts. Even scholars expert in the manuscript tradition by and large approach the ancient texts imbued with the systematic, totalizing purposes of modern textual criticism.

Before the fifteenth century, literary texts, whether Greek or Roman, Chinese or Arab, were produced by scribes. The attitudes toward scribal work in the Middle Ages reflected a Christian sensibility, but the basic technological situation remained consistent with that of antiquity. The texts produced by the scribal tradition varied from copy to copy, the quality depending on the attentiveness and ability of the scribe. With the introduction of moveable type and the printing press in the fifteenth century, however, the fundamental character of the book changed. It became possible to produce vast numbers of identical copies of texts, and this change affected every aspect of literary work – including composition, format, dissemination, and reading.

Modern translations of most ancient authors are the product of the cumulative labor of scholars in the five centuries since Gutenberg. The possibility of manufacturing widely disseminated standardized texts led to the characteristic practices of modern scholarship and the systematic art of the textual critic. The printed texts that we now cite as evidence for our histories are not the raw materials of the literary tradition, the ruinous "monuments" of ancient authors exemplified by the venerable and imperfect manuscripts surviving to us, but finely honed implements of scholarly research. The texts have been collected, sanitized, and homogenized for the use of the general scholarly public: examples of the manuscript tradition have been converted to authoritative documents. When modern historians appeal to the evidence of ancient authors in modern editions, they refer to processed and technical tools of academic research, not to the socially embedded relics of ancient writers. In their pursuit of the author's original words, modern editors conceal the corruptions and mistakes and damage that characterize any particular manuscript of the text, consigning them to the oblivion of footnotes or critical apparatus, and in the case of most translations omitting them entirely. The political and cultural significance of the text resides not in what the author intended, but in its reception. Consequently the modern reader who wants to make historical sense of an ancient author needs to be equipped to pierce the armature of modern scholarship and recover some sense of the nature of the ancient book. This ability will have the reflexive result of enhancing sensibility of the social context of modern, printed literature as well.

Writing and Early Literary Texts

The Greeks learned to write from Phoenicians about 800 BC. From Greece the alphabet passed to Italy and the Romans by about 700 BC, and thence it was conveyed to western Europe. Writing systems existed earlier and independent of the Greek alphabet. Sumerian cuneiform was in use by the middle of the fourth millennium BC, Egyptian hieroglyphics by the middle of the third millennium. Independent of these, Meso-American civilizations invented a writing system in the first millennium AD. Inhabitants of the Greek mainland used a syllabary called "Linear B" in the second millennium BC; it perished with the palatial political organization of the Bronze Age, around 1200 BC. Knowledge of Linear B was restricted to a scribal class; it was used chiefly for record keeping. With the fall of the palaces, the context for the use of writing vanished, and so the Greeks "forgot" how to write for about 400 years. The event is instructive: writing is not simply an intellectual matter, but requires a social base for its development and continuation. The introduction of the alphabet at the beginning of the eighth century was implicated with the emergence of a new political environment, the Greek polis; the practice of writing would not henceforth be so much restricted to the political and economic ends of government, but more integrated with society in general. Among the earliest Greek texts we possess are snippets of poetry, such as the metrical text, incised on a vase: "who now of the dancers sports most shamelessly:" perhaps a prize for dancing (Jeffery, *LSAG*, 15–16, 68, 76). Another text on an early vase alludes to the Homeric poems: "I am the cup of Nestor" (*ML* 1).

The use of writing to support the circulation of literary writing needs to be understood in the context of the society of the polis. Texts of authors were being copied and circulated in Greece by the sixth century BC. The few details known about the specific circumstances of their production and dissemination suggest a world alien even by the standards of later Greco-Roman scribal culture. Thus, for example, we hear that the philosopher Heraclitus dedicated his book of philosophy in the sanctuary of Artemis at Ephesos (Diogenes Laertius, *Lives*, 9. 6). The Athenian tyrant-family, the Peisistratids, supposedly had a copy of the Homeric poems written down, either as a check on the inconsistent performances of rhapsodes, who recited it from memory, or in order to glorify Athens and their own regime (if we can believe Cicero, *De Oratore* 3.137). The compositions of the fifth-century dramatists were evidently memorized by the actors through oral instruction; texts later regarded as authoritative were lodged (as dedications?) in the Athenian Shrine of the Mother Goddess, the Metroon. How these scripts originally came to be written down is a mystery: the received texts show signs of "actors' interpolations." The texts of authors of the archaic and early classical periods were at some point copied and disseminated: they would not otherwise have survived in any form, fragmentary or otherwise. The details of the process are elusive until the later fifth century.

Although the earliest surviving Greek literary manuscript is a papyrus scroll of the late fourth century BC, discovered in a grave at Derveni in Macedon, books may be seen on vase paintings of the sixth and fifth centuries; by the end of the fifth century we find references to booksellers in Athens (e.g. Eupolis frag. 305 K). By this time, we also know that books were being exported from Athens. It is also clear from vase paintings that books were being used in schools for basic instruction in reading; Plato and other philosophers gave readings of texts they had written. Collections of texts ("libraries") are likewise attested late. We first hear of book collections from the Athenian comic playwrights. From the fourth century Plato's Academy and Aristotle's Lyceum both possessed "libraries," though details of them are benighted.

In Rome the early evidence for book production suggests a situation somewhat different than in Greece. Earliest uses of writing are dedicatory, funerary, and administrative – religious regulations in particular are among the earliest texts known. Use of writing to disseminate texts in multiple copies is only attested rather late, and clearly under the influence of Greek models. We first hear of texts being copied and circulated (as opposed to inscribed and displayed) in Rome in the middle of the third century BC – and these are Greek texts. It would not be surprising if other Greek texts circulated somewhat earlier. Latin texts notoriously were not written for circulation until the end of the third and beginning of the second century, again clearly under Greek influence. Thus the earliest Roman poets, such as Ennius, write Latin only pursuant to Greek. The earliest Roman prose authors wrote in Greek, and the first to write in Latin, Cato, protests too much his contempt for Greek literature and for those Romans who do not find their own language good enough for literature.

Alexander's conquest of Egypt and the foundation of the Ptolemaic monarchy mark a watershed in our knowledge of Greek literary production. Because of Egypt's dry climate ancient papyri have survived in quantity; books are found whole in jars, cut in strips and used to manufacture cartonnage (papier-mâché) to encase mummies; or they are found discarded in ancient city-dumps. Henceforth we are very well informed about the appearance of ancient books and the circumstances of their production.

The Library at Alexandria was founded by the first of the Ptolemies and expanded by his successor. It is said to have contained at its peak anywhere from 100,000 to 700,000 books, and the Ptolemies were notoriously unscrupulous when presented with an opportunity to add to the collection. Boats entering the harbor at Alexandria, for example, were supposedly searched for books, and desirable copies were confiscated for the library. Not only books in Greek, but in any language, were collected and examined: for example the translation of the Hebrew Bible into Greek by "The Seventy," the Septuagint, is reputedly owed to the patronage of the Ptolemies.

The Ptolemies also supported writing and study in an institution known as the "shrine of the Muses," the Museum. The great library at Alexandria may have had some connection with this Museum, and the fact is interesting, because we know that the individuals associated with the Museum were concerned among other things to improve the quality of the texts. The endeavor is best attested in connection with Homer. Before the period of Alexandrian scholarship, the circulating texts of the Iliad and Odyssey were surprisingly heterogeneous. The rare earlier papyri of these texts include passages, for example, that are unknown to the later manuscript tradition. Scholars of the Museum took an interest in sanitizing Homer and their work had a substantial impact on the later reception. The Alexandrians created the text subsequently transmitted.

After the foundation of the Library and Museum at Alexandria other Hellenistic Kingdoms, perhaps in emulation, also established libraries; scholars are sometimes known to have been associated with these collections. The most famous and largest was the collection at Pergamum. Others too are known, such as that of the last autonomous king of Macedon, Perseus.

Public libraries in Rome are not known until the first century BC. Private collections certainly existed. The conqueror of Macedon, L. Aemilius Paullus is said to have removed the library of Perseus to Rome after 167. The sybaritic Lucullus is said to have possessed a large collection of books, as did Cicero. The first "public library" in Rome, however, was not founded until the end of the first century by the wealthy and independent historian of the age of Augustus, Asinius Pollio. Augustus himself soon followed suit and established two libraries.

Circumspection is warranted when gauging the influence of libraries on the transmission of ancient books. Certainly books at these libraries were consulted, and some influential individuals may have been able to borrow texts; but the extent of circulation and the nature of the clientele are uncertain. And despite the evident contributions of scholars of the Alexandrian Museum to the text of Homer, it is far from clear that books in libraries were used as authoritative copies to check corruptions in the general book-trade.

Appearance and Production of Ancient Books

The Greeks and Romans wrote on practically all materials that could conceivably bear writing, including fronds, fabric, leather, and wood. For literature, however, the two most important materials were papyrus, whence derives the modern word "paper," and parchment.

Papyrus was used for writing in Egypt from the third millennium BC. It is made from the triangular stalks of the papyrus plant, which is indigenous to the marshes of Lower Egypt. The rind is removed and the fibrous pith is peeled away in strips. Two layers of these strips are laid down at right angles to one another and hammered together, releasing a sap that cements the layers together. Thus the one side of the finished sheet, typically used in the first instance as the writing surface, has plant fibers running horizontally; the back has fibers running vertically. From Hellenistic times the size of these sheets was a fairly uniform nine by nine inches. About 20 of them would be pasted together to make a scroll.

Parchment, on the other hand, was made from animal hides. The difference between leather and parchment depends on the tanning process. Leather is cured using tannin, parchment with alum and chalk. The finest parchment is scraped to translucency; either side of the sheet might be used for writing, though they were of unequal quality. In the case of coarser parchments, the difference may be immediately distinguishable to the touch. The "hair" side of parchment is typically rougher; the "meat" side has a smoother texture.

Although papyrus grew only in Egypt, material for parchment was available everywhere animals grazed. Both materials are light and strong, though parchment is considerably more durable. The raw materials for papyrus were cheaper, though the Egyptian monopoly might inflate the price. Nevertheless, papyrus was far the more common writing material in antiquity; parchment did not displace it as the material of choice until the fourth century AD, in connection with the spread of the codex format – that is, the modern book-form.

Ancient books took the form of scrolls, long sheets of paper that were stored in rolls. Text was written on one side of the scroll, laid out across the scroll from left to right, in columns called "paginae," whence comes the modern word "page." So readers could unroll the scroll to display a single column entire and after finishing roll on to the next. Scrolls had to be read with two hands; readers passed the text before their eyes by unrolling it with their right hand and re-rolling it with their left. Knobs of wood or metal marked the ends of the roll. The length of rolls varied considerably; the "books" into which ancient literature has come down to us divided presumably reflect a conventional size: an ancient book of poetry typically runs between 700 and 900 lines.

In contrast to modern books, scrolls are awkward to store and liable to be crushed; they are not easily portable, nor can they conveniently be read without a large table. Casual consultation of sections of them is difficult; one cannot simply flip to the page desired, but must roll through the entire work. A dictionary written on a scroll, for example, would be very cumbersome to consult. Students may compare the difference between a videotape and a DVD. A videotape, like a scroll, rolls through the entire movie; it is difficult to sample various scenes, and only the kind trouble to rewind after a viewing. By contrast, one can jump easily from place to place on a DVD, as one can in a book.

With the advent of the codex-form in the fourth century AD, text was written on sheets that were folded to form individual pages, called folia, or "leaves." The group of pages formed by the fold is called a "quire." A number of quires would then be sewn together to form the codex. Writing was arranged on front and back of each page in a column or two. A codex easily contains the writing of many scrolls. Furthermore, since sheets were sandwiched together flat rather than rolled, the codex is more durable than the scroll. The codex is also more versatile than the scroll, since one can easily and quickly leap from place to place in it by simply turning a stack of pages. These advantages have made the codex the most common form for organizing writing in the world today.

As the codex triumphs, parchment replaces papyrus as the preferred material for books. The change is doubtless related to the adoption of the codex form, because papyrus, when repeatedly folded and bent (as is necessary for the construction and reading of a codex) will finally break. Supple parchment better suits the codex form, and indeed the few surviving fourth century AD parchment manuscripts remain usable after more than 1,500 years.

In early times Greek and Roman books were typically written in capital, or block letters. Later deluxe copies of literary texts continued to be written in capital letters. Cheaper copies of literary texts, like utilitarian records, were often written "long-hand," in a flowing and rapid cursive. Punctuation and word-divisions are seldom to be found at all in ancient writing; consistent usage of punctuation gradually came into being with the introduction of printing.

The general circumstances of book production were constant throughout Greco-Roman antiquity, and indeed elsewhere, down through the Middle Ages. There was only the most rudimentary institutional support for the making and distribution of texts. Certainly there was nothing like the modern profession of the "publisher"; that is to say, in antiquity no one took the position of middleman between author and public, paying the writer for the right to sell and distribute a work and receiving in return a monopoly over reproduction of the text. Nor did the ancients have anything like modern copyright law, which was first promulgated in the early modern period, not to protect the intellectual property of authors, but the investments of printers. Once an ancient author "released" the book it could be copied and disseminated promiscuously. The ancient Greek word that corresponds most closely to our modern "publication" is *ekdosis*, and it means something much more like "release" or even "abandonment." It is possible that authors made some money when they handed over the initial copy of the work; at that point they still had something to sell. But once the work was in circulation it became, from the author's point of view, valueless.

What incentive then did authors have to "publish" their works at all? Political writers, such as Cicero, circulated their works to sway public opinion and justify themselves. Historians may have had similar motives, if we think of history as an extension of ancient political activity. But surely such motives must have been far removed from the thoughts of poets? How did writers who were not wealthy support themselves? Some tangible benefits likely accrued from the release of a book. Thus we know that at the time of Augustus a number of authors, including Vergil, were supported by the patronage of the wealthy; presumably the reputation that came from the circulation of a work played its part in convincing a wealthy man like Augustus' friend Maecenas to support him. Presumably too authors supported themselves by giving recitations of their works; and reputation will have helped them drum up other patrons or pupils.

Copyists, by contrast, had a product to sell: actual texts, which they produced on commission. Some popular texts were evidently produced in numbers for general sale or distribution. We occasionally hear for example of copies produced by dictating to a number of copyists, in order to produce a "run" of a book for general distribution quickly.

Prices varied considerably, depending on the quality of the book. Papyrus, for example, came in various qualities; a roll might cost 2–4 drachmas, the equivalent of several days' pay for an unskilled laborer. Labor costs also varied. Copyists billed by the line, and charged more for certain styles and presentations. A cursive, for example, was faster and therefore cheaper to produce than a laborious block style. Legibility cost extra. Flourishes, illustrations, and rubrics for example, added to the price of the book as well. Average costs of books are impossible to know, and prices were probably not standardized. We hear of short, cheap books in the second century AD that cost as little as 5–6 drachmas, more than a day's wage for a skilled craftsman. A deluxe copy might cost several times as much, and a collectible or rare text could command almost any price.

Copyists were generally small-time craftsmen of low social status. They might be, but need not be, slaves. Wealthier individuals employed their own scribes. Political authors such as Cicero were able at need to get access to numbers of scribes for quick production and distribution of their work. Free men might work independently in a stall in the market, working at a "piece rate," on commission. Others still might be attached to workshops at the service of an office or library or bookseller. Booksellers frequently doubled as book producers. For example, the Roman poet Martial speaks of bookshops in the Forums of Rome that had books scrolls hanging up for display on their awnings. Such shops produced their own books and might employ or own a number of scribes. We also hear of itinerant booksellers who hawked books door-to-door, much as Bibles and encyclopedias used to be sold in America.

Reading

In the pre-industrial world the vast majority of the population lived and farmed in the countryside. There was no public education; those who wished to read had to teach themselves or pay someone else to teach them. Comparative evidence suggests that the literacy rate produced in such circumstances must have been low, perhaps somewhere between 10 and 20 percent of the population. Literacy was the preserve of the upper classes and of professionals, such as scribes. The point is perhaps confirmed by the expense of texts. Acquisition of books, never mind a library, was beyond the reach of all but a few.

Reading and writing in antiquity were often practiced in groups rather than individually, in private. The group practice of reading was reinforced in educational methods. Those children who did attend school learned to read and write by a process of memorization. A well known text was memorized, and once it was familiar it was puzzled out on the page. Writing was practiced by taking dictation in the manner of scribes. The teacher read out the text and the students wrote it down. Likewise scribes also sometimes made multiple copies of books by taking dictation as a group. Highly literate individuals, such as Cicero and Caesar, often composed by dictating to a scribe rather than working alone with pen in hand.

In more public environments texts were often "performed." So when reading is portrayed in vase painting it is frequently in the context of a group. Public postings and inscriptions sometimes include a provision that they be read aloud to those interested. More commonly we hear of recitations of literary works being offered by the authors and others. Even when reading to oneself, it was common to read aloud, not to read silently as we do today. Of course, some people may have read silently to themselves, but ancient literature was written to be heard rather than read.

Oral reading suited the circumstances of the ancient book. In an era when books could not easily be produced in great numbers, when literacy was limited, it increased the accessibility of the text. At the same time, group reading contributed to the sense of community: the experience of reading in the ancient world was social, not private.

Continuity of the Manuscript Tradition

In antiquity books owed their survival to the tastes of the elite and the work of scribes. In the eastern half of the Mediterranean there is continuity from the late Roman Empire to the Byzantine period. Political continuity provided a stable environment for the production and reading of literature, and the transmission of ancient Greek literature for this reason continued largely uninterrupted down to the time of the crusades. Manuscripts of ancient authors continued to be produced and preserved by the wealthy. Certainly there was decline in learning; and the conversion of the elite to Christianity played a part in decisions about what to preserve. Yet the essential techniques of book production and distribution remained unchanged. In the west the situation is somewhat different. The disintegration of the Roman Empire disrupted the elites who had traditionally collected books. Even here the methods of book production remain the same: books continue to be produced by scribes. But they are now produced for different people.

In the fourth century AD Ammianus remarked on the book collections possessed by the great Roman aristocratic families (14.6.19). Two centuries later these libraries had vanished, replaced by collections of the Christian Church. The church, of course, preferred Christian writings to pagan writings. Nevertheless, substantial numbers of manuscripts containing the writings of the old Roman writers found their way into the collections of monasteries and churches. How and why this happened is a mystery.

There is also a geographical division in the preservation of literature. As the Romans acquired their empire in the eastern half of the Mediterranean in the second century BC, they continued to use the existing political language, Greek, for administrative purposes. By the beginning of the fourth century AD the linguistic division hardened into an administrative one. The empire itself was divided into halves, one Latin-speaking, the other Greek-speaking. Latin literature was more widely read in the west, Greek in the east. With the collapse of the west in the fifth century AD the division was exacerbated. During the Middle Ages Greek was largely forgotten in Italy and Greek manuscripts vanished from collections.

The introduction of the codex in the fourth century AD created a kind of "bottleneck" in the transmission of manuscripts. Scrolls were discarded; works that were to survive had to be transferred to the new format. Not every manuscript was judged worthy of the time and trouble of recopying. So the tastes of the fourth and fifth century AD dictated to an extent what survived to the modern world. A comparable bottleneck, occasioned by the popularization of a new script, occurred in the ninth century AD. Whereas before literary texts had typically been written in block letters (majuscule), henceforth texts would generally be written in a more economical format, the minuscule. Again at this time some authors fell out of the tradition.

In the west, from roughly the sixth century AD to the eleventh century, the preservation of ancient literature is owed almost entirely to the Christian Church. The copying of manuscripts in this environment became a religious discipline. Monks gathered in monastic scriptoria to copy texts. The choice of what was preserved and recopied and what was allowed to rot was determined by the ideals of Christianity. In the eleventh century "scholastic" culture emerges; with the growth of large cities, the first medieval universities take shape and learning and books move from the monastery back out into the secular world. The leading academic discipline of the day was law.

From this environment spring the "humanists" of the fourteenth century and the Renaissance. These scholars cultivated traditional areas of learning: grammar, rhetoric, history, poetry, and moral philosophy. The language of learning was Latin, and eloquence on the model of the ancients, especially Cicero, was highly valued. Wealthy and politically powerful individuals used history and the critical examination of texts as a weapon in political feuds. Monastic libraries were rifled for new copies of old texts, and texts that were so far unknown.

At this point, though, learning was almost exclusively a matter of the Latin tradition. The Greeks, though highly regarded, were known only by their reputation among the Roman authors. The west rediscovered Greek literature as a result of the Crusades; the most famous of these, the Fourth Crusade of 1204, led to the sack of Byzantium and the export of booty to the west, including perhaps some Greek manuscripts. The main export of Greek literature and scholars to the west came with the destruction of

Byzantium by the Turks in 1453. The core of the repertory of Greek and Roman authors now available was disseminated in Europe after this time.

Printing Press and Modern Books

The introduction of moveable type and the printing press in Europe in the fifteenth century introduced in its essentials the book in the form that continues to be familiar today. The fundamental difference between ancient and modern books lies in the fact that modern books are printed. Printing imposes a particular logic on the production of books. The labor involved in setting type is greater than that of manually copying a single book. The payoff comes from the fact that setting type allows the press to manufacture in principle an unlimited number of books with minimal additional labor. The only cost in running off additional copies is the raw materials: paper and ink. So the average cost per book falls precipitously as each additional book is printed. Savings flatten as the cost per volume approaches the cost of the raw materials for the book. As large numbers of books are produced the chief investment becomes the materials. If books are not sold, the press will lose money on its investment in materials. So, in producing books by print, presses are pressured by twin imperatives: to bring down costs of labor by producing many books, and to limit the risk incurred by investment in materials. Typically presses produce books just to the point that labor costs begin to approach the cost of materials. If more books are required, a second printing can be undertaken. Thus profit margins increase with the number of books sold. Early print runs were thus typically small, by modern standards. The initial run of the Gutenberg Bible produced only about 160–180 copies, and for the first centuries of printing most runs were comparable. Today press runs of academic books are of about the same order; one thousand copies of my last book were printed by the University of Texas Press. The initial run of this book will be about 1,500 copies, Blackwell wagers that it can sell copies to libraries and instructors of classes.

Early printed books were influenced by the prestige of the older manuscript form. Thus about a quarter of the first run of the Gutenberg Bible was printed on traditional (and expensive) vellum rather than on the cheaper paper. Typefaces imitated scribal hands; illuminated letters and illustrations were sometimes added by hand. Nevertheless, the technology of reproduction exerted continuing pressure to bring aspects of book appearance into line with its potential, capacities, and advantages.

It is not only the economy of production and sales that change with the introduction of moveable type. Printing facilitates new developments in the nature of reading itself. For example, print made possible the production of cheaper copies. Profit lay in the number of copies sold rather than in the high prices of a deluxe copy. The logic of mechanical reproduction dictated attempts to decrease the risk associated with investment in materials. Production costs were brought lower still by using cheaper materials: paper, which had been imported from China in the tenth century. Cheaper inks were devised. Book producers had an incentive to sell larger numbers of books, and so to produce a wider "reading public."

Cheaper editions, designed to sell to large numbers of people were designed. Portable, "travelers' copies," became increasingly popular. Books before the fifteenth century as a rule were cumbersome and unwieldy. As we have seen, scrolls required two hands and a table. Books tended to be large and heavy. With the introduction of the "pocket book" the traditional environment of reading came unhinged. It was no longer necessary to read in a particular place, say the library. Readers could easily take books with them anywhere, read them in restaurants or on riverbanks, as it pleased them. The habit of reading was reconfigured from a group activity to an individual activity. Because books were portable, reading became a private individual activity rather than the traditional social activity it had been.

Reading practices changed as well. In antiquity and the medieval world reading was predominantly an oral activity. Authors composed by dictation to scribes; scribes copied works not by looking at the page, but by listening to a reader; and readers read by voicing the text aloud, to others or to themselves alone. The development of a common practice of "silent reading" can be observed for several centuries before the introduction of the printing press. Now instead of voicing the text, writing is comprehended silently, internally. The change in reading is complicit with a vast shift in the conception of the individual and society, and even of consciousness and conscience. At the grossest level, the spread of silent reading destroys the communal practice of reading and encourages the mass dissemination of books and literacy. A single book for a community is not enough. Every individual must have a book. At the same time, apprehension of meaning comes to be thought of as a personal, individual matter rather than as something shared: in the early medieval period God is shown making His word known to men by giving them dictation; by the later Middle Ages, He is represented as handing over a book.

There is unsurprisingly a political aspect to this change. Traditionally reading had a group ethic; it was practiced in the open, together with other members of the community. Now it became something to be done alone. Seditious literature and critical free thinking flourished in this environment. Silent reading contributes for good and ill to the breakdown of the community and the rise of the individual. To take a contemporary parallel, until relatively recently, to watch a movie it was necessary to go to a theater, where one enjoyed the film alongside other members of the community. Television brought movies out of the theaters and into the home; later still videotapes and DVDs and portable players made it possible to watch movies anywhere at any time. The effect of this has been to remove the medium from the constraints of the group. Most people are more comfortable watching culturally condemned material like pornography alone than before the eyes of their neighbors.

The spread of silent reading encouraged changes in the appearance of books. Traditionally writing had been laid out continuously on the page, without word divisions or punctuation. Such texts are more easily read by sounding them out than by simply glancing at them. Silent reading required a text that was accessible to the eye rather than the voice. Some such visual cues – chapter headings and rubrics, for example – are as old as Greek and Roman writing. By the high Middle Ages we see the beginnings of the trend toward making the written text visually rational in a more thorough-going way: word divisions begin to be marked, punctuation is standardized, paragraphs are divided. It becomes possible to take in whole sentences at a glance.

One of the most obvious and important changes associated with printing is the standardization of the text of books. Literature had always existed and circulated in copies. These copies, however accurately scribes may have copied them, were not identical with one another. Substantive copying errors, garbling or omission of passages, misspellings and so on, accrued. Each successive copying of a text was only another opportunity to further corrupt a text. Furthermore, scribal copies could never even aspire to uniformity except with regard to content. Reproduction of page layout, illustrations, and so on, was never an object. With printing, a run of books was identical in terms of pagination. Complex diagrams and illustrations could be accurately reproduced. Errors in content could be corrected, and so a subsequent copy – or as we can now call it, an edition – could be an improvement on the last. Because books can now be widely disseminated in identical copies, it now becomes possible for readers to "synchronize" their references. The text of an author can be cited by page number, paragraph number, sentence number, with the expectation that readers on the other side of the world can pull down the same text and go to the same page, paragraph, and sentence and find the same text. The standard forms of reference to most classical authors were devised at this time, usually on the basis of an early and prestigious printed book. For example, the sixteenth-century French scholar Henri Estienne (in contemporary French, Étienne: his surname was Latinized as Stephanus), published widely-disseminated and highly-regarded texts of a number of classical authors, and it became common to cite these texts according to his editions of them. Thus for example, even today, when a scholar refers to Plato's *Symposium*, 173 a, the number refers to the "Stephanus page," that is it refers to a page in Estienne's edition of Plato (Geneva 1578).

The standardization of texts makes possible not just common reference, but the undertaking of scholarship as a group activity. Now it becomes possible to make the collections of evidence that serve as the foundation for the common historical research, and the essential conception of the modern document becomes thinkable. It is from the Renaissance that the long process of collecting and standardizing evidence begins. The culmination of the process and the apotheosis of the modern notion of the document will not occur until the nineteenth century; the idea, however, would have been – was – unthinkable in a manuscript culture. Printing is the technical foundation for the modern notion of the document.

Textual Criticism

Since antiquity literature had circulated in handmade copies. Errors naturally accumulated as copy was made from copy. It can be difficult for modern readers, accustomed to the printed book, to appreciate how often ancient manuscripts contain mistakes, omissions, and utterly confounded passages. Such errors accumulate in a process of transmission that lasted for more than a thousand years. The old party game, called "Whisper down the Lane" or "Telephone" provides an analogy illuminating the process of corruption. A sentence or story is whispered from one participant to the next and as it goes it subtly changes. At the end the story, sometimes radically transformed, is compared with the original.

The correction of scribal errors was left to the reader; such corrections occur wherever there is writing. In Roman Late Antiquity we have an outstanding set of subscriptions that provide an example of how the process of correction in a scribal culture worked. After the copy was made, the reader read the new text, sometimes introducing corrections merely on the basis of sense and their command of the language, at other times with reference to the text from which the copy had been made, sometimes even with reference to other copies of the same text, and made corrections. These corrections were generally introduced on top of the copied text – in the margins or between the lines. No attempt was made to produce a new "clean" manuscript with corrections fully integrated, as modern editions do.

The ancient practices of correction remained common down to the time of printing and beyond. In the Renaissance, for example, scholars hunted down manuscripts in monasteries and libraries, in hopes of finding new texts or better copies of texts that were already known. Corrections were made by comparing texts with one another, or by the simple intuition of the editor, through unsupported conjecture. So long as texts continued to be circulated in scribal copies, there was no remedy for the situation. Every reader had to be a corrector, and every text had to be read critically for errors.

The printed text changes the situation fundamentally. When a text is printed, all copies of the run are identical. There is no point in perusing each copy for errors. Corrections need to be introduced not to the various copies of the book, but to the original from which they are made, the prototype of the edition – what used to be called "galleys." With printing, correction is no longer left to the reader. A new job is created: the editor.

As printed versions of the ancient authors were issued, the aims of correction changed. Traditionally the aim had been to produce a single reliable copy for one's own use. Now it became possible to try to produce an accurate text for general distribution. Attention shifts from the specific text in one's own possession to an attempt to reconstruct the original text – the authorial manuscript copy of say Vergil or Livy – from which the manuscript tradition of these authors derived. In a scribal culture it would be pointless to try to produce an authoritative text, because every copying introduces new error: flawlessness cannot be reproduced, only produced on each specific occasion. The goals and effects of correction are necessarily limited by the nature of book production.

Early printed texts of classical authors were frequently simply copied from an existing manuscript, then "proofread" by the printer or his employees. Of course scholars of the age understood that gains were to be realized by comparing one manuscript with another, and some printed texts were produced on the basis of a comparison with two or more manuscripts. The texts of the classical authors improved over the following centuries as the fruits of learning accumulated in print, as conjectures were suggested and disseminated, debated, and then accepted or rejected. From the time of the Renaissance, textual criticism was frequently characterized as an art rather than a science, and the supreme example of the editor's art was the ability to make a conjectural emendation; to put one's finger on the page and say "thou ailest there;" and then to correct the corruption. The Cambridge scholar, Richard Bentley (1662–1742), stands as the culmination of this tradition. The process of correction in these years was not in essence different from that used in Roman antiquity. The application, however, was different, in that the changes introduced to the texts could now, through printing, be fixed; this application carries with it the seeds of a new method.

It is not until the nineteenth century that the principles of modern textual criticism were devised. These principles are a foreseeable extension of the changes and potentials introduced by the practice of printing, and developed over the five centuries after the Renaissance. The essence of the method is consistent with other scholarly developments of the nineteenth century: manuscripts must be treated systematically rather than individually. The crucial information to be discovered is their relationship to each other. From the point of view of this new science the beauty or intrinsic historical value of a given manuscript is irrelevant. Textual critics spend much time inveighing against earlier editors who preferred manuscripts simply because they were early or physically impressive. To the textual critic what matters is not the specific manuscript, but its place in the tradition. An illuminated codex, once in the possession of Charlemagne's adviser Alcuin, for all its intrinsic interest as an object, may be of less value for reconstructing the tradition of the text than an ugly, poorly written scrap from the sixteenth century.

The foundation of modern textual criticism is normally held to have been laid in Germany in the early nineteenth century. Though many contributed to the development of the method, Karl Lachmann (1793–1851), with his edition of the Roman poet Lucretius (Berlin 1850), is usually granted the status of founding hero. Lachmann, like earlier scholars, valued the unteachable and unmethodical genius epitomized in the conjectural emendation; this ineffable virtue of the textual critic continued to be praised in the late nineteenth century by the belligerent (and wickedly brilliant) A. E. Housman (1859–1936), and is still revered by textual critics today. Lachmann, however, introduced a method. Before the genius of the critic can be allowed to flower, a basic text needs to be established. Recension, the systematic comparison ("collation") of known manuscripts, determines relationships and allows the establishment of a composite text. The relationships of the various manuscripts are determined by looking at their shared errors and corruptions: common error suggests a common source. What is right derives from the original; what is wrong, from the tradition. Thus manuscripts are grouped together and the relative value of their witness for the text of an author determined. The results of collation are typically represented by a genealogical "family tree" of the manuscripts, or stemma; hence the method is sometimes known as "stemmatic criticism." In this way the surviving manuscripts can be combined and used to recreate the original from which they derived: the archetype. The composite then serves as the basis for the conjectural emendations of textual critics; conjecture, however, can only be admitted once the evidence of the manuscript tradition has been thoroughly evaluated. Conjectural emendation is the last resort.

The method produced spectacular results; Lachmann was able to reconstruct a vanished manuscript of Lucretius, down to its line and page lengths. The success was also due to the new aims of editing, which were in turn produced by the medium of printing: that is, the production of clean, authoritative texts that would be mass distributed. Furthermore, the essence of the method, that is the treatment of evidence systematically, was "in the air" at the time. This is the period when evidence itself is rethought in light of the possibility of reproducing and disseminating it, and when we also see the move from valuation of individual items of evidence to an insistence on their systematic appreciation. At the same time historical evidence is increasingly reproduced and disseminated in books. The process of reproduction itself facilitates the segregation of the evidence from a specific social milieu. Modern readers share no common environment, and that isolation is perhaps the essence of the modern experience of literature.

Conclusion

Every modern reader will have an intuitive grasp of the "documentary" qualities of the printed book. The formal qualities of the printed text, even our techniques of reading, predispose us all to think of literature primarily as content. Consideration of the "objective" qualities of the specific text, however – the circumstances of its making, the vicissitudes of its survival – open a window onto its "monumental" significance: its implication in the making of politics and a developing tradition, as opposed to its role as a simple reporter of them.

There are material reasons why we today tend to think of books more as contents than as concrete objects. Most of the texts we encounter these days are disposable; they carry with them an intentional impermanence. A newspaper is probably the supreme example of this kind of printing. Penguins, with their shoddy bindings and flimsy paper-stock, provide another case-in-point. A more extreme case than either would be a digital text, which exists only when called up onto the screen of a computer. Such texts have no history, or no history that matters. They are absolutely the same from one to the next, and being without differentiation, they are as interchangeable as money. Consequently what matters is the very thing, the only thing, that such texts preserve: homogenized, definitive content.

Yet time and human interaction can "monumentalize" anything. Even a Penguin can become a relic. One way this can happen is through destruction. Penguins exist in countless numbers, identical with one another. As the bulk of them are destroyed, the survivors may become more valuable – such a thing happened with the western pulp magazines of the 1940s and 1950s and old newspapers, for example. Another way is through "customization." For example, the (authenticated) contact of someone famous (or only meaningful to the collector) with the book might be enough to make it collectible. Sylvester Stallone's annotated copy of "The Love Song of J. Alfred Prufrock" might conceivably be as interesting and valuable as Petrarch's copy of Cicero.

When we read we direct our attention from the text before us to what the text refers to. If we wish to consider the "monumental" nature of the text, we need to shift our attention from this distractionary meaning back on to the text as a *thing*. In the case of the book before you at this moment you might, for example, contemplate the relationship between what I am writing, academic presses, and university instruction. Or again, a famous text such as the Declaration of Independence or The Magna Carta may exist in many copies. It may even be possible to buy more or less exact facsimiles of the manuscript, reproduced on parchment with appropriate signs of aging precisely applied. Nevertheless, there would be a difference between burning a facsimile of the Declaration of Independence and burning the autograph copy. That is why the Declaration of Independence is kept in a case in the National Archives that would be impervious to a direct hit by a nuclear bomb; the physical circumstances of the autograph tell us something about the relationship of the text to contemporary American politics.

In a manuscript culture, each copy of a book is itself unique, and as it endures it accumulates the damage and history that makes it, in its very physical presence, a vehicle of tradition. A medieval copy of Vergil preserves not only the words of the ancient author, but in the wear and in the vicissitudes of its history, it reflects the place of Vergil in the western tradition – down to the time that the manuscript is mothballed in the rare book room of some academic library. The monumental qualities of the manuscript abide precisely in the story of its embedded endurance in history. This ineffable quality is destroyed by mass reproduction; it is perhaps the most significant way that our experience of texts differs from the ancient. The Penguin, by contrast, communicates the words of the author, but at the price of obscuring its monumental significance. The removal of later textual accretions is the goal of modern textual criticism, as the elimination of anachronism is the object of historicism. The consequence of both is the alienation of past from the present. The gains realized by the printing revolution and the techniques of modern textual criticism are patent and undeniable, but they have come at a cost. Of course readers should grasp the content of the texts they read, but they need also to have some cognizance of the place of these texts in present and past society.

Bibliographical Essay

Generally on the classical manuscript tradition there is the nonpareil introduction by Leighton D. Reynolds and Nigel G. Wilson, *Scribes and Scholars: an Introduction to the Transmission of Greek and Latin Literature*, 3rd edn., Oxford 1991. On ancient books see various works by Eric Turner, including *Athenian Books of the Fifth and Fourth Century* BC, London 1977; *Greek Papyri*, Oxford 1980; and *Greek*

Manuscripts of the Ancient World, London 1987; more recently cf. William A. Johnson, *Bookrolls and Scribes in Oxyrhynchus, Studies in Book and Print Culture Series*, Toronto 2004; for scroll and codex, Colin H. Roberts and Theodore C. Skeat, *The Birth of the Codex*, Oxford 1983. Brief accounts of ancient books are to be found at the beginnings of the two volumes of the *Cambridge History of Classical Literature*, vol. 1; Patricia Easterling and Bernard M. W. Knox, *Greek Literature*, vol. 2, Cambridge 1985; E. J. Kenney, *Latin Literature*, Cambridge 1982. For various technical aspects of production see e.g. Laurel N. Braswell, *Western Manuscripts from Classical Antiquity to the Renaissance: a Handbook* (*Garland Reference Library of the Humanities*, 139), London 1981; Bernhard A. van Groningen, *Short Manual of Greek Palaeography*, 4th edn., Leiden 1967; Bernhard Bischoff, *Latin Palaeography: Antiquity and the Middle Ages*, Cambridge 1993. For the histories of the transmission of particular authors, see Leighton D. Reynolds, ed., *Texts and Transmission: a Survey of the Latin Classics*, Oxford 1983. The series *Approaching the Ancient World* includes two books devoted to the historical interpretation of various literary texts: Christopher Pelling, *Literary Texts and the Greek Historian*, London 2000, and David Potter, *Literary Texts and the Roman Historian*, London 1999.

On medieval manuscript culture see Michael T. Clanchy, *From Memory to Written Record*, Harvard 1993; Rosamund McKitterick, *The Carolingians and the Written Word*, Cambridge 1989; various works by Paul Saenger, e.g. *The Space between Words: the Origins of Silent Reading*, Palo Alto 1997.

For the printing revolution see Lucien Febvre and Henri-Jean Martin, *The Coming of the Book*, London 1976; Elizabeth Eisenstein, *The Printing Revolution in Early Modern Europe*, Cambridge 1983; on the form and production of the modern book Philip Gaskell, *A New Introduction to Bibliography*, Oxford 1972; for a survey of problems associated with the modern book, Robert Darnton, "What is the History of Books," in *The Kiss of Lamourette: Reflections in Cultural History*, New York 1990, 107–35.

There are few academic websites devoted to manuscript culture: a good gateway is sponsored by Georgetown, *The Labyrinth: Resources for Medieval Studies* (labyrinth. georgetown.edu), section on "manuscripts;" cf. *Interpreting Ancient Manuscripts*, from Earlham (www.earlham.edu/~seidti/iam/interp_mss.html); *The Digital Scriptorium* (sunsite3.berkeley.edu/Scriptorium); *Ductus* (www.medieval.unimelb.edu. au/ductus).

Critical texts of literary authors in Greek and Latin will be of little use to those without Greek and Latin; nevertheless students should be aware of the two major series: *Oxford Classical Texts* (abbreviated *OCT*) and Teubner (printed in Leipzig). Some authors, such as Homer and Vergil, exist in many English translations, others in few. Translations of certain authors, even important ones, may be difficult to find. Where does one go to find, for example, a translation of Varro? The bibliography cited at the end of articles in the *OCD*³ will in many cases offer guidance (not much on Varro); as a last resort, students should consult the *Loeb Classical Library*, which provides Greek or Latin texts of ancient authors with facing English translation.

Only some of the literary works written in antiquity have survived to the present; many others are known through snippets and summaries. Collections of such fragments have been published for various literary genres and authors. Students of history will most frequently encounter references to the standard collections of the fragments of the Greek and Roman historians: for Greeks, Felix Jacoby, *Die Fragmente der griechischen Historiker*, Berlin and Leiden 1923– (*FGrH*; Brill is currently undertaking to publish a "New Jacoby"); for Romans, Hermann Peter, *Historicorum Romanorum Reliquiae*, Leipzig 1906–14 (abbreviated "Peter" or *HRRel*; a new edition of this collection has been announced by a team led by Tim J. Cornell). Collections of fragments pertaining to other genres and authors can be found in the bibliographies provided to the articles in the *OCD*³, e.g. "tragedy, Greek" or "Tullius Cicero, Marcus." These again will be difficult to use for students without Greek and Latin.

Citation of classic older texts or even influential modern texts poses a problem: over the years they have been issued in many different editions, which as a rule will have different paginations. Current conventions of citation regularly lead students (and even scholars) to commit such monstrosities as "Plato 2000, 122," or "Vergil 1956, 103," or "Machiavelli 1922, 12," or "Freud 2004, 193." In the first place, the dates are misleading; furthermore, the page references are useless for someone who does not happen to have the same edition of the text. Ancient texts have standard forms of reference. Poetry is cited by work, book, and line number: for example, Vergil, *Aeneid*, 4.101 refers to the fourth book of the *Aeneid*, line 101. Prose works are divided into paragraphs, usually on the basis of some early modern edition of the author. Thus Thucydides 1.22 refers to the first book of the historian's *History of the Peloponnesian War*, paragraph 22. Such citation has the virtue of being intelligible and useful to all readers, no matter which editions or translations of the author they may happen to have in hand.

Penguin history

For "primary evidence" see See Arnaldo D. Momigliano, "Ancient History and the Antiquarian," in his *Contributo alla storia degli studi classici*, Rome 1955, 67–106; Moses I. Finley, "The Ancient Historian and His Sources," in *Ancient History: Evidence and Models*, New York 1985, 7–26.

Writing and early literary texts

For a recent survey of the massive bibliography on the origins of classical Greek writing see e.g. Roger Woodard, *Greek Writing from Knossos to Homer*, Oxford University Press 1997. For a survey of world writing systems see e.g. H.-J. Martin, *The History and Power of Writing*, Chicago 1994, chapter 1. On Linear B, see the concise statement in Oliver T. P. K. Dickinson, *The Aegean Bronze Age*, Cambridge 1994, 193–7. For essays on the context of various palatial writing systems see Maria Brosius, ed., *Ancient Archives and Archival Traditions*, Oxford 2003; for Homer and early writing: cf. Barry Powell, *Homer and the Origin of the Greek Alphabet*, Cambridge 1991; for the Derveni Papyrus, André Laks and Glenn W. Most, *Studies on the Derveni Papyrus*, Oxford 1997.

On ancient libraries see Lionel Casson, *Libraries in the Ancient World*, Yale 2001; for the library at Alexandria there is the entertaining book by Luciano Canfora, *The Vanished Library: a Wonder of the Ancient World*, Berkeley 1989; on the culture of Alexandrian scholarship, Rudolph Pfeiffer, *History of Classical Scholarship from the Beginnings to the End of the Hellenistic Age*, Oxford 1968, and Alan Cameron, *Callimachus and his Critics*, Princeton 1995. For the early history of the texts of the tragic poets, Denys L. Page, *Actors' Interpolations in Greek Tragedy*, Oxford 1934.

Reading

On ancient literacy see William V. Harris, *Ancient Literacy*, Harvard 1989; for techniques of reading and writing see Bernard M. W. Knox, "Silent Reading in Antiquity," *Greek Roman and Byzantine Studies* 9 (1968), 421–35; Theodore C. Skeat, "The Use of Dictation in Ancient Book Production," *Proceedings of the British Academy* 42 (1956), 179–208; Jesper Svenbro, *Phrasikleia: an Anthropology of Reading in Ancient Greece*, Ithaca 1988. On ancient education, Henri-Irenée Marrou, *A History of Education in Antiquity*, New York 1956; Frederick A. G. Beck, *An Album of Greek Education*, Sydney 1975; aside from its substantial intrinsic interest, Raffaella Cribiori, *Gymnastics of the Mind: Greek Education in Hellenistic and Roman Egypt*, Princeton 2001, offers further bibliography.

Continuity of the manuscript tradition

On the survival of ancient literary culture into the middle ages, it used to be thought that Christian aristocrats such as Cassiodorus formed a bridge: see Herbert Bloch, "The Pagan Revival in the West," in Arnaldo D. Momigliano, ed., *The Conflict Between Paganism and Christianity in the Fourth Century: Essays*, Oxford 1964, 199–244, esp. 240–1. This view has now been discredited, and no solution has been offered in its place: see James J. O'Donnell, *Cassiodorus*, Berkeley 1979. For the continuation of the classical literary tradition in Byzantium see Nigel G. Wilson, *The Scholars of Byzantium*, London 1983. The bibliography on medieval and Renaissance libraries is enormous: one of the greatest experts was Paul Oskar Kristeller: to get a sense of library holdings and catalogues see his *Iter Italicum*, Brill 1977–; for other aspects see his collection, *Studies in Renaissance Thought and Letters*, Rome 1956; James Westfall Thompson, *The Medieval Library*, Chicago 1939; Roger Chartier, *The Order of Books: Readers, Authors and Libraries in Europe between the 14th and 18th Centuries*, Cambridge 1993. On the scholastic culture of the high medieval period see the classic book by Charles H. Haskins, *The Renaissance of the Twelfth Century*, Cambridge, Mass. 1927.

Textual criticism

See James E. G. Zetzel, *Latin Textual Criticism in Antiquity*, New York 1981; Charles W. Hedrick, Jr., *History and Silence: Purge and Rehabilitation of Memory in Late Antiquity*, Austin 2000, chapter 6; for activities in Renaissance publishing houses, see Martin Lowry, *The World of Aldus Manutius*, Oxford 1979. For modern textual criticism, its methods and history, see e.g. Paul Maas, *Textual Criticism*, Oxford 1958; Martin L. West, *Textual Criticism and Editorial Technique Applicable to Greek and Latin Texts*, Stuttgart 1973. For a critique and attempt to view nine-teenth-century textual criticism contextually, Sebastiano Timpanaro, *The Freudian Slip: Psychoanalysis and Textual Criticism*, London 1976, repr. 2002; *La genesi del methodo di Lachmann*, Padua 1981. For more general criticism of textual criticism, see G. Thomas Tanselle, *A Rationale of Textual Criticism*, Philadelphia 1989; Jerome McGann, *A Critique of Modern Textual Criticism*, Chicago 1983, and *The Textual Condition*, Princeton 1991.

Conclusion

On reproduction and tradition see Walter Benjamin, "The Work of Art in the Age of Mechanical Reproduction," reprinted in the collection of his essays edited by Hannah Arendt, *Illuminations*, New York 1968.

5

Records

Introduction

In the filing cabinet to the side of my desk at home I keep my personal records, including a set of my tax returns going back to 1984, the year I left graduate school for my first teaching job. I filed some tax returns before then, but I did not keep copies and when I think of it now I am slightly chagrined that the set is incomplete. My wife pesters me from time to time to throw them out, emphasizing that the statute of limitations for the audit of back tax-returns expires after six years – the same limit that applies in America to prosecution of crimes, with the exception of murder. She is right, and I am not sure why I keep them; I suppose I am simply too inert or sentimental or obsessive to part with them.

If I described my set of tax returns as "documents" or an "archive" it would smack of pretension. Certainly they could become "documents" or an "archive" if some future historian should realize my importance and use them to reconstruct my life. As they are, however, gathering dust in my cabinet, they would more accurately be described as "records," or "files:" that is, they are instruments rather than historical sources. The returns that are more than six years old have outlived their practical usefulness and might be regarded as something other than records. I keep them not because of their present usefulness, but because of my sentimental attachment to them and my perception of them as links to my personal past. This significance is more "monumental" than "documentary."

Papyrology has been defined as a field that takes as the object of its study ancient texts that have "no pretensions to permanence," that is to say written instruments, or records. In this way the purview of papyrology can be conveniently distinguished from that of epigraphy. The boundary is nevertheless imprecise. "Impermanent" texts may be written on various materials – including not only papyri, but also sturdier materials such as wood, metal, leather,

or broken pieces of pottery, or ostraca – and the texts written on such materials are sometimes treated as a problem for epigraphers, at other times as
the proper province of papyrologists. If there is one formal, practical criterion
for assigning texts to one field or the other, it is the style of the writing:
papyrologists have special expertise in deciphering scripts – handwriting –
whereas epigraphers typically deal with monumental forms of writing – capital
"block" letters. In antiquity as today, block letters were associated with the
more formal texts that stood on public display, sometimes permanently, and
handwriting was associated with "written instruments," texts that were oriented toward ephemeral, particular situations.

Horace remarked that he had, through his poetry, erected a monument
"more lasting than bronze" (*Odes* 3.30). Among the texts studied by papyrologists are works of literature (above, chapter 4), and these certainly do
have pretensions of permanence. Although they may not be intended to
endure in any particular, individual copy, they may yet outlast monuments
by being copied and recopied. Nevertheless, the elementary distinction
observed by papyrologists between "literary" and "documentary" texts is
essential; it finds some historical support in the fact that distinguishable styles
of handwriting were often used for each by ancient writers. Literary papyri
generally offer the courtesy and convenience of legibility to the reader, as
do certain kinds of "documentary" papyri, such as petitions to officials; most
documentary papyri are by contrast written in a fast illegible cursive, and
presume that the reader already knows what is being communicated. Furthermore, the existence of the literary text in multiple copies diminishes its
situational significance. Works of Homer and Sappho circulated simultaneously in many copies among ancient readers. What makes a text "literary" is
its generality. By contrast, the essence of the "documentary" text is its par-
ticularity. A receipt for payment on a loan, for example, even if completely
formulaic, takes its meaning as much and more from its situational use as
from its content: each receipt serves as a chit to prove that a particular person
satisfied a particular debt owed to another particular person. For this reason
editors conceive of literary texts as copies which, if corrupt, need "emendation" to conform to an ideal, if usually inaccessible, original; they reproduce
"documents," because every document is an original.

This papyrological distinction between the "literary" and "documentary"
is also to some extent arbitrary: it is clearly possible to treat literary texts as
"documentary" and "documentary" texts as literary. A particular manuscript
of Virgil, for example, might be understood as having played various specific
parts in its long life – perhaps, for example, an instrument of aristocratic
competitive gift-giving. A tax bill, on the other hand, might be treated as an
instance of a literary genre, exemplifying the more general, formulaic rhetoric of bureaucracy. The distinction is guaranteed by contingent but nonethe-

less rigid cultural values – that is, by history. American readers, for example, would be as unlikely to read the dossier of my tax returns for formal or esthetic delectation as they would be to scrutinize a particular paperback copy of a novel by Stephen King for its pragmatic function: the status of each is not intrinsic, but is determined by prevailing patterns of social use.

Papyrologists' use of the word "document" does not correspond to the definition I have adopted in this book; consequently I have marked it with "scare" quotes, and will henceforth refer to such texts where possible as records. This common use of the word "document" confounds the distinction between the ancient written instrument and the contemporary historical source. The assimilation of ancient record to modern source is motivated: it leads scholars to disregard the political imperatives that underwrite the creation of ancient texts, and reinforces the contemporary illusion of the independent status of objects that are created by exercise of modern method, so validating the method itself. Modern historians – and papyrologists – are always at risk of foisting their methods of research onto the past. The ancients had their letters and receipts, tax returns and depositions, as we do; such things become documents only when they have exhausted their usefulness and, abstracted from the files of their owners, come to be taken as evidence for the past instead of instruments for present use. Obviously historians in antiquity could have used ancient letters and tax receipts and so on as documents of past life, though they seldom did so and certainly never collected them for general study, as modern papyrologists do. The controversial exceptions date to the early Empire: the Roman historian Tacitus made use of senatorial records in writing his history, and his contemporary, the imperial biographer Suetonius, used texts, including private letters, from the imperial files. These cases, it seems to me, are only apparent exceptions; the use of such sources is tied to the social status of the author: Tacitus was a senator who was interested in telling the story of the degradation of the senate of his day, and Suetonius was an imperial functionary, whose duties included maintenance of the emperor's correspondence.

Papyri in the Ancient World

Most of the surviving records of the Greco-Roman world have been discovered in Egypt, written on papyrus or ostraca. Survival of Egyptian papyri is undoubtedly due in large part to the climate: the aridity of the climate outside of the Nile valley itself makes possible the preservation of organic materials that would have perished elsewhere. This fact also accounts for the survival pattern of papyri in Egypt. Very few papyri have been recovered from the great population centers, such as Alexandria, for the reason that these centers are located near the river, in the path of the annual inundations of the Nile, or in proximity to Mediterranean shore and the corroding sea.

Ostraca were also frequently used for the writing of records. A curved fragment of broken ceramic was more awkward to use than papyrus, and was certainly less portable. On the other hand, it was free and available anywhere people broke clay pots – which is to say, everywhere. Fired clay is practically indestructible, but the ink applied can easily be worn away. Written ostraca, like papyri, are seldom found in the Nile valley; they are often found in the desert, however. An impressive variety of records were written on potsherds, some quite substantial.

Egyptians kept their records in the various languages of the country. Thus we find texts written in the monumental Hieroglyphic characters, or in the bureaucratic Egyptian script called Demotic, which develops after about 650 BC. Egypt was conquered by Alexander in 331 BC and established as an independent kingdom by his general Ptolemy in 305; subsequently the dominant political language of the land was Greek, and remained so through Roman times. Relatively few Greek papyri have been preserved from the Ptolemaic period. In the Roman period, the majority of the preserved texts were written in Greek, though the use of Demotic by natives continued in this period. Coptic texts (the old Egyptian language written in Greek characters) are found from the late second century AD, and in increasing numbers from the fourth. Coptic texts account for a small percentage of the surviving texts of the Greco-Roman period. A few rare Latin texts have been recovered.

The number of papyri now preserved in modern collections amounts to somewhere between a million and a million and a half. Some of the largest collections have not even fully catalogued their holdings. Only a fraction of these, something on the order of 75,000, have been published. And the discrepancy grows: more new papyri are discovered each year than are published. The variety of these texts is rich, and attempts to draw them together in conventional categories, while useful and even necessary, have the effect of minimizing their range and idiosyncrasy. Thus, as we have seen, papyrologists typically begin by discriminating "documentary" from "literary" papyri. "Literary" papyri are comparatively rare – in 1965 only about 2,000 were known – but these include samples of most of the major genres, from philosophical, historical, and antiquarian essays; to oratory; to epic, dramatic, and lyric poetry; to dictionaries. The number of literary texts must now stand at some multiple of that number. "Documentary" texts are likewise categorized according to content. At the most general level papyrologists distinguish between private and public records; that is, texts concerning private individuals, as opposed to those sent from or addressed to individuals in official positions. The Loeb collection of "Select Papyri," for example, divides private "documents" into Agreements, Receipts, Wills, Disownments,

Letters, Memoranda, Invitations, Orders for Payment, Agenda, Accounts and Lists, Questions to Oracles, Prayers, Charms, and Horoscopes; it divides public "documents" into Codes and Regulations, Edicts and Orders, Public Announcements, Reports of Meetings, Official Acts and Inquiries, Judicial Business, Petitions and Applications, Declarations to Officials, Nominations and Appointments, Contracts and Tenders, Receipts, Orders for Payment, Accounts and Lists, and Correspondence. As impressive as this list may appear, it is far from exhaustive. Where, for example, are Recipes? School Exercises? Curses? At the same time, the apparently simple categories disguise a mass of heterogeneous material. Under private documents, for example, the category "Agreements" includes marriage contracts, deeds of divorce, deeds of adoption, emancipations of slaves, contracts of apprenticeship, contracts of hire, property rentals, deeds of sale, leases, divisions of property, settlements of claims, indemnifications, and loans – and I have simplified the list. Some agreements do not fall conveniently into these categories: for example in one text a widow contracts with another woman to raise her daughter; in another an employee swears to be honest on pain of financial penalties; in other a person provides sureties that a peasant will remain on the land and will not run off.

Most of the surviving Egyptian papyri date from the Roman period, and especially from the second and third centuries AD. Papyri dating to the Ptolemaic period, that is, from the establishment of the reign of the Ptolemies at the end of the fourth century BC down to the conquest of Egypt and queen Cleopatra in 30 BC by the future emperor Augustus, are surprisingly few in number, particularly in view of the substantial number known before (in the Saite-Persian period) and after. The majority of these are owed to one chance find, a dossier of texts known as the "Zenon archive," an early third-century collection of about 1,800 texts from the office of the estate manager of the second Ptolemy's minister of finance, Apollonios. While the "Zenon archive" accounts for a disproportionate part of the documentation of the Ptolemaic period, it is also sufficient to suggest that the bureaucratic habit was not alien to Ptolemaic society. The significant number of Ptolemaic Greek texts written on ostraca that have been recovered support this conclusion.

The difference in the preserved numbers of papyri from Ptolemaic and Roman times is almost surely not due to a difference in the numbers that were produced, but rather to the circumstances of preservation and excavation. Most of the great Ptolemaic centers were located in the most fertile, low-lying sections of Egypt; subsequent settlement and the Nile inundations led to the destruction of papyri in these places. In the period of the Roman Empire, however, more intensive irrigation brought settlements up into the desert. With the end of the Roman period these irrigation projects were abandoned and many of these settlements returned to desert – subject neither to the depredations of future generations of townsmen and farmers, nor to the more insidious threat of the annual floods of the Nile. When excavators of the later nineteenth century turned their attention to the recovery of papyri, they went precisely to these Roman desert settlements.

The extent of the surviving papyrological evidence in Egypt is unparalleled elsewhere in the ancient world, and many have consequently wondered whether Egypt is simply exceptional, different than the rest of the Greeks and Romans when it comes to its habit of bureaucratic writing: perhaps the peculiarities of the long tradition of centralized Pharaonic and then Ptolemaic taxation and bureaucracy led to a habit of writing that was never duplicated elsewhere in the ancient Mediterranean world? The discussion breaks down along disciplinary lines: papyrologists tend to argue that Egyptian writing habits are typical of the rest of the Greco-Roman world, while historians of, say, Classical Greece or Roman Gaul tend to argue that Egypt is exceptional. Most have always been willing to grant that the patterns of bureaucratic writing of the Roman administration in Egypt are typical of broader, empire-wide patterns. But the extent of the participation of the populace seems extraordinary. Surely farmers in say France and Britain were not so implicated in bureaucratic culture as farmers appear to be in Egypt? If they were, why has no evidence survived? It might be argued that records written on ephemeral materials have not survived in Britain because of the climate. But why, then, have comparable caches of papyri or ostraca not emerged in, say, North Africa? And if there was a comparable record-keeping culture in antiquity in southern Europe, why has no trace of it survived, say through reference in inscriptions or the texts of the literary tradition?

The arguments for "Egyptian exceptionalism" still remain, I think, dominant among scholars, though their strength has eroded significantly lately in light of new discoveries. To be sure, no place has yielded – or is likely to yield – records in the numbers that they have been found in Egypt, yet examples that are perhaps representative of a more pervasive practice outside of Egypt have emerged, many of these in the last decade, especially from desert areas of the Near East, from the Dead Sea to the Caspian. These texts are written on materials similar to those used in Egypt in a bureaucratic language quite like that used in Egypt, while preserving local peculiarities of nomenclature. There can be little doubt that in the later Roman period records were everywhere kept of important transactions.

The first ancient papyri that captured the attention of the European world were discovered in Italy, not Egypt: this was a philosophical library, unearthed at Herculaneum in the eighteenth century. But these are literary. Records have also long been known from Herculaneum and Pompeii (though most of these are written on more durable materials, such as metal and clay, wax tablets and notebooks of wood). "Documentary" texts from Petra and Dura-

Europus have been known since the 1920s. Increasingly papyri and ostraca have been found and published from the desert surrounding the Dead Sea. The spectacular discovery of texts written on wood at a Roman army base at Vindolanda in Britain, by Hadrian's wall, dating to the second/third century AD show that the habit of writing was carried by the Romans to the extreme limits of their imperial possessions. The papyri from Egypt themselves sometimes provide evidence for writing habit beyond the bounds of Egypt. Thus, for example, letters directed to Egyptians from Italy have been recovered in Egypt (cf. P. Mich. 8.491 = Rowlandson 105). Formal collections of literary letters, such as that of Pliny the Younger, preserved via the manuscript tradition, confirm the point. There can be no reasonable doubt that the habit of letter writing was pervasive even among the non-elite (and even non-literate) population throughout the Roman Empire.

In Egypt itself, large numbers of texts dating before the Hellenistic period have yet to be discovered, though Greeks occupied certain sites, such as Naukratis, from the archaic period. In other words, the letter writing, bureaucratic contracts, and so on may be linked to the particular social and political situation of the Greco-Roman period; or perhaps the lack is simply an accident of preservation. Nor do the papyri fail with the end of antiquity: for a time after the Arab conquest of 642 texts continue to be written in Greek, but in the course of about a century the language of official records becomes Arabic. The Egyptian language proved more resilient than the Greek: texts in Demotic and Coptic continued to be written through the years of Arab occupation, and Coptic survives as a living language to this day.

In the Greco-Roman world at large the use of writing for private, practical purposes can be shown to date not long after the introduction of writing itself in the eighth century; and many have reasonably suspected that the adoption of writing was made precisely for practical reasons. Allusions to instrumental writing are found in many Greek authors: already Homer, for example, refers to a message written in *semata lugra*, "baleful signs" (whether or not this refers to the Greek alphabet, *Iliad*, 6.168–70). Thucydides and Herodotus allude on occasion to correspondence. Actual records are thin on the ground, and those we have owe their survival to having been written on some enduring material such as metal. The earliest known Greek letter is a business letter of the sixth century, incised on lead, discovered in the region of the Black Sea, at Berezan (*SEG* 26, 845). So there is no question that writing is used for common, practical purposes from the archaic period, though the details of how it was used and the pervasiveness of the practice is controversial.

In the absence of widespread literacy, records, like literary texts, were written by specialists. The evidence furnished by Egyptian papyri throws unaccustomed light on the problem. As a rule officials were literate. Illiteracy, however, was no bar to participating in the advantages of writing: if, for example, an illiterate or semi-literate person wished to send a letter they might go to a better educated neighbor and have them write for them, perhaps laboriously signing their name to the text produced for them. People who made their living by writing – scribes – might also be employed. The position of scribe was lucrative enough to be desirable, and we actually hear of *scribes* whose skill in writing was rudimentary, or even non-existent. In one case a scribe named Petaus actually accuses another scribe of being illiterate.

In Europe, as in Egypt, instrumental use of writing does not cease at the end of antiquity: Greek in Byzantium, Latin in the west, is adopted by new regimes for their record keeping and other purposes. There are certain continuities – in formulaic language, writing forms, and techniques for example – from the bureaucratic culture of antiquity to that of Byzantium and the western Middle Ages.

Modern Study of Papyrology

Papyrology is the youngest of the ancillary disciplines associated with classics. Study and collection of papyri does not begin until the late nineteenth century, and it is from its beginnings under the sway of the modern methods of the scientific history that were developed at beginning of the nineteenth century. This situation is to some extent to be expected. Before the nineteenth century historians were interested in monumental remains from antiquity; and scrappy records from this perspective seemed trivial. They did not appear to have anything to contribute to the narrative of great memorable events, nor were they of any evident significance for the grand narrative of what mattered in the past. When papyri first came to the attention of the European intellectual community, they fascinated precisely because of the promise they seemed to hold of fresh additions to the store of literature from antiquity. Scholars hoped to find new plays of Sophocles and fresh biblical texts in the ancient scrolls. The point is well illustrated by the occasional early dealings that scholars had with papyri before the later nineteenth century.

At Herculaneum a philosophical library of some 800 rolls was recovered from the devastation wrought by Vesuvius in AD 79. Although the papyri were otherwise unharmed, the heat of the volcanic flow that buried Herculaneum had carbonized them, and they could not be unrolled without destroying them. Attempts were made to decipher them, with only limited success. Thus the antiquarians of the day were confronted with a spectacular collection of physical books from antiquity, but these texts remained for them objects; for the most part they could not be read.

One of the earliest Egyptian papyri to attract attention in Europe was the so-called Borghesi papyrus, an impressive meters-long scroll given to Cardinal Stefano Borgia in 1778. Its display in the family's library in Florence stirred great interest; the decipherment and publication (by Nicolaus Schow, 1788), however, was an anticlimax. The text was not literary or philosophical, but a list of men liable to conscription for work on the irrigation system of the Fayyum, a fertile, watered pocket to the west of the Nile, in 192 AD.

Over the next hundred years Egyptian papyri gradually accumulated in European collections, such as Berlin, Vienna, and London. These were acquired chiefly through the antiquities trade: chance finds made by farmers were sold to dealers and thence were brought out of the Egypt to Europe. Publications of these begin in the teens and twenties of the nineteenth century; and while records were not neglected in these early publications, broader interest in the work was focused on the recovery of literature.

European archaeological excavations in Egypt date to the 1850s; in the 1870s research accelerated considerably. Most of this work was motivated by the search for impressive monumental discoveries – however the archaeologist Flinders Petrie (1853–1942) was notable for his anticipation of contemporary attitudes toward archaeological excavation. Along with their other discoveries, these excavations recovered numbers of papyri that were duly shipped back to collections in Europe. One of the most productive of these expeditions was undertaken by Wallace Budge in 1888. From his excavations in the Fayyum he shipped boxes of ancient papyri home to his sponsor, the British Museum. These included some of the most famous of all papyrological finds. Not least of these was an almost complete text of a previously lost essay, Aristotle's *Constitution of the Athenian State*, which was published by Frederic G. Kenyon in 1891.

Publication of such discoveries spurred further expeditions; these now were organized with the express purpose of recovering texts. In the dry climate of Egypt, many papyri are preserved unprotected in the ground; archaeologists find them lying among the ruins of past settlements. One common source of papyri is ancient rubbish dumps. This soil is relatively rich and has been used by farmers to enrich their fields since antiquity; the search for fertilizer led to the discovery of many of the papyri that found their way into the antiquities market. Another significant source of ancient papyri is mummy cartonnage. The Egyptians made a kind of papier-mâché (moldable cardboard), in early times from linen, but later using layers of recycled papyrus, to make a form-fitting sheath for the embalmed bodies of the dead. These papyri sometimes bear writing, and with steam and chemicals the layers can be disentangled and read.

In 1895 the English "Egyptian Exploration Society" sent three excavators, David G. Hogarth, Bernard P. Grenfell, and Arthur S. Hunt, to Egypt with the express purpose of recovering papyri. In the following two years they visited a number of sites in the Fayyum. They were still motivated by the goal of recovering literary materials: as Grenfell noted in explaining the attention they gave to the Nome capital of Oxyrhynchos, they imagined that "it must have been the abode of many rich persons who could afford to possess a library of literary texts." Here they unearthed an enormous quantity of papyri, recovering for example "thirty-six good sized baskets" in one day's work, and another 25 on the following day. They left Egypt after this first expedition with more than 280 boxes of papyri, fewer than a tenth of which were literary.

The work of Grenfell and Hunt inaugurated a new era in papyrology. Now the antiquities trade was supplemented by archaeological investigation. Hunt would return to Egypt repeatedly, at first with Grenfell and later alone, to excavate and discover papyri. The great university collections of Europe and North America stem from excavations at this time. The bulk of the texts discovered by Grenfell and Hunt at Oxyrhynchos is now lodged at Oxford, but hundreds of pieces were also distributed to other institutions that had supported their excavations. In America the core of the University of California at Berkeley's collection comes from Tebtynis, which was excavated for them by Grenfell and Hunt; the collection of the University of Michigan is founded on materials discovered in their own excavations at Karanis and Socnopaiou Nesos from the mid 1920s to the mid 1930s. Also in these years universities began to acquire collections in a systematic manner by buying on the antiquities markets of Cairo and Alexandria.

At all times recovery of instrumental texts vastly outweighed the numbers of literary papyri; nevertheless, the literary papyri have always attracted disproportionate attention and have been regarded as more important. With the expansion of collections from the 1870s on, scholars became increasingly interested in "documentary" papyri and their significance for history. In Vienna, Carl Wessely was a pioneer. Grenfell and Hunt are notable because they attended to the publication not only of the literary papyri they had discovered, but also of the "documentary" papyri. Doubtless the greatest name in papyrology of this or any era, Ulrich Wilcken wrote his dissertation in 1885 on the history of Egypt on the basis of "documentary" papyri. In this interest he was following the same principles and interests that had dominated classics since the turn of the nineteenth century and the days of August Boeckh. Wilcken would go on to dominate and organize the publication of papyri from his position at Berlin until his death in 1945.

Early collectors were chiefly interested in relatively complete texts, objects that by their physical size and general appearance produced an impressive effect on viewers. They were also overwhelmingly concerned with literary texts. Their interest was certainly reasonable: the discoveries of papyrology offered the opportunity to read snippets, and occasionally large chunks, of works that had not survived through the manuscript tradition; in other cases the papyri threw light on the history of the transmission of texts of authors preserved in the manuscript tradition. Nevertheless, the fact remains that many classicists then (and now) care only for papyri to the extent that they preserve literary texts, for the reason that such texts have maintained a "monumental" prestige in western tradition down to modern times. Appreciation of literary texts does not depend (at least not entirely or essentially) on placing them in an historical context; that is, they need not be read in a systematic relationship with analogous texts of the period. Before the historical revolution of the nineteenth century it was universally held that great works of literature and philosophy exemplified eternal, transcendental values. The notion remains very much alive today. The interest of scholars in literary papyri reflects this traditional assessment of the value of great literature. Records have no such pretensions. They take their interest rather from their place in an historical context, for what they reveal of a general historical process. To understand them – even, in a pragmatic way, simply to decipher them – presupposes an interest in the historically contingent rather than in the philosophically eternal. At a pragmatic level, this means a willingness to understand them systematically, in and against other documents.

Archives, Ancient and Modern

Historical interest in records is characteristically modern. The papyri we characterize as "documents" were in fact written instruments, to be discarded when their usefulness was exhausted. It may be inevitable that we apply the concepts of our own methods to the objects of study, as if there is no difference between the two. Yet the imposition of ourselves onto the past always brings with it a tension. The point can be illustrated by considering the use of the word "archive" by papyrologists.

Modern historians convert records to documents in part by institutionalizing them, depositing them in dedicated repositories. Valued historical documents today are housed in modern collections, "archives," which isolate and preserve them. Archives also "bring together" such texts and make it possible to consider them systematically. In the modern world, the archive is a place where written instruments are enshrined as historical sources, that is, as documents. Archives authorize knowledge about the past; by being lodged in archives texts are vested with a social prestige that allows them to serve as the authoritative basis of knowledge. The archive accomplishes this work precisely by segregating the instrument from the context of its usefulness or local meaningfulness.

As soon as historical research became affiliated with the archive there arose
the danger of confusing the modern scholarly collections of sources with
past repertoires of records, as if the collections of the archive are not to be
understood as modern concoctions, but can somehow be granted an historical validity as well. The archive is one of the central institutions of modern
professional historical practice, and has been at least since the 1830s when
the German historian Leopold von Ranke set the students of his seminars to
work with the rallying cry, "back to the archives!" Ranke was applying the
methods of classical philology to the modern world; he was inspired by the
work of classicists with inscriptions, notably August Boeckh. The resource
he took advantage of, humble records, did not seem available to classicists
at the time. In the wake of Ranke's successes, the emergence of the great
papyrus collections seemed a glorious and unanticipated gift. Ancient historians might now be able to do the same work as modern historians, and
achieve comparable results. In this light, the use of the word "archive" by
papyrologists from the dawn of the discipline in the 1870s scarcely seems
unmotivated. So collections of related texts from antiquity were commonly
described as "archives," whether these texts had been united in antiquity, or
whether they had been united by some modern papyrologist. Thus, if a
number of papyri were discovered that had originally been in the possession
of the engineer Kleon, this dossier was described as an "archive." If texts
were discovered that mentioned this same Kleon, even if they originated
from elsewhere than the dossier that had been in Kleon's possession, they
might also be collected and described as part of the same archive.

Doubtless the choice of the word "archive" to describe papyrological
dossiers was suggested by the nineteenth-century prestige of the idea of the
archive among historians of the modern world. And in using the word indif-
ferently to describe ancient and modern collections they were conforming
to established usage. The modern word "archive" in common usage may
describe any collection of texts – texts accessioned in an official public archive
or museum collection or as informally and haphazardly held as those in my
filing cabinet. In recent years papyrologists have become uncomfortable with
their use of the word, and have argued that collections of papyri made in
antiquity need to be distinguished from those made by modern scholars.
Thus increasingly papyrologists use the word "archive" for ancient collections of texts, while other terms, such as "dossiers" and "repertoires" are
used to describe modern collections.

The current attempt to distinguish ancient from modern collections of
texts reflects an awareness that methods of study and objects being studied
affect one another. Yet the definitions now proposed, it seems to me, are
precisely backwards: for historians, archives are collections of documents,
that is collections of records that have outlived their useful lives and so can

be consecrated as historical authorities. Such collections are by their nature anachronistic, made after the event. Furthermore, they exist for the purposes of historical study: historical archives are meant to be consulted as evidence for the past; reading rooms are provided and the collections are systematically surveyed and catalogued. For modern historians ancient collections of papyri are not to be regarded as archives, but as collections of instruments, like my collection of tax returns.

The English word "archive" derives from the Greek word *archeion*, meaning "magistrate's office," which was later Latinized as *archiva*. Etymology suggests then that an ancient "archive" was originally a collection of written instruments housed in a magistrate's office. Historical evidence seems to bear out this interpretation. Where we hear of "archives" they are associated with rulers, groups of officials, and particular administrators. Thus in the Greek east we know of "archives" in the keeping of Hellenistic kings, town councils (*boulai*), and particular officials. In Rome the censors kept an "archive," as did the senate.

The earliest use of the word *archeion* to describe a collection of texts occurs in the context of the regimes of the Hellenistic kings and dates to the end of the fourth century, and such collections are well attested in the Hellenistic and Roman periods. The collections are not always called "archives," but frequently take their names from the building where they are housed. Thus for example the archive of the Roman senate was called the "Aerarium." The earliest certainly known "archive" in the Greek world is the collection of the council (*boule*) of Athens, called the Metroon for the building in which it was kept certainly from the mid-fourth century and most probably from the end of the fifth century. The Hellenistic archives provide the example for the Romans. The relationship between the Athenian Metroon and the Hellenistic archives is unclear.

Holdings of ancient archives included especially texts generated by the office with which they were associated. Thus the Athenian Metroon held examples of treaties and other actions undertaken by the Athenian council; so too did the Roman Aerarium. The most vivid evidence for ancient "archival practice" comes from Egypt and the city of Tebtynis, where a number of texts discarded from the local notary office (*grapheion*) archive dating to the reign of the emperor Claudius (41–54 AD) have been recovered. The preserved texts included both lists of contracts executed over a period of more than two years, and longer abstracts of some of these contracts. Contents of ancient collections of texts were various, depending on the nature and function of groups that kept them. Lodged in the temple of the Vestals in the Roman forum was notoriously a collection of wills registered with the Vestals. We know that various groups – the family, the army, offices of the state – kept collections of records.

Such official ancient "archives" were collections of instruments, not documents. They were kept not because they were historically authoritative, but because they were socially authoritative, that is to say, useful, and were tied to the present functioning of the institution that kept them. When they ceased to be relevant they were not kept as evidence of the past, but were discarded; as we know happened with the records of the office at Tebtynis. There was in the ancient world no question of institutionalizing or preserving or reproducing such texts because of their historical significance, as in the modern world. Ancient historians seldom allude to them, though they have an obvious significance for the reconstruction of the past.

Modern archives, by contrast, are depots into which superannuated instruments are retired; in the modern world we associate them with the sources for history. The archive is the place where the historical source is institutionalized. The connection dates to the beginning of the nineteenth century. It is generally considered that the first of the modern archives was the French Bibliothèque Nationale, which was opened to the public in 1720. The US National Archive opened considerably later, in the nineteenth century. Such institutions gathered and preserved under one roof a mass of disparate material; the debris of the national past. The various national archives of modern Europe and America were certainly founded in large part as the result of a nationalist impulse: the US archives exist to preserve the heritage and history of the American nation. It is no accident that soon after the various national archives were founded, professional historical scholarship, sponsored by the nation, arose.

These institutions did not appear out of thin air. For example, various institutions of the medieval period – churches, towns, monasteries – kept superannuated records, though not to serve as resources for historical work. These were regarded rather as "monuments" of the institutions that had created them: so Cicero, in a remarkable passage, refers to the records of the Roman Senate as the "monuments of this order," *monumenta huius ordinis* (*Philippic.* 5.17). From the Renaissance on scholars and antiquarians became increasingly interested in these. The most famous early essay would be the declamation of Lorenzo Valla (1407–57) exposing of the "Donation of Constantine" as a forgery: among his arguments Valla pointed to the historical mistakes linguistic infelicities contained in the text. Such humanistic research culminated in the great work by Jean Mabillon (1632–1707), *De Re Diplomatica* (1681), a general account of methods for determining the authenticity of official texts – charters, deeds, and the like – to be found in these medieval institutions. By doing this work, Mabillon and others were treating records as "documents," though the collections were not yet "archives" in the modern sense, and the texts within them had yet to be institutionalized as "documents." With the establishment of the great national archives from the end of the eighteenth century, texts, ancient and contemporary, begin to be set aside with an eye to their future use as historical sources. Henceforth documents will not be produced out of the raw materials of society by the labor of scholars like Mabillon. Instead they will be presented to the historian in the environment of the archive, already isolated from society, pre-constituted as documents.

The discarding of records is perhaps the best indication of the difference between the archives of the ancient world and modern historical archives. If we look at the so-called "family archives," that is informal collections of texts associated with particular individuals or households, it does not appear that texts were kept long. Certainly there are exceptions: texts bearing on long term property interests, such as deeds of sale for property and marriage contracts, might be kept for longer periods. Even so, collections of papyri found in particular houses at Karanis were generally restricted to about a 30-year period, suggesting that earlier materials had not been judged worth keeping; only what was instrumental, or perhaps of sentimental value to the current occupant, was kept. There is ample evidence that papyrological texts were discarded in antiquity, either thrown away, reused for other texts, or recycled as mummy cartonnage. And the texts from the notary archive at Tebtynis were also discarded in antiquity, while the office was still in operation. The evidence is imperfect. It is possible that by oversight or sentiment or regard for an especially famous name some records were preserved for long periods of time, but there is no evidence that there was any systematic concern to preserve obsolete material, and there are substantial indications that the contrary was the case. In fact, if we exclude from the account texts that had an enduring usefulness, it appears that few records in ancient Egypt were kept for more than five years before they were reused.

Conclusion

The "archives" of antiquity have more to do with the disheveled stacks of paper on my desk and in my filing cabinet than they do with the systematic and indexed collections of modern archives. To be sure, we know of people and institutions in antiquity that kept papers over generations. In some cases this was because the text, say a deed or a loan, remained effective. In a few instances, though, texts that had outlived their functions were preserved. Roman senatorial families, for example, kept texts pertaining to their august ancestors – notebooks (*commentarii*) kept when holding office and the like. These, however, should be regarded more as monuments than documents. They take their meaning more from their relation to status and prestige of the present group than from their role as historical sources. Of course, it is possible to convert such texts from monuments of a family to historical sources; this is precisely what papyrologists do when they lodge their texts in modern archives, libraries, and museums, reproduce them in journals and scholarly collections, and treat them as sources for their histories rather than as monuments of a vital tradition. Such texts could not have been institutionalized as documents in the ancient world; the social and physical apparatus to do so did not exist. It would have been possible for historians to treat such texts as objective evidence for the past; they seldom do so. Even such apparent exceptions as Tacitus conceive of records in the first place as heirlooms that only become evidence for events through the labor of the historian. Certainly it would never have occurred to any historian in antiquity to consider records systematically, as a group, though as we have seen, had they wished to do so the material might have easily been gathered.

Bibliographical Essay

The specialist discipline that deals with ancient records, particularly as they are preserved on papyrus and potsherds, or ostraka, is papyrology. Eric Turner with his *Greek Papyri: an Introduction*, Oxford 1968, served for many years as the standard English introduction; students should now supplement it with Roger Bagnall, *Reading Papyri, Writing Ancient History*, London 1995; students who have no fear of Greek can also profit from P. W. Pestman, *The New Papyrological Primer*, 2nd edn., Brill 1994. For the history of the discipline of papyrology, see the *New Pauly*, vol. 15/2, s.v.; cf. Peter van Minnen, "The First Century of Papyrology," *BASP* 30 (1993), 5–18, available online with the title "The Century of Papyrology (1892–1992)," at the *Duke Papyrus Archive* (see below). Bibliography of topics relevant to the study of papyri and ostraka can be obtained through Marcel Hombert et al., eds., *Bibliographie papyrologique*, Brussels 1932– (now available on CD-ROM).

Many papyri and ostraka are initially published in corpus volumes. Principles of nomenclature for these are relatively consistent: P. or O. for P(apyri) or O(straka), followed by an abbreviated form of the name of the collection to which they belong. These typically refer either to the name of the place where the papyri were discovered (e.g. Oxy. for Oxyrhynchos, a metropolitan city, that is a regional capital, located on a branch of the Nile about a hundred miles south of Cairo), or to the name of the place where the modern collection is housed (e.g. Lond. for London, that is, the British Museum), or less commonly for some other reason (e.g. Petr. for the Flinders Petrie papyri, named in honor of the great archaeologist and housed in Dublin). Texts not included in the corpus volume of some collection may be published in many specialist journals. These texts are subsequently collected in a German reference work, the *Collection of Greek Documents from Egypt* (Friedrich Preisigke et al. eds., *Sammelbuch griechischer Urkunden aus Ägypten*, at my last count in 24 vols., Strassburg 1915–, abbreviated *SB*), which then provides them with a standard form of reference. For resolution of mysterious abbreviations see the online *Checklist of Editions* (below).

It is important to bear in mind that modern editions of papyri, as of any ancient texts, have been substantially doctored by scholars: ancient papyri are sometimes the work of careless scribes; their texts may contain difficult abbreviations; they may have been seriously damaged. The following editorial conventions will be frequently encountered by beginning students: square brackets [enclose material "restored" by the editor, which is thought to have been present at some time in the text but which has been lost for some reason]; round brackets (enclose letters provided by the editor to resolve an abbreviation); and angle brackets < enclose material provided by the editor, either because the ancient writer omitted them or wrote something else in error >.

The best collection of translated documentary papyri is Jane Rowlandson, ed., *Women and Society in Greek and Roman Egypt: a Sourcebook*, Cambridge 1998; the Loeb collection remains useful: Arthur S. Hunt and Campbell C. Edgar, *Select Papyri*, 2 vols., *Loeb Classical Library*, Cambridge 1932–4. The following histories make exemplary use of papyrological evidence: Naphtali Lewis, *Greeks in Ptolemaic Egypt*, Oxford 1986; the same, *Life in Egypt under Roman Rule*, Oxford 1983; Michel Chauveau, *Egypt in the Age of Cleopatra*, Ithaca 2000; Roger Bagnall, *Egypt in Late Antiquity*, Princeton 1993; Alan K. Bowman, *Egypt after the Pharaohs: 332–AD 642, From Alexander to the Arab Conquest*, rev. edn., Berkeley 1990.

Papyrology is better served with web-based research resources than any other specialist discipline in ancient history. The best English gateways to this material are the homepage of the *American Society of Papyrologists* (www.papyrology.org); *APIS: Advanced Papyrological Information System* out of Columbia (www.columbia.edu/cu/lweb/projects/digital/apis/); the *Duke Papyrus Archive*, from Duke University (scriptorium.lib.duke.edu/papyrus/); and Traianos Gagos' *A Select Bibliography of Papyrology* (www.lib.umich.edu/pap/tools/bibliography/bib_main.html). Links to the following especially noteworthy items can be found from the home page of the Duke Papyrus Archive: the *Duke Databank of Documentary Papyri*, a searchable corpus of the documentary papyri (also available on CD-ROM); and the *Checklist of Editions of Greek, Latin, Demotic and Coptic Papyri, Ostraka and Tablets*, which provides an account of the myriad collections of texts, along with their abbreviations.

Introduction

Roger Bagnall, *Reading Papyri, Writing Ancient History*, London 1995, provides a succinct definition of the field at 9–10. On the very interesting question of the general connotations of styles of script see notably Stanley Morison, *Politics and Script: Aspects of Authority and Freedom in the Development of Graeco-Latin Script from the Sixth Century* BC *to the Twentieth Century* AD, Oxford 1972, and various essays by Armando Petrucci, such as his *Public Lettering: Script, Power and Culture*, Chicago 1993. For a general account of writing in the ancient world, see *The Beginning of Understanding: Writing in the Ancient World*, Ann Arbor 1991, adapted on the web by Peter van Minnen at *Duke Papyrus Archive* (above). On ancient Latin scripts there is now the superb survey by Bernhard Bischoff, *Latin Palaeography: Antiquity and the Middle Ages*, Cambridge 1990. Students may be interested to examine, even if they cannot read, the examples collected in Eric Turner and Peter Parsons, *Greek*

Manuscripts of the Ancient World, BICS Suppl. 46, London 1987, or, for Latin, Alan K. Bowman's various publications of *The Vindolanda Writing Tablets* (available on the web, *Vindolanda Tablets Online*, vindolanda.csad.ox.ac.uk). For the difference between the editing of a "document" and that of a literary text see G. Thomas Tansell, *A Rationale of Textual Criticism*, Philadelphia 1989. For Greek and Roman historians and their disregard of documents and archives see Moses I. Finley, "The Ancient Historian and His Sources," in *Ancient History, Evidence and Models*, Penguin 1985, 7–26; for a review of the famous controversy surrounding Tacitus' use of "documentary sources," see Timothy D. Barnes, "Tacitus and the Senatus Consultum de Cn. Pisone Patre," *Phoenix* 52 (1998) 125–48.

Papyri in the ancient world

On the numbers of papyri published and preserved in collections, Peter van Minnen, "The Millennium of Papyrology (2001–)?" in Hermann Harrauer and Bernhard Palme eds., *Akten des 23. internationalen Papyrologenkongresses*, forthcoming. On the literary papyri, see the catalogue of Roger A. Pack, *The Greek and Latin Literary Texts from Greco-Roman Egypt*, 2nd edn., Ann Arbor 1965. I use the Loeb edition to illustrate the types of papyri because of its easy accessibility; for a more recent, scholarly categorization see a recent volume of the *Sammelbuch* (above). On the Zenon archive see the brief summary by Rowlandson (above), 95–8, or the *OCD*[3] s.v. On Egyptian exceptionalism see e.g. Roger Bagnall, *Reading Papyri, Writing Ancient History*, London 1995, 11–13. For ancient letter writing, the *New Pauly*, s.v. epistle; Patricia Rosenmeyer, *Ancient Epistolary Fictions: the Letter in Greek Literature*, Cambridge 2001. On literacy and illiteracy see William V. Harris, *Ancient Literacy*, Cambridge, Mass. 1991, Harris touches on the illiterate scribes at 278; cf., Herbert Youtie's famous article, "*Bradeos graphon*: Between Literacy and Illiteracy," *GRBS* 12 (1971), 240–3.

Modern study of papyrology

On the texts from Herculaneum, Marcello Gigante, *Philodemus in Italy: the Books from Herculaneum*, Ann Arbor 1995; the library has recently (2004) been the subject of a PBS documentary, "Out of the Ashes: Recovering the Lost Library of Herculaneum." For the tendency of papyrologists to disregard historical and archaeological context, Peter van Minnen, "House-to-House Enquiries: An Interdisciplinary Approach to Roman Karanis," *ZPE* 100 (1994), 227–51.

Archives, ancient and modern

The best survey of the history of the modern archive is in French: Robert-Henri Bautier, "Les Archives" in Charles Samaran, ed., *L'Histoire et ses methodes*. (Encyclopédie de la Pléiade 11), Paris 1961, 1120–66; more recently, generally, and in English, see Carolyn Steedman, *Dust*, Manchester 2001. Jacques Derrida's publication of *Archive Fever: a Freudian Impression*, Chicago 1996, has provoked a deluge of theoretical publication. The bibliography on ancient archives is scattered: generally Ernst Posner's very outdated essay on *Archives in the Ancient World*, Cambridge 1972, may be recommended by virtue of its comprehensiveness and the fact that it is written in English; on the Near Eastern tradition see Maria Brosius, ed., *Archives and Archival Traditions: Concepts of Record-Keeping in the Ancient World, Monograph Series of the CSAD*, vol. 1, Oxford 2003, with a notable contribution on Greece by John K. Davies; James P. Sickinger deals with the Athenian Metroon in his *Public Records and Archives in Classical Athens*, Chapel Hill 1999; for Hellenistic archives it is necessary to go to an Italian article, Michele Faraguna, "A proposito degli archivi nel mondo greco: terra e registrazioni fondiarie," *Chiron* 30 (2000), 65–115; on Roman archives a pair of books in French are available: Ségolène Demougin, ed., *La Mémoire perdue, à la recherche des archives oubliées, publique et privées de la Rome antique*, Paris 1994, and *La Mémoire perdue, recherches sur l'administration romaine*, (*Collection de l'École française de Rome* 243), Rome 1998. For the evidence attesting the engineer Kleon and its association with various collections, see Naphtali Lewis, *Greeks in Ptolemaic Egypt*, Oxford 1986, 37–45. For the rethinking of the use of the term "archive" by papyrologists, A. Martin, "Archives privées et cachettes documentaires," in *Proceedings of the 20th Congress of Papyrology*, Copenhagen, 1994, 569–77. For collections of texts found in houses at Karanis, see again Peter van Minnen's essay on "House-to-House Enquiries" (above); for examples of the reuse of archives in cartonnage, see Naphtali Lewis, *Greeks in Ptolemaic Egypt*, Oxford 1986, 58 and 104–23; for the amount of time that documents were generally retained before reuse see Eric Turner and Peter Parsons, *Greek Manuscripts of the Ancient World* (*BICS* sup. 46), London, 1986, 18–19.

6

Public Writing

Introduction

The most notable inscription in Oberlin, Ohio is a war-memorial, which stands in a park in a residential area at the edge of the older part of the town. Oberlin is a college town, set in farming country about 45 minutes outside of Cleveland. The college and city were founded at the same moment, in 1833, by a utopian religious movement. The permanent residents of the town number about 9,000; faculty, staff, and transient students of the college run to about 4,000–5,000. The college's preeminence in the town is reflected in the layout of the city center. The heart of the town is occupied by a park, owned by the college but accessible to the general public. The college surrounds the park on three sides and the "First Church" stands among the college buildings. The small commercial "Main Street" of the town lies along the fourth side of the park.

The city of Oberlin is located in a rural area of a conservative state. The college, by contrast, draws many of its students from urban areas and boasts a long tradition of liberalism and social activism. Two years after the college was founded, almost 30 years before the Civil War, black students were admitted; women joined the college two years later, in 1837. From its origins Oberlin was an abolitionist center; during the Civil War it became a notorious stop on the "underground railroad." Since the 1870s the college – and the First Church – have sponsored social and missionary programs in China. In some respects the college sets the tone for the community: for example, most of the city's essential services – utilities, library, and cable television, for example – are cooperatives, managed by citizen boards. Inevitably, however, there is some tension between "town and gown."

Oberlin's "Soldiers' Monument" took shape piecemeal, as the inconsistency of its materials and lettering attest. Inscriptions of various periods are set into a brick retaining wall. At top center a marble plaque designates the wall a memorial to fallen soldiers. The earliest texts are the largest and most central: four weathered marble tablets occupy the middle zone of the wall and name the casualties from the Civil War, a total of 96 names. Below these, similarly lettered marble plaques list the battles in which the soldiers died. Four marble plaques of various dates are arranged along the top of the wall, each naming one of the wars in which men of the town fought, from the Civil War to the Second World War. Two marble plaques set at the bottom of the wall at either side provide quotes from Thucydides' Funeral Oration. Casualties incurred after the Civil War are written on small bronze plaques affixed to the wall: 11 in World War I, 16 in World War II, two in Korea, and two in Vietnam.

Something of the general history of the monument can be reconstructed even from its present appearance: for example, the oldest plaques suggest that originally the memorial must have been four-sided and commemorated only casualties of the Civil War. But such speculative reconstructions are unnecessary; the local newspapers and the college's archives provide a detailed history. The original Civil War memorial was a Gothic spire, erected in 1871, which stood on campus in the heart of town, at one corner of the park, on the boundary between the college and the town's business district. The monument in time became a meeting place both for townspeople and college students: students described it as "the sunken church." A local crisis erupted in 1934 when these two groups came into conflict around the monument. Student pacifists, protesting against US military expenditures, disrupted the town's Memorial Day observances, draping the monument with signs urging the need for schools rather than battleships, and proposing the transfer of war funds to needy students. Soon afterward the college, pleading the dilapidation of the monument, had it dismantled and put the inscribed marble tablets and plaques in storage.

In 1943 the town acquired the inscriptions; instead of restoring them to a monument at the center of town, near the college, they built the new monument in a park in a residential area, blocks away from the college. The American Legion at this time took up the maintenance of the monument. The inscriptions thus became once more the focus of the town's commemoration of Memorial Day and the Fourth of July.

The removal of the monument from the area reflects some hostility of the townspeople toward the college. The attitude is also expressed in the casualty lists subsequently affixed to the monument. Whereas the monument lists almost a hundred casualties from the Civil War, only about 30 are named from all wars since. The list of Civil War casualties includes both townspeople and students of the college; subsequent lists are restricted to townspeople. The college lost many students and alumni to World War II, but these are commemorated with a separate monument, which is located on the campus.

At the same time Oberlin College students have long been ambivalent about war and the motivation for commemorating it. Pacifist protests by students seem to have been among the causes that precipitated the dismantling of the Civil War memorial. The college's World War II memorial was dedicated only in 1997 through the efforts of older alumni and even then a point was made of including the names of alumni who died fighting on the *Japanese* side. Another campus monument, a memorial arch commemorating local missionaries who died in the Boxer Rebellion in China, was dedicated in 1903; in 1994 a plaque was added to specify that the arch also commemorated the Chinese who died at the time.

Tensions between residents and students continue to be articulated around the town's "Soldiers' Monument." A few years ago, while visiting at Oberlin College, I took a class to look at the monument. Neighbors summoned the police to supervise. As the officer explained, the town had spent a sum of money to renovate the monument, and there was concern that students might vandalize it.

Most older communities in the United States display war memorials in some public location – a town square or a park. The story of the Oberlin "Soldiers' Monument" for all its peculiarities illustrates some of the common and remarkable features of public writing. Inscriptions are monumental: permanent and enduring markers, they work to articulate the meaningful public space of the community, and their simple physical presence matters as much as, and frequently far more than, the written texts they bear; in fact, the contemporary social significance of an inscription need have little or nothing to do with the text it bears. The significance of monumental writing is deeply socialized and markedly contextual: its significance is grounded in a particular and developing relationship to the local community.

In the case of the Oberlin "Soldiers' Monument" the texts of the inscriptions, the specific names recorded, are only marginally relevant to the social significance of the monument. A scholar might use the inscriptions to discuss, for example, numbers of casualties, nomenclature in the mid-nineteenth century, conscription patterns of Union Regiments, or Thucydides' place in the culture of a college town. Such academic problems are a matter of indifference to the contemporary citizens of Oberlin. The ongoing uses of the monument by townspeople and students, on the other hand, would be irrelevant to this reconstruction of the historical significance of the inscriptions – worse, for an historian they would be a distraction, or even an anachronistic perversion of the monument's status as a document of the past, no more relevant to the inscriptions' historical significance than an eighteenth-century peasant's understanding of a fifth-century BC Greek inscription.

The present significance of public inscriptions is tied to their many and sometimes conflicting uses by various groups in the community. They serve as landmarks, meeting places, public bulletin boards. They may serve as focal points for nationalist ritual: Memorial Day picnics, Fourth of July barbecues. Local organizations such as the American Legion may take a proprietary interest in their maintenance. The Oberlin inscription became a lightning rod for local conflict. Does it reflect the values of the community, and commemorate the sacrifice of local families and Oberlin's historic contribution to the abolitionist cause? Or is it an attempt by government to promote a jingoistic glorification of war?

Public inscriptions are created and cultivated to serve the monumental needs of the community, not the documentary convenience of historians. In fact, documentary practice and monumental function are at odds. Historians appropriate monuments for use as their sources at the expense of the meaningful engagement of the past with present life. If it were felt that the text of the Oberlin monument had some extraordinary significance as a source for the Civil War, it would doubtless be protected: fenced off, or even replaced by casts, so that the originals might be removed and displayed in a museum. Such measures would safeguard the inscription, but at the expense of severing its meaningful connection with the life of the community. Just so, when historians isolate inscriptions in museums and reproduce their texts in corpus volumes, journals, and other publications, they convey the content of the inscription, but lose its living, evolving connection with society.

Ancient Inscriptions

The modern study of ancient public writing is called "epigraphy," which derives from the Greek word for "inscription." As a practical matter, epigraphy takes in more than only public writing. Disciplinary definitions are always hazy at the boundaries. "Epigraphers" or "epigraphists" study writing on all sorts of durable objects, including for example bricks, pottery, bronze, and lead sheets, whether or not such texts were ever destined for public display. In this chapter, I will restrict discussion to public writing.

Marx and Engels described Greece and Rome as civilizations of slavery; the eminent French epigrapher Louis Robert described them as "civilizations of the inscription." By contrast Robert's idea may seem trivial or at least overstated, yet it contains enough truth to provoke thought. Almost all societies that use writing display it publicly for various purposes. In the modern world it is to be seen everywhere: street signs, billboards, graffiti, and so on. Yet most of this writing is ephemeral and consequently severely functional in character. Display of permanent, monumental writing is by and large restricted to the graveyard, dedicatory inscriptions on buildings and the rare monument. The Greeks and Romans displayed ephemeral texts too, but they also set up permanent texts of all sorts in far greater numbers than we do today.

On the order of 100,000 Greek inscriptions are known. The habit of displaying writing in permanent monumental form, however, derives from Egypt, if it is not an independent Greek innovation. The earliest examples of writing are found around 800 BC, often on pots; within the century the various states have begun to inscribe texts on durable surfaces, especially stone, lead, and bronze, for public display. By the sixth century substantial inscriptions of all kinds, and notably the texts of laws, are preserved. Numbers of known inscriptions remain relatively sparse until the fifth century; from the 450s Athens inscribes public texts on a scale not previously seen before. Substantial numbers are attested throughout the Greek world from the fourth century on. Inscriptions are henceforth found for as long as the Greek civic culture remains healthy. They decline and virtually cease by the end of the third century AD.

Inscriptions are an urban phenomenon in the Greek world (contrast Runic inscriptions from northern Europe, which were mostly displayed in the countryside, or hieroglyphic inscriptions from Egypt, which are found particularly clustered around shrines). Athens produces far the largest proportion of Greek inscriptions. Some 20,000 inscriptions are known from Athenian territory alone, in the neighborhood of 20 percent of the total number of all Greek inscriptions. Other large cities and sanctuaries, such as Ephesus and Delphi have also produced numerous inscriptions, though nowhere near so many as Athens.

Perhaps as many as 280,000 Latin inscriptions have now been published. The Romans learned to write from the Etruscans. The Etruscans learned about writing and inscriptions from the Greeks, and their earliest inscriptions date to around 700. The Roman alphabet too is a modified form of a version of the Greek alphabet. Very few Latin inscriptions dating earlier than the first century BC have survived. Roman authors claim knowledge of inscriptions of the fifth and even sixth centuries BC. In a famous passage, for example, Livy claims to have seen the dedicatory inscription for the original temple of Jupiter Optimus Maximus, which would date to the late sixth or early fifth century BC (7.3, 8). The dates of the earliest surviving inscriptions are usually difficult to determine. The famous *Lapis Niger*, for example, a stone found in the Roman forum, evidently recording religious regulations, is dated variously to as early as the sixth and as late as the fourth century (*CIL* I^2, 1). More inscriptions survive from the late Republic, but not many more; only about 2,000 Latin inscriptions are known for the period of the entire republic, though the number would be somewhat higher if it included inscriptions erected in Greek by Romans as they conquered the eastern Mediterranean. With Augustus and the Empire the number of surviving inscriptions expands rapidly, spiking in the middle of the second century AD, then declining rapidly in the third, never to recover.

As in the Greek case, inscriptions are associated with population centers. Not surprisingly, the great political centers produced the greatest numbers of texts. Rome itself has predictably furnished the greatest numbers, between 30,000 and 40,000.

The Greeks wrote in Greek wherever they went. The Romans, after the spread of their empire, favored two languages. As a rule, inscriptions were written in Latin in the western Mediterranean. East of the Italian peninsula, however, Greek was favored for inscriptions and administration. Of course the Mediterranean world contained more than the Greeks and Romans, and inscriptions in other languages have also been found. In some cases the influence of the Greco-Roman "epigraphical habit" is obvious, in others a local tradition of monumental writing is known; in still other cases the history of the tradition of monumental writing is more obscure. So for example, inscriptions in Phrygian, Egyptian, Gallic, Semitic, and other languages are known from areas of Greco-Roman political control.

The variety of inscriptions defies brief summary; a general typology is possible, though. In antiquity, as in the contemporary world, the most common type of stone inscription was the gravestone. Honorific inscriptions were also very common: the Greeks and Romans placed inscriptions honoring benefactors and donors on public works, buildings, and monuments, or wrote them on freestanding *stelai*, which were erected by the hundreds in town squares. Other sorts of inscriptions do not find ready parallels in the modern world. Public texts, such as decrees and laws were commonly inscribed. Texts associated with religious activities, regulations and dedications for example, were frequently carved in stone. Lists of war dead, public accounts, records of temple holdings – all might be recorded in stone. Many elements of society – particularly of urban society – are reflected in the inscriptions: political figures, priests, soldiers, women, slaves, and freedmen all figure in the dedication or matter of inscriptions. Nor are the subjects of epigraphy exhausted in what we nowadays describe as the "documentary." Discursive texts of a more "literary" flavor, such as poems, wills, excerpts from books, and the like might also be inscribed for display. The length of inscriptions is also immensely variable. A tombstone or graffito may comprise only a word or two. The largest epigraphical texts from antiquity, such as Augustus' account of his "Deeds" (*Res Gestae*), or the Epicurean teachings commissioned by Diogenes of Oenoanda, or Diocletian's "Edict on Maximum Prices" run to many pages in printed editions – they are the size of small books, or pamphlets.

We probably have a representative sample of the kinds of inscriptions that the Greeks and Romans displayed. It is hard to estimate how many inscriptions were ever erected in the ancient world. We have no way of estimating what percentage of inscriptions that ever existed has been recovered.

Monumental Texts

Publicly displayed texts in the ancient world, as in the modern, can usefully be distinguished according to their permanence. Some texts, incised for example on soft metal, written or painted on wooden boards or other white-washed surfaces, were intended to serve a limited purpose, then to be destroyed or reused for another message. Other texts, frequently cut in stone, were made to last. Anyone who has posted flyers will readily understand why texts with limited relevance are written on perishable materials. Once the bicycle is sold, the apartment rented, the lost cat found, the flyer becomes pointless, another bit of clutter defacing the community's walls, and it is a public service to pull it down and throw it away. Less obvious is the justification for carving certain texts in bulky permanent stone. These texts – laws, treaties, contracts, and the like – may have on-going authority and pertinence, and so may reasonably be made to last. Many monumental texts, however, had no such lasting relevance. What was the point of inscribing (and then every fourth year inscribing anew) an inventory of dedications lodged in a temple?

The relevance of the content of any text is linked to the context for which it was produced – and context is ephemeral. Impermanent texts are intended to serve a practical and immediate end, and they are destroyed when the situation changes. Enduring inscriptions by contrast are monumental: in time they outlive whatever practical relevance they may have had, and become associated with something more general: tradition. Impermanent texts were displayed to be read. Permanent texts may of course also have been read, as modern scholars read them, but they possess in addition an exaggerated symbolic dimension. Impermanence emphasizes the importance of content, permanence detracts from it, and over time content becomes less and less relevant to the significance of the monument.

A public text can be written by anyone with the desire and a magic marker or a can of spray paint. Graffiti were as common in the ancient world as they are today in New York City. Ancient graffiti are perhaps best illustrated by the various scrawls that grace or deface the walls of buildings at Pompeii; weightier texts were written by professionals. In Greece, through the archaic period inscriptions seem to have been carved by sculptors. The chief evidence is a dossier of statue bases from the Athenian Acropolis on which artists "sign" their names, taking credit for statue or inscription or both. By the fifth century in Athens official texts were inscribed in a beautiful, uniform "chancery" style, which bespeaks accomplished, specialized stonemasons. From the fourth century on it is possible to identify the "hands" of various carvers and their "schools."

We are considerably better informed about the carving of Roman inscriptions – which is not to say that the evidence is adequate to support a social analysis of the profession of stone carver. One often-reproduced inscription from Palermo (*CIL* 10.7296) provides a bilingual advertisement for a stone-cutter's workshop: "inscriptions laid out and carved here for religious buildings and public works." Neither the Greek nor the Latin text of this inscription is entirely grammatical or fluent, though the lettering is quite nice. The stonemason, though a fine carver, is evidently not the possessor of a refined literary sensibility.

As this text illustrates, in both Greece and Rome the carving of inscriptions, even public inscriptions, was normally contracted to private individuals. The text to be inscribed would as a rule have been provided to them. Public decrees, for example, might be drafted by those who proposed them; we hear that Demosthenes, for example, amazed his colleagues by his ability to compose such texts on short notice. In other cases secretaries or other functionaries might be entrusted with the work. In certain instances stonecutters themselves might furnish texts for their customers. We know, for example, that some books of appropriate and formulaic funerary epitaphs circulated among stonemasons in the Roman Empire.

Once the text was in hand, a calligrapher would lay the text out on paper – Romans called this step the "ordinatio." Once suitably arranged the text would be transferred to the stone in chalk or charcoal. The mason would then carve over the drawn text. Finally the incised letters were colored, often in red.

Punctuation and word divisions were generally lacking in Greek and Roman inscription. Marks might occasionally be added to indicate abbreviations or significant breaks in the text. The end of a thought (what we would call a paragraph) is sometimes indicated on inscriptions by a line-break or a design such as a leaf, for instance. A raised dot sometimes marks an abbreviation in Roman inscriptions. But such notations are sporadically used. Layout of text is not consistently rationalized. In some cases, in fact, the layout positively seems designed to combat rational division of the text. In state decrees of the classical Athenian democracy, for instance, a grid was laid out on the stone, and letters were evenly spaced horizontally and vertically (this is the famous "stoichedon" style).

Inscriptions were applied to rocks and metal plaques of various shapes. One of the most common, a stele, for instance, is (in modern usage) a free-standing stone shaped roughly like a door; a cippus is a low, cylindrical or box-shaped marker, used especially for gravestones. The variety is endless;

ancient inscriptions are found on everything from statues to buildings to boulders.

A monumental style of lettering emerges early in the course of the sixth century in Greece. By the fifth century in Athens a distinctive lettering style for public inscriptions has developed. Classical Greek inscriptions, however, make few concessions to the circumstances in which public texts were seen. Letters are made very small and shallow. The Romans put considerably more effort into the monumental appearance of their inscriptions. The supreme example of the Roman monumental style is traditionally taken to be the inscription on the column of Trajan. The monumental qualities of the lettering of Roman stone inscriptions can be appreciated by considering the lettering used for their ephemeral notices: these are typically painted, written, or incised in a manner with affinities to hands used for record keeping and book writing, the "actuary style."

Stone inscriptions were expensive. A modern stonemason may be able to inscribe three hundred letters a day. Even the writing of an ephemeral poster represents a considerable commitment of time. The carving of a substantial ancient inscription then, represents many days' work of a skilled craftsman; and this calculation does not include the cost of materials.

Public writing was "published" by displaying it, whether in a single place in one copy, or with multiple copies, in several places. The entire population then has access to the text. In societies like those of Greece and Rome, where the economy was agrarian and the literacy rate probably did not exceed 10 to 20 percent of the population, the intent and effect of such displays is questionable.

It is remarkable that permanent inscriptions were often displayed with little regard for their legibility. The inscriptions displayed near the Royal Stoa in the Agora of Athens may serve as a case in point. Here were particularly displayed inscriptions honoring ex-magistrates (archons). In time a virtual forest of stelai sprang up, which effectively obscured one another and cluttered up the open space required for readers to decipher the texts. In addition the stelai themselves stand very low to the ground. Many of the texts displayed are at knee-height, which again makes them difficult to read, unless one lies on one's stomach.

By contrast, provisions for the posting of ephemeral texts frequently spell out requirements for their display that are intended to make them easily accessible to readers. So, for example, when Caesar reformed the Roman grain dole, he required that recipients declare their eligibility to the consul, who kept a list of their names. This list was to be copied "in black letters on a white board and displayed in the forum during the greater part of every day at the place where the grain is distributed to the people, so that it may be plainly read from the level of the ground" (*ILS* 6085 = *Roman*

Civilization Vol. 1 161, p. 409). On the rare occasions when we can discern the actual places where such texts were displayed, a comparable concern for legible display is apparent. So at Athens postings were displayed on the base of the Monument of the Eponymous Heroes in the Agora. The area where the texts were displayed was fenced off and fronted an open space where crowds could congregate to read. Such a posting place is represented on a fresco from Pompeii, and a roofed, whitewashed writing surface has been recovered on one of the walls of a building fronting a public square.

As a form of mass communication such texts remain problematic if not everyone could read. The chief problem is that modern scholars tend to think of reading as an individual activity, such as they themselves practice, rather than as a group activity. Thus, in modern reconstructions of the Monument of the Eponymous Heroes we see represented one or two people standing sedately and reading to themselves. We might better imagine a more lively scene: one person bends through the fence, finger to the text, calling the words up to another fellow standing on the rails, using his hands as a megaphone to call out to a jostling mass of people around them. In one of his letters (*Letters to Atticus* 2.21.4), Cicero hints at such a scene: decrees of Roman magistrates were commonly "posted" in impermanent form (the Latin word is *propono*) for informational purposes. Some were so amusing for their invective that they attracted huge crowds of readers that impeded foot-traffic. We infrequently hear that particular texts are to receive regular public readings. So, for example, when the Romans make a treaty with the small Greek state of Astypalaia, they order that a copy of the treaty be "set up in a public and easily visible place where most of the citizens pass by, and it be given a public reading each year in the assembly" (*IG* XII 173 = *Roman Civilization* V. 1, no. 132, p. 331). And of course it was always possible for the illiterate to seek help from their reading neighbors. So, an inscription from Sulmo in Italy addresses "whoever may read it, or listen to someone read it" (*Supplementum Italicum* N.S. 4, no. 58, 78–84).

It was possible to get access to the content of a text even if one was illiterate. But inscriptions would only have been "read" to the extent that they were of some interest. Utilitarian postings had an obvious pressing relevance, and on occasion even hoary old texts were summarized by Athenian orators and others. Again, however, the value of the inscription has more to do with tradition than pragmatic usefulness.

Epigraphical Scholarship

Epigraphists of the nineteenth century had a vivid and correct sense that they were doing something entirely new – rigorous, scientific, and modern.

"It was the work of one great scholar, August Boeckh, to raise Greek epigraphy to a science." Boeckh (1785–1867), a scholar whose influence was felt
in practically every field of the classics, had inaugurated the first modern
corpus of ancient inscriptions, the *Corpus Inscriptionum Graecarum* (1828–
77; abbreviated *CIG*). "In the Corpus Boeckh had settled forever the
methods of Greek epigraphy." On the Roman side, two Italians were credited
with breaking from the past. Gaetano Marini (1742–1815), who was known
for his book on the Acts of the Arval Brethren, "opens a new era of truly
critical and scientific handling of inscriptions;" but "his disciple and successor Count Bartolommeo Borghesi (best known for his work on the Roman
consular fasti) may rightly be called the founder of the modern science of
Roman epigraphy." Borghesi (1781–1860) was in turn the mentor of
Theodor Mommsen (1817–1903).

Scholars had given attention to inscriptions long before the nineteenth
century. Historians, both Greek and Roman, quote them as evidence in their
histories: Thucydides quotes public decrees notably in Books 5 and 8 of his
History; Polybius begins his account of the second Punic War by quoting
inscribed treaties between Rome and Carthage (3.22–27); Livy mentions
many Latin and Greek inscriptions. Many authors, Greek and Roman, took
an interest in epigraphy, describing and quoting notable inscriptions. Greeks
collected inscriptions as early as the fourth century BC. The earliest known
collection of Latin inscriptions was made by a Christian pilgrim to Rome
around 800 AD. From the Renaissance on, humanists reproduced ancient
inscriptions in notebooks and paintings; diplomats and traders, like Cyriacus
of Ancona (1391–1452), noted antiquities that they encountered in their
travels. By the beginning of the sixteenth century the first collections of
inscriptions were being printed. By the beginning of the seventeenth century
Jan Gruyter (or Janus Gruter, 1560–1627) and Joseph Scaliger (1540–1609)
compiled and published the first corpus of all Roman inscriptions known at
that time. Antiquarians of the seventeenth and eighteenth centuries produced erudite explanations of particular texts and continued to compile
inscriptions, expanding earlier corpora and correcting the texts in successive
editions and polemical counter-editions and reviews.

In what respects, then, was the research of the nineteenth century new
and different from what had gone before? We should begin by excluding
collections made before the Renaissance. Such works were not made "for
the use of scholars" (*in usu scholarum* is a common phrase heading collections and academic essays from the Renaissance on). Krateros' compendium
of decrees was doubtless intended to illustrate noble monuments of the
Athenian state, perhaps focusing on texts associated with the names of
famous statesmen. A pilgrim's collection, like that of the "Anonymus

Eisiedlensis," collected inscriptions only incidentally, insofar as they were part of the sights of the holy city, and so were of interest to those pilgrims who came to Rome. Collections made before the Renaissance may be useful as resources of otherwise unknown inscriptions, but though they are sometimes treated as if they belong to a tradition that leads directly to the great modern epigraphical corpora, they do not.

More interesting and difficult is the question of how nineteenth-century work differed from work done from the fifteenth century on. Scholars of the day typically pointed to their rigor (as opposed to the sloppiness and gullibility of their predecessors). In fact, they claimed that they developed their methodology precisely as an antidote to the inaccuracies and falsifications that had crept into earlier epigraphical collections. In the nineteenth century epigraphers worked in accordance with narrowly defined and generally agreed rules. Copies of inscriptions were viewed with mistrust; autopsy of the stone itself was sought wherever possible. Editing and interpretation of texts was to be done in accordance with accepted practices of philological textual criticism.

Claims such as these seem in retrospect vague, general, and self-serving. Surely scholars before the nineteenth century aimed to produce precise and accurate texts of inscriptions. If there is a difference between the nineteenth century and earlier eras in this respect, it is a matter of degree, not of kind. The essential difference can be seen in their techniques of interpretation, which is avowedly systematic. This new, systematic orientation is reflected in the new rules for the organization of the collection of inscriptions.

Rather than reading an inscription as simple evidence for an event, they insisted that it should be considered first in the context of other inscriptions. Boeckh put the point well in his polemical introduction to the *CIG*: "it is necessary to be familiar with many inscriptions, if you want to explain individual ones." Inscriptions can be understood only if they "explain themselves." The sentiment has remained current. It is still a commonplace in epigraphy that inscriptions do not mean anything until they are put in relation to other inscriptions.

The organization of the new epigraphical corpora illustrates this attitude. As Boeckh remarked, before the nineteenth century corpora were commonly organized thematically. Henceforth it would be an unalterable rule that inscriptions should first be grouped according to geographical criteria, then chronological. Only then would the organization of the corpus move on to thematic criteria. In the older organization, inscriptions had been grouped thematically, according to the type of text. Such organization continues to be used in the famous nineteenth-century selections of inscriptions, such as the *ILS* and the *SIG*, and of course in specialized genre studies

(Verse-Inscriptions or Legal Inscriptions for example). In the newer corpora, however, texts were put into relation with other inscriptions of the same place, time, and type. Again, the organization is part of the shift to systematic interpretation. The historicist unities of place and time are imposed on the organization of evidence as well.

The *CIG* was the first modern corpus of inscriptions, and the works that came to replace it were modeled on it. The current standard collections of inscriptions, the *Corpus Inscriptionum Latinarum* (founded by Mommsen, first volume published in 1873), and the *Inscriptiones Graecae* (abbreviated *IG*, begun by Koehler in the 1870s and re-founded in its present form by Wilamowitz in 1902), are the direct descendants of the *CIG*. The principles enunciated by Boeckh in his preface spawned two centuries of research. The influence was already clear in the nineteenth century. Epigraphers of the day acknowledged the primacy of the *CIG*: "out of the publication of the *Corpus* there grew up a new school of students." The institutional success of Boeckh's corpus is not the least of his achievement. By establishing clearly defined principles of interpretation, he incorporated inscriptions into the flowering professional society of history. The attraction of specialized students is the very definition of the creation of a professional standard of epigraphical interpretation. The *CIG* marks the beginning of professional scholarship on inscriptions.

The impulse behind the new collections of inscriptions was the desire to make the texts widely available in a standard format; in other words, the point was to create inscriptions as "documents," resources for historical research. The new methods contributed to this development: philological criticism aimed to reconstitute the original meanings of texts; later connotations and uses of these monuments were ignored, in favor of the original meaning of the text. Inscriptions were understood in terms of their content, not as unique objects that occupied a certain space and function in the tradition. Scholars of the nineteenth century projected their contemporary vision of the inscription onto the past: "The primary value of the inscription (i.e. even in antiquity) lay in its documentary evidence." The attitude remains vital: many continue reflexively to think that inscriptions were displayed to be read in the same way that archival texts are now stored to be consulted. Monumental functions that they may have had are incidental.

In a related development, the collection of texts for the corpora coincided with the physical collection of the inscriptions in private collections and museums. In his 1927 introduction to epigraphy, John E. Sandys could remark, with some surprise, that few inscriptions remained in their original places; most had already been removed to private collections or museums. Thus the modern project both figuratively and literally removed or "abstracted" ancient inscriptions from their living social context. Between the

covers of a book, or on the wall of a museum, inscriptions were no longer
public texts, but specialized scholarly resources.

Conclusion

Late in his *History* (6.54), Thucydides digresses to give an account of the
tyranny of the Peisistratids a century before. He writes to correct certain
widespread misapprehensions of the Athenians about the tyranny and to
show "that the Athenians are not more accurate than the rest of the world
in their accounts of their own tyrants and of the facts of their history." He
notes that the tyrant family took care to have their own men hold the chief
magistracy of the Athenians, the archonship.

> Among those that held the yearly archonship at Athens was Peisistratos, son
> of the tyrant Hippias and named for his grandfather, who dedicated during his
> term of office the Altar to the Twelve Gods in the Agora, and that of Apollo
> in the Pythian sanctuary. The Athenian people later added onto and expanded
> the altar in the market place, and erased the inscription; but the one in the
> Pythian sanctuary can still be seen, though with faded letters, and it says the
> following: "Peisistratos son of Hippias, set up this record of his archonship in
> the precinct of Apollo Pythias."

Thucydides is certainly using this inscription as evidence, though he is
hardly writing "in the modern academic manner," as many modern academics like to think. He writes avowedly to correct a prevalent popular tradition;
to do this he does not appeal to esoteric books and evidence. He sends his
readers instead to objects that exist in their own city, available to anyone
who happens to be passing by. He makes no attempt to "contextualize" the
text, but expects that its significance will be obvious to all who note it. He
combats an errant popular tradition with a popular monument.

The altar of the younger Peisistratos was recovered in 1877, near the
Ilissos river, where the ancient sanctuary of Apollo Pythias was located. It is
now on display in the Epigraphical Museum in Athens (*IG* I^3 948). The
principal scholarly controversy about it has to do with the date of the
younger Peisistratos' archonship, and the character of the letter forms on
the altar, which seem to be too developed and mature to suit such a date:
other letter forms of the period have a markedly archaic flavor to them (cf.
ML 11). This discussion displays the typical characteristics of modern, historicizing work: the text is interpreted in light of other contemporary texts.
What is lost is the association of the monument with the community's tradition – an association which, though now long extinguished, was very much

alive in the tradition that Thucydides criticizes, and in the arguments that he uses against that tradition.

Bibliographical Essay

There are a number of introductions to epigraphy in English. For Greek epigraphy see A. Geoffrey Woodhead, *The Study of Greek Inscriptions*, 2nd edn., Oklahoma 1992; Bradley McLean, *An Introduction to the Greek Epigraphy of the Hellenistic and Roman Periods from Alexander the Great Down to the Reign of Constantine (323 BC–AD 337)*, Ann Arbor 2002. For Roman epigraphy, Arthur E. Gordon, *Illustrated Introduction to Latin Epigraphy*, Berkeley 1983; the old essay by John E. Sandys, *Latin Epigraphy: an Introduction to the Study of Latin Inscriptions*, Cambridge 1927 (2nd edn., rev., Groningen 1969), remains serviceable. John P. Bodel, *Epigraphic Evidence: Ancient History from Inscriptions*, (*Approaching the Ancient World*), London 2001, deals with both. For the history of epigraphy, see the soon-to-be-translated entries in the *Neue Pauly*, s.vv. "Inschriftenkunde, griechische" (vol. 14) and Latinische Inschriften" (vol. 15/1). The most detailed narrative of the history of the discipline of Greek epigraphy is still to be found in Wilhelm Larfeld, *Handbuch der griechischen Epigrafik*, 2 vols., Leipzig 1898–1907. In English see the general textbooks cited above, particularly Sandys and Gordon. Bibliography pertaining to the study of inscriptions is usefully and accessibly collected in François Bérard et al., *Guide de l'épigraphiste: Bibliographie des épigraphies antiques et médiévales*, 3rd edn., Paris 2000. Armando Petrucci has done fascinating comparative work on the general history of inscriptions: see e.g. his *Public Lettering: Script, Power and Culture*, Chicago 1993, and *Writing the Dead: Death and Writing Strategies in the Western Tradition* (*Figurae: Reading Medieval Culture*), Stanford 1998.

Many inscriptions are initially published in specialist or local journals, sometimes obscure even by professional academic standards. Various publications are devoted to the ongoing collection and review of such publications. For Greek inscriptions there is the French "Bulletin épigraphique," issued annually as part of the *Revue des études grècques*, Paris 1888–; many of these have been collected and published as a series of books, with thorough indices (abbreviated *Bull. ép.* or *BE*); the Latin and English *Supplementum Epigraphicum Graecum* (abbreviated *SEG*), vols. 1–25, Leiden 1923–71, vols. 26– Amsterdam 1979–. And for Roman inscriptions, *L'Année épigraphique*, Paris 1888– (abbreviated *AE*). Once reproduced in the *SEG* or *AE* the inscription is provided with a readily accessible number, which will be commonly used to refer to it in academic publications (for example in chapter 5, *SEG* 26, 845 refers to the *Supplement*, vol. 26, lemma number 845, the lead letter from Berezan). In time, inscriptions are gathered into corpus volumes. The most famous and frequently encountered of these are the *Inscriptiones Graecae*, 13 vols., some in second editions, one in a third, Berlin 1873 (abbreviated *IG*), and the *Corpus Inscriptionum Latinarum*, 18 vols., some in second editions, with many supplements, Berlin 1863– (abbreviated *CIL*), though there are numerous others, which can be found listed in the general introductions cited above (I point in the first instance to Bodel, 153–74).

Some collections cherry-pick the most famous inscriptions. The most frequently cited of these include Wilhelm Dittenberger, *Sylloge Inscriptionum Graecarum*, 3rd edn., 4 vols., Leipzig 1915–24 (*Selection of Greek Inscriptions*, abbreviated *Syll.*^{3} or *SIG*^{3}); Russell Meiggs and David Lewis, eds., *A Selection of Greek Historical Inscriptions to the End of the Fifth Century* BC, 2nd edn., Oxford 1988 (abbreviated *ML* or Meiggs-Lewis), and now its companion volume, P. J. Rhodes and Robin Osborne, eds., *Greek Historical Inscriptions 404–323*, Oxford 2003 (including English translations); Hermann Dessau, *Inscriptiones Latinae Selectae*, Berlin 1892–1916 (*Selected Latin Inscriptions*, abbreviated Dessau or *ILS*); and there are many others as well, which again can be found discussed in the general bibliography cited above.

As with papyri, modern editions of inscriptions are presentations of ancient stones, often substantially edited. The most frequently encountered editorial signs are the same as those found in the papyri (above, bibliographical essay to chapter 5).

Translations of inscriptions are available from many "source-books." The fine series, *Translated Documents of Greece and Rome*, series editor Robert K. Sherk, Cambridge includes the following five volumes: vol. 1, Charles Fornara, ed. and trans., *Archaic Times to the End of the Peloponnesian War*, 2nd edn., 1983; vol. 2, Philip Harding, ed. and trans., *From the End of the Peloponnesian War to the Battle of Ipsus*, 1985; vol. 3, Stanley M. Burstein, ed. and trans., *The Hellenistic Age from the Battle of Ipsos to the Death of Kleopatra VII*, 1985; vol. 4, Robert K. Sherk, ed. and trans., *Rome and the Greek East to the Death of Augustus*, 1984; (no vol. 5 appeared); vol. 6, Robert K. Sherk, ed. and trans., *The Roman Empire: Augustus to Hadrian*, 1988. The famous and expansive collection of inscriptions and other evidence by Naphtali Lewis and Meyer Reinhold remains evergreen: *Roman Civilization*, vol. 1, *The Roman Republic and the Principate of Augustus*, vol. 2, *The Roman Empire*, 3rd edn., New York 1990. Late antiquity is poorly served: Brian Croke and Jill Harries have furnished a (lamentably out of print) survey of *Religious Conflict in Fourth-Century Rome: a Documentary Study*, Sydney 1982.

There are a number of academic websites devoted to the study of Greek and Latin inscriptions. Useful gateways are provided by: the *American Society of Greek and Latin Epigraphy* at Chapel Hill (asgle.classics.unc.edu); the *Center for Epigraphical and Palaeographic Studies* at Ohio State (omega.cohums.ohio-state.edu/epigraphy); and the *Centre for the Study of Ancient Documents* in Oxford (www.csad.ox.ac.uk). A useful site for epigraphical bibliography is to be found (in Italian) from Bologna: *Fonti Epigraphiche* (www.rassegna.unibo.it/epigrafi.html).

Introduction

The Oberlin "Soldier's Monument" is discussed in Geoffrey Blodgett, *Oberlin Architecture, College and Town: a Guide to Its Social History*, Oberlin 1985, 207–8; photographs of the various incarnations of the inscription can be found on the college's *Oberlin Through History* website (www.oberlin.edu/external/EOG; steer in via the category "places"). A substantial bibliography deals with the living relationship of monuments and society: start with David Loewenthal, *The Past is a Foreign Country*, Cambridge 1985; cf. the debates surrounding the commemoration of the Holocaust, treated for example in James E. Young, *The Texture of Memory: Holocaust Memorials and Meaning*, Yale 1993.

Ancient inscriptions

The quote from Louis Robert derives from his famous introduction to Greek epigraphy (unfortunately in French): "L'épigraphie grècque," published in Charles Samaran, ed., *L'Histoire et ses methodes* (*Encyclopédie de la Pléiade*, 11), Paris 1961, 453–97 (Robert's essay was republished separately in German with an expanded bibliography under the title *Epigraphik der klassischen Welt*, Bonn 1970). For the numbers of Greek inscriptions and their distribution, see Charles W. Hedrick, Jr., "Democracy and the Athenian Epigraphical Habit," *Hesperia* 68 (1999), 387–439; on the numbers of Roman inscriptions, Ramsay MacMullen, "The Epigraphic Habit in the Roman Empire," *AJP* 103 (1982), 233–46; Gordon (cited above), 7.

Monumental texts

For the monumental qualities of public texts and the distinction between them and ephemeral public texts, see Charles W. Hedrick, Jr., "For Anyone Who Wishes to See," in *The Dance of Hippocleides: a Festschrift for Frank J. Frost*, R. Frakes and D. Toye, eds., special issue of *The Ancient World* 31 (2000), 127–35; see further Rosalind Thomas, *Oral Tradition and Written Record in Classical Athens*, Cambridge 1989. For Roman temporary postings on tabulae, see now Elizabeth Meyer *Legitimacy and Law in the Roman World: Tabulae in Roman Belief and Practice*, Cambridge 2004, who makes a different point than mine here. On graffiti see Armando Petrucci, *Public Lettering: Script, Power and Culture*, Chicago 1993, 117–29. On the role of Archaic sculptors in carving inscriptions, see Antony Raubitschek, *Dedications from the Athenian Akropolis; a Catalogue of the Inscriptions of the Sixth and Fifth Centuries* BC, Cambridge 1949; Stephen V. Tracy has authored several landmark studies, including his *The Lettering of an Athenian Mason*, Princeton 1975. For the production of Roman inscriptions see Gian Carlo Susini, *The Roman Stonecutter: an Introduction to Latin Epigraphy*, Oxford 1973, and many essays by Arthur E. Gordon, including his essay with Joyce S. Gordon, *Contributions to the Palaeography of Latin Inscriptions* (*University of California Publications in Classical Archaeology* 3, 3), Berkeley 1957. On the monumental qualities of the lettering of Greek inscriptions, cf. Henry Immerwahr, *Attic Script: a Survey* (*Oxford Monographs on Classical Archaeology*), Oxford 1990; for Latin lettering, Joyce and Arthur Gordon (cited above). The controversy between Jean Mallon and Louis Robert about the relationship between epigraphical and manuscript hands can be most easily pursued in their essays in Charles Samaran, ed., *L'Histoire et ses méthodes* (*Encyclopédie de la Pléiade*, 11), Paris 1961. Evidence for the cost of inscribing Athenian inscriptions is now collected in William T. Loomis, *Wages, Welfare Costs and Inflation in Classical Athens*, Ann Arbor 1998; other useful information can be gathered from W. Kendrick Pritchett, *Greek Archives, Cults and Topography*, Amsterdam 1996. The famous evidence comes from Delphi, on which see *SIG*³ 275 and 252 n.13. For Roman inscriptions, see

Susini (cited above). For a taste of the problems involved in the reading of inscriptions: William V. Harris, *Ancient Literacy*, Harvard 1989; Charles W. Hedrick, Jr., "Reading, Writing and Democracy," in Simon Hornblower and Robin Osborne, eds., *Ritual, Finance, Politics: Athenian Democratic Accounts Presented to David Lewis*, Oxford 1994, 157–74; Rosalind Thomas, *Oral Tradition and Written Record in Classical Athens*, Cambridge 1989; Jesper Svenbro, *Phrasikleia: an Anthropology of Reading in Ancient Greece*, Ithaca 1993. The problem has long occupied Roman historians: see e.g. Zvi Yavetz, "The *Res Gestae* and Augustus' Public Image," in Fergus Millar and Erich Segal, eds., *Caesar Augustus: Seven Aspects*, Oxford 1984, 8–14.

Epigraphical scholarship

Unattributed quotes in the section on the history of scholarship are from Ernst Huebner's essay on "Inscriptions," printed in the *Encyclopedia Britannica* from the 9th edition (1875) through the 12th edition (1922).

Conclusion

For a more elaborate treatment of the tradition of the expulsion of the Peisistratids (with a different emphasis), Rosalind Thomas, *Oral Tradition and Written Record in Classical Athens*, Cambridge 1989, chapter 5.

7

Coins

Introduction: Love and Money

No one is sentimental about cash, which is famously not fuzzy and warm, but cold and hard. The flinty hearts of economists may wobble and turn to gelatin when their hosts contemplate investment and compound interest; misers may swoon at the thought of wallowing in bathtubs of silver and scrip; yet their love remains very general. Pieces of money are made to be identical and hence exchangeable: commensurability is the essence of money, and if ever we begin to value individual coins and bills, they become distinguishable and their transactional usefulness is undermined. Consequently we love money as we love the impossibly the aerobic sex-gods of the media: more in the abstract than in the particular.

The ubiquity of money and the pervasive commercialism of modern culture have perhaps diminished our sensibility of the uncanniness of cash. Its peculiarity remains obvious in certain highly charged ethical situations, such as dating. Consider the traditional scenario: a young man asks a young woman to dinner. He has romance on his mind and wants to call on her with a love-gift. Should he pour his heart out in a poem? Or should it be flowers? The poem is beyond price, but perhaps she is a Philistine whose icy heart is proof against the hot passion of his verse? Poetry is too risky: he chooses the conventional pledge of a twenty-dollar bouquet. By some mischance, however, on the way to her house the flowers are destroyed, and he arrives at the door with nothing in his hands but his poem and wallet, and after an excruciating stab at recital, he gives up and presents her with a twenty-dollar bill, suggesting she buy herself something with it. In the context of a date, even a Philistine must regard such a present as entirely inappropriate, no matter that the bouquet cost as much. There is nothing special about a twenty-dollar bill: money makes a poor emblem of affection and a worse memento; it is the accepted vehicle of rational economic exchange, and suggests that the young man is trying to initiate a commercial rather than a personal relationship. The couple limps off to a restaurant. Dinner ends, the check arrives. If the date has gone well, the young woman might thank the young man for dinner and volunteer to pay the next time they go out. By doing this, she is treating the dinner as a gift rather than as an expenditure of 45 dollars plus tip. As such, it opens a relationship, and imposes subsequent obligations and counter-obligations. If, on the other hand, the date has not gone well and the young woman has decided that the young man has obnoxious political views and poor personal hygiene and that she does not wish to see him again, she might propose that they split the tab. Such an arrangement puts a period to the relationship. Dinner becomes an economic transaction, and cash balances the books.

Objects that serve as vehicles of tradition – mementos, souvenirs, monuments, historical sources – are understood as having individual values in and of themselves: this poster was given to me by my college girlfriend; I acquired that camel whip on a 1974 trip to Cairo; this stone marks my grandfather's grave. Such things are not interchangeable because they are unique, or have through their history become unique. As such they are, like the young man's poem, incommensurable, beyond price. Money, for formal and practical reasons, resists such treatment. Nevertheless, even specific coins and bills may become bearers of symbolic or historical value: storeowners, for example, occasionally sign, frame, and display the first dollar they earned in the business; as issues pass out of circulation collectors accumulate rare or pristine specimens; and historians treat coins as historical sources. But these are transformations of money from a vehicle of exchange to a symbolic token of something – and money, more than almost anything else, resists such treatment.

The study of coins (numismatics, from the Greek word for coin, *nomisma*) has a peculiar history. To contemporary historians, coins may seem a negligible source. Yet numismatics has one of the most venerable traditions of any of the so-called "ancillary" disciplines. Ancient coins have been collected and studied since the Renaissance, and they played a central part in the study of antiquity through the nineteenth century. Consequently the development of the modern conception of evidence can be seen especially clearly here.

Connotations of Money

Although particular bits of money may be viewed strictly in terms of their transactional use, money in general does have certain common connotations. These are usually based on its perceived antagonism to personal relationships and morality. For example, money is unsurprisingly associated with money-earners: merchants and tradesmen. Whereas the behavior of the upper class is typically imagined as governed by considerations of honor and shame, merchants are often portrayed as being driven by nothing but the desire for base profit. Furthermore, dependence on a wage is frequently equated with social subservience. Since Freud it has been observed by the observant that money is associated with excrement: filthy lucre. Ancient authors frequently expressed such views. Those who depended on money for their livelihood were condemned. The noble and appropriately wealthy were supposed to take their wealth from other sources, notably farming. So, from the archaic period Greek authors expressed contempt for the acquisitive professions. In Rome senators were notoriously expected to abstain from commerce.

One of the most obvious connotations of money lies in its overt association with the state. A coin is, in a way that is obvious and immediate for all, a sign of the sovereignty of the state. The state issues coins, images of the state decorate them, and so they are obviously imagined as property of the state. Thus, to take only the most famous example, we hear in the Bible that Jesus, when asked by his disciples whether or not they should pay their taxes, held up a coin to show them the image of Caesar on it, and admonished them to "render unto Caesar what is Caesar's, and render unto God what is God's" (Matthew 22:17–22). The association of money and state is clear from the beginning, and remains a constant feature throughout antiquity and down to the present day. Political understanding of the significance of coins can be traced in various ways. For example, in certain coin hoards it is clear that the person who has deposited the coins preferred images of certain emperors to others. Or again, when a ruler was discredited after death and suffered the "damnatio memoriae," his coins might be re-struck or overstruck and so defaced. In this practice we see an implicit acknowledgment of the political message that the coin bears.

Something of the complexity of the political significance of coins can be seen in the contrast between Roman Republican coins and Imperial ones. In the Republic the minting of coins was in the charge of three junior magistrates, the *tresviri monetis faciundis*, who had the discretion to determine the designs that adorned the faces of the coins; consequently at this period devices on coins often refer to the situations and allegiances of these magistrates and their families. The devices are not infrequently complex and their interpretation abstruse. As coins circulate they may come into anyone's hands. Who would have been equipped to understand the politics of this message? By contrast, with the establishment of empire, the emperor's face comes to dominate coinage. The devices on the coins become at once simpler and more consistent. The political message of the coin is made more accessible to the general populace.

These are some very general connotations of coins. At the same time, coins can obviously be used as evidence for the past, and it is clear that various ancients were sensitive to this significance. The attitude crystallizes by Late Antiquity, when Cassiodorus is able to remark that coins, by virtue of the images of rulers impressed upon them, "will remind future ages of our times" (*Varia* 6, 7).

Ancient authors speak often and intelligently of coins. From the earliest times, they are aware that coins can be used as evidence for the past. Consequently historians may use coins to illustrate stories – and so, presumably, may also use coins as evidence for their stories. Already in the sixth and fifth centuries BC, Greek philosophers and historians were interested in the origin of coinage, attributing it to the neighboring people of Lydia. Herodotus (1.94), following Xenophanes, remarked that the Lydians, not the Greeks, invented coinage. Among later Greek writers, coins were frequently mentioned in the "constitutions" of various states that were supposedly written by Aristotle, out of interest in the local significance of their devices and the names given them. Roman historians, in their accounts of various emperors and leaders of the past, not infrequently mention the coins that they minted.

Evidence for collection and study of coins is somewhat rarer. In both Greek and Roman contexts, a variety of coins of many different periods were amassed in sanctuaries. In several places Herodotus, for example, specifies that coins were kept in treasuries and other locations at Delphi (e.g. 1.50, 1.92). Coins frequently comprised a substantial part of the booty that Romans brought back from their military campaigns and dedicated in sanctuaries, or kept in houses as keepsakes. Ancient authors frequently mentioned the coins kept in sanctuaries; such dedications evidently prompted observation and reflection. Only one individual from antiquity is known to have kept a coin collection: the emperor Augustus had a collection of coins, including ancient, regal, and foreign examples, that he kept to illustrate for himself the histories of the various kings and potentates of the world (Suetonius *Augustus* 72.3 and 75).

A sense of the historical value of coinage may have been nourished by the variety of coinage in circulation at any time. The worth of ancient coins was tied to their intrinsic value as metal. They were valuable anywhere; political boundaries, for example, discouraged no one from hoarding foreign issues. Older and foreign coins might circulate alongside contemporary and local issues. The coins themselves occasionally hint at a general historical appreciation of older coinage. For example, some coins "cite" earlier issues. The emperor Trajan for example imagined himself as the restorer of Roman peace and legitimacy after years of rule by the degenerate Domitian. As a way of driving this point home, his coinage boasts of a *renovatio* (renewal) and imitates earlier coinages of the emperor Augustus.

The end of antiquity did not mean the complete disappearance of its coinage. Governments of the Middle Ages continued to show familiarity with the coinages of the past, and occasionally construed them in ways that show an appreciation of their historical value. Again, the coinage of the day some-times hints itself at such an understanding. Thus classical coins occasionally served as models for coins issued by medieval rulers. The references to coinage in the Bible predictably had an effect on medieval understanding of classical coinage. For example, the disciple Judas sold Jesus to the Romans for thirty pieces of silver (Matthew 26:15). Ancient coins, including some that dated to the classical Greek period and were of gold, were shown in the reliquaries of various churches as if they were some of the infamous 30 pieces. One Syracusan gold piece has survived, which has been set in a ring and inscribed with the motto "because it was the price of blood" (*quia pretium sanguinis*).

Trends that would culminate in the modern study of numismatics date from the Renaissance. Petrarch (1304–74) was arguably the first modern collector of coins, and he describes his reasons for studying them in a letter accompanying a coin that he sent as a present to a nobleman. "Here," he said, in the face on the coin, "you see your predecessor, whom you should emulate and admire, after whose image and example you should judge your-self" (Petrarch, *Opera* 19. 3, 1004). The emphasis on the importance of emulation of the past, and the assimilation of numismatics to that goal, is entirely consistent with the traditional values of history: we study to learn the virtues to emulate and the vices to avoid. Coins are a useful adjunct to the reading of history in that they put faces to the great exemplary figures of the past. Pictures of rulers, like stories of them, can provoke rulers of the present day to aspire to the same glory as their predecessors.

Petrarch's comment exemplifies antiquarian interest in coins throughout the Renaissance and Baroque. Images of coins were frequently produced in conjunction with printed texts of lives of famous men, as a sort of portrait gallery. The notion finds its echo in practices of collection and display. In the antiquarian period, from roughly the sixteenth through the eighteenth centuries, coins were collected for reasons of connoisseurship. Markers of status and learning, they were collected increasingly as the "Grand Tour" of Europe became popular. Henry Peacham, in his *Compleat Gentleman* (1634) expatiates on the value of the study of ancient statues, inscriptions, and coins for men of breeding (ch. 12, 104–24). Coins, unlike many other antiquities are "much easier to come by," because of their numbers, portability, and affordability; any can possess a collection. Furthermore they are worthy of study by virtue of their intrinsic interest – money is the price of all things and the general of all wars. Not least, "it is no small satisfaction to an ingenuous eye to contemplate the faces and the heads, and in them the Characters of all these famous Emperours, Captaines and illustrious men whose actions will bee ever admired, both for themselves, and the learning of the pennes that writ them" (p. 124, all spellings *sic*). Coins and medallions were part of the necessary furniture of a gentleman's library, displayed in a "cabinet" for the delectation of the owner and guests (the term "cabinet" continues to be used in older European museums to describe their numismatic collections). Ideally one might display a long series of, say, Roman emperors, which visitors could admire as they might paintings.

Such interests did not preclude erudition: in this period scholars such as Ezechiel Spannheim (1629–1710) wrote erudite treatises on ancient coins. In the age of the "conflict between the ancients and moderns," some argued that more detailed information could be derived from the coins. Such accumulations of knowledge were, however, trivial, and could only be despised by the discerning. In his *Dialogues Upon the Usefulness of Ancient Medals* (1726), that eloquent champion of the ancients, Joseph Addison (1672–1719), dismissed such pedants with the comment "Should I tell you gravely that without the help of coins we should never have known which was the first of the Emperors that wore a beard, or rode in Stirrups, I might turn my science into a ridicule."

Proper interest in coins, as in other things, in the early modern period was founded on their exemplary value. Joseph Addison again commented on the great numbers of coins surviving from antiquity, and suggested that their sheer numbers and the vividness of their images gave them a unique position among the survivals of antiquity. Because they were produced in such numbers they were proof against time's vandalism, and their freshness seemed to bring us face to face for once with the great men of antiquity, across a divide of 2,000 years or more. They were, he said, the "truest monument of antiquity."

The modern study of coins begins at the end of the eighteenth century. The watershed essay was Joseph Eckhel's *Doctrina numorum veterum* (1792–8). Eckhel's interests, like those of other methodologically oriented scholars of the day, were essentially taxonomic. Other scholars had earlier attempted general essays and collections of numismatic evidence, the greatest of these being Spannheim. Earlier work, however, even when it liberated itself from the tyranny of the exemplary view of the past, nevertheless organized collection in a most rudimentary way, breaking coins down chiefly according to material and size. Provenance was usually listed alphabetically, without consideration of regional relationships. Eckhel insisted on more nuanced articulation, and above all that coins should be treated in accordance with the historicist unities of space and time. A properly considered taxonomy necessarily leads to and presumes the idea that coins must be dealt with in terms of their historical relationships. This articulation produced the categories of investigation and proper field of numismatic research: in a word, method; and without method, as Eckhel's biographer says, "our knowledge is merely a farrago of notions clinging to memory." The importance of

Eckhel's work was straightway acknowledged, leading his contemporaries to characterize him as the founder of the science of numismatics, as Charles Linné (Linnaeus) had been the founder of the science of botany.

Ancient Coins

Modern scholarship on coinage dates from the late eighteenth century and is characterized by an interest in general, systematic issues, especially problems of production, dating, and circulation. A coin is conventionally defined as a standardized piece of metal issued by some sponsoring agency; the coins of a particular issue will all be of the same weight and quality of metal, and they will bear an imprint of some sort reflecting the authority that issued them. The front of the coin is called the obverse (the "head") and the back, the reverse (or the "tail"). Some ancient coins, but far from all, will also bear an inscription, or legend, frequently much abbreviated. These legends frequently run in a circle around the rim of the coin, or in straight lines across the face.

From the very beginning and ever after, coins have been made using techniques of mass production. With the industrial revolution of the nineteenth century this technique of manufacture became routine; before this time it was the exception, and mass-produced objects were exceedingly rare in the ancient world. The technique is not otherwise unexampled in the ancient world: certain pots, for example, formed from molds, were mass-produced. The essence of money is that it is exchangeable, and so it must be uniform and indistinguishable. If coins are not conceived as identical, if some are heavier, more valuable, or prettier than others, their potential for use in rational transactions is undermined. For this reason, the techniques of reproduction support the function of coinage. For this reason too, it is a mistake to speak of the "originals" of coins. Of course coins were designed by someone, and modern scholars have spent much ingenuity on discussion of their design, style, and artistic merit, but it makes no more sense to speak of ancient coins as copies of some original than it does to speak of a modern Volkswagen or Barbie-doll as a copy. Mass produced objects are made from "prototypes," not originals. The cast or die that was used to manufacture the issue was made to produce coins, not to have any independent esthetic status. A coin's original is a tool of production, not an autonomous work of art.

Ancient coins were sometimes cast (i.e. made by pouring metal into a mold), particularly when the coin was large. Normally, however, coins were struck: an engraving of the mirror image of the obverse of the coin, a die, was set into an anvil, and a die of the reverse was set into a punch; a disk of metal (a "blank"), heated or cold, was placed between them, and "struck" with a blow from a hammer or mallet.

Careful consideration of the production of a particular issue of coins provides much more information than might be imagined. Study focuses on the sequence of dies (Stempel-Sequenzen, or in English "die-studies") used for a coin's issue. This technique was worked out by the Swiss numismatist Friedrich Imhoof-Blumer (1838–1920), in the second half of the nineteenth century. The die fixed in the anvil, being supported and stationary, tended to last rather longer than the die set into the punch; for this reason the two tend not to be replaced at the same time. Thus in a given issue of coins one can observe a progression of dies in the changing couplings of obverses and reverses. By studying the connections between the various obverses and reverses a sequence can be established. It is also possible on this basis to estimate the general size of the issue. By modern estimates, which are based on experiment, a die might typically produce anywhere from 5,000 to 30,000 coins before wearing out. This range is obviously vast, but at least provides some sense of the range of possibility. If an issue is made using ten obverse dies, the number of coins produced lies somewhere between 50,000 and 300,000.

Modern money is fiduciary, that is, it has a token value: its face worth is guaranteed by the state, not by any intrinsic content of metal. An American dollar bill is simply a piece of paper, in itself worth a fraction of a cent; the US Treasury guarantees its face value, until recently with gold held in reserve. American pennies used to be made of copper, but when the metal content came to be worth more than the face value of the coin it was replaced with zinc. Ancient coinage, by contrast, is commodity money. The coin in principle is worth the metal it contains and there is an implicit assurance that the coin's face value is matched by the quantity and quality of the metal of which the coin consists. Earliest Greek coins were made of electrum, a mix of gold and silver; Greek coins of the classical period were typically of silver. Gold coins came into common use with Alexander.

Precious metal for issues of coins was obviously ultimately obtained from the earth. Athens' rise to prominence in the fifth century was notoriously due in part to the discovery of a rich vein of silver in her territory. But not all states were fortunate enough to possess mines in their territories. Some states acquired metal for their coinage issues indirectly. Aegina, for example, which was one of the leading trading powers of the sixth century BC, produced one of the most widely used and influential coinages of the sixth century BC, though it had access to no natural supply of silver. It obtained its silver from the island of Siphnos, doubtless through trade. Another common source of revenue was warfare. In conquering the Persian Empire, Alexander got possession of the Persian treasury between 333 and 330. These provided the material for a series of gold issues; earlier, Greek coinage had been almost exclusively minted of silver. Roman issues from the third century BC were certainly produced to a significant degree from bullion exacted as war booty. Coins were also produced by re-striking existing coins. The process of preparing coins for recirculation might be as simple as "over-striking" the existing coin with an additional sign or image, or as elaborate as melting them down for fresh minting. In a famous case of the fifth century BC, we hear that the Athenians required their allies to bring their coins to the Athenian mint to be re-struck as Athenian coins (*ML* 45).

The principle that the face value of the coin was an expression of its intrinsic worth was frequently flouted in antiquity. For example, one of the problems with precious metal coinages is that its intrinsic worth is so great that a coin that would be of use in day to day transactions, such as the purchase of a loaf of bread, would have to be unmanageably small, perhaps the size and weight of a fish scale (as Aristophanes jokes, *Wasps*, 790–1). Such miniscule coins would have been difficult to handle; so in Greece by the fourth century BC smaller denominations ("fractional coinages") were represented by sizeable tokens of baser metals, often bronze, which were not worth their face value. In the extraordinary case of Ptolemaic Egypt, foreign currencies were not allowed into the country: visitors were forced to exchange their money for the local currency, which was often devalued to the point of being token. At various times, state emergencies led to devaluations of coinage: that is, the weight or quality of the metal was decreased without a corresponding drop in the face value of the coin. Sometimes existing coins were simply struck with new denominations, giving them higher values. Sometimes too a silver wash might be applied over a base core (e.g. billon, a mix of silver and other components). The most notorious devaluation of coinage in ancient history dates to the so-called "crisis of the third century" AD, when the Roman Empire faced political and economic collapse.

Surprisingly, such devaluations did not necessarily lead to inflation, though it does appear that they prompted increased hoarding of good money, thus taking valuable metal out of circulation. On one occasion the Roman state actually refused to accept its own currency in payment of taxes, requiring that taxes be paid in older, purer metal coin. But individuals evidently accepted (as they had to) money at its face value. The rulers of the state themselves as a rule made it a priority after times of fiscal emergency to return to solid currency, evidently prompted less by economic constraint or prudence than by self-imposed moral considerations.

Ease of exchange requires a common standard of weights and measures and the coinages of particular states are necessarily internally coherent; coins of the same denomination weigh the same, and they are linked to other denominations by a consistent system of fractions or multiples. It may not, however, be presumed that coins of different states observe the same system of weights and denominations, any more than it should surprise anyone that the subdivisions of the present day Euro or Rial do not correspond in any one-to-one way to the value of the dollar, quarter, dime, nickel, and penny. In antiquity coins were traded among states as bullion rather than as currency. Foreign coins tendered at the market of a given state might have been weighed rather than counted.

It is nevertheless true that at any given time the money of states preeminent in politics or trade might have an extraordinary position in international trade, becoming a kind of international standard, as the American dollar has today. Thus in the sixth century BC the coinage of a great trading power, the island of Aegina, served as a standard to which the coinages of many other states came to conform. In the fifth and fourth centuries BC the coinage of Athens was in common use throughout the eastern Mediterranean, and had a hegemonic influence on the weight standards of other states' coinages. After Alexander seized the Persian treasury his coinage became highly prized and widely used; his issues later served as a model for his successors and their Hellenistic kingdoms. The Romans dominated the entire Mediterranean. In the west, traditional denominations of Roman coins were used; yet, in the east, Greek denominations survived.

Hoards and Chronology

Coins of the Roman imperial period were sometimes inscribed with information that allows them to be dated: for example the titulature of a Roman emperor, or the number of years that he had held tribunician power, or a reference in the image or legend to an historical person or event. Such information is seldom encountered on coins of other periods. Traditionally, many coins were dated using stylistic criteria: by comparing, for example, the style of the representation of a head with prevailing styles in sculpture. Such practice is useful and broadly reliable in some cases. For example, the Athenians issued a coinage with Athena's head on the obverse and her owl on the reverse, from the sixth century through the fourth. The difference between the archaic and classical styles of representation is apparent at a glance. Such a method, however, yields only the most general date, and is not infrequently misleading. The foundation of modern numismatic chronology is the coin hoard.

A hoard is a collection of coins that was buried, perhaps in a pot or a purse. Money was buried in antiquity chiefly for safekeeping, as some Americans after the depression did not trust banks and so kept their savings in their mattresses. There might be various motives for wishing to keep money safe: a merchant might bury his money to preserve it from thieves, as thieves might bury their booty to preserve themselves from apprehension. The owners of hoards would in the normal course of things have recovered their money. The hoards that archaeologists discover today are deposits that the owners never returned to carry away; these generally date to periods of violence and upheaval, for example when a city is under siege by an army. If a town is taken and destroyed, many owners would never have recovered their caches because they did not survive to do so. From an archaeological point of view, there is a positive side to the annihilation of a town. Such a destruction will be generally datable, or, if attested in a literary source, even precisely datable. Such a context provides a precise date for the deposition of the hoard. In a case such as this, the destruction of the town provides a *terminus ante quem*, "a boundary before which," for the coins contained in the hoard; that is, the coins in the collection must all date before the destruction.

Coins in hoards tend to be of higher denominations, since they usually represent savings. By contrast, coins found by archaeologists in isolation, perhaps because they were lost, tend to be of lower denominations. People will look longer and harder for a mislaid 100-dollar bill than for a penny. The coins collected in hoards tend also to be a heterogeneous mix in terms of date and type, in part because their owners accumulated them over time, but also because of the circulation patterns of ancient coins. Since the value of coinage was determined by its intrinsic constitution, a coin issued by a foreign state was as worthy of preservation as those of the local state, and so coin hoards often preserve a substantial mix of coins from various states. A coin hoard may also contain coins as much as a century or two older than the date of its deposit. Today the government regularly recycles paper money so it is unusual to encounter paper money more than 15 years old. Modern coins are also removed from circulation at a certain point. It is now a rare event to find, say, a "wheat penny," that is a Lincoln Head penny, with sheaves of wheat on the reverse (issued 1909–58), in one's change.

With these provisos a coin hoard provides a snapshot of coins in circulation at a particular moment in time. Within the coin hoard, various considerations help determine the relative chronology of coins. As a rule, the more recent the coin, the more copiously attested it will be in the hoard. Another clue to the relative chronology is provided by patterns of wear. The longer a coin has been in circulation the more wear it will accumulate. The most recent coins in a hoard, by contrast, may appear sharp and fresh. These criteria are only general guides; in specific cases they may prove misleading. An accurate assessment will derive from the evidence of many hoards.

Origins of Coinage

Economic transactions did not begin with coinage. Gift exchange preceded monetary exchange, and continued alongside it in the ancient world; it survives today in our highly monetized economy. Even monetary transactions can be colored by the ethics of gift exchange. Gift exchange is a transaction that is "embedded," to use Karl Polanyi's word, in its social and political situation. Giving and receiving of gifts creates or confirms a relationship: the one who gives more acquires greater status and imposes a status and obligation on the other. Young adults may think of their relationships with their parents: they may gladly take presents from them and make little or no return; the situation reflects their subordination to them. With equals they might feel compelled to maintain some balance of gift-giving.

In a pre-monetary economy there is no general standard of value, like money: objects of exchange are unique and for this reason at best imperfectly commensurable. The situation is perfectly suited to the ethical quality of gift exchange. Coinage, by contrast, is an egalitarian innovation: it provides an abstract, finely articulated standard by which the value of anything – labor, cows, wheat – can be equated. Everything is comparable according to this standard, and so transactions can be undertaken from a position of equality: pay corresponds to service rendered, with no remainder. Political subordination and ethical obligation is banished from the economic transaction.

Before the introduction of coinage there are certain standardized forms of exchange from which money develops. Thus, for example, in some places standard measures of grain served as a basis for exchange or taxation. Such a standard of value was presumed in the legislation of Solon in Athens as late as the beginning of the sixth century BC; there he classes the population according to income calculated in bushels of grain. Cattle have been the basis for computing wealth in many societies, from Africa to Europe, and traces of this history survive in various languages. Thus the English word "fee" derives from the same stem as the German "Veh," sheep; the Roman word for money, "pecunia" is related to the Latin word for herd-animal, "pecus." More to the point, common systems of weights and measures developed to serve in the exchange of bullion lead to the essential notion of coinage as a piece of metal of standard weight and purity.

As we have seen, according to ancient tradition, Greeks borrowed the idea of coinage from a neighboring people of western Anatolia, the Lydians. The surviving early coins lend some support to this notion, but whether or not it is true, use of coinage flourished and was passed on through the Greeks, not the Lydians. Something about Greek political society was amenable to use of coinage, and it spread in this culture rapidly. Greek states produced many coins, and these became the dominant tender for centuries throughout the Mediterranean. Thus the Romans learned of coinage somewhat later, about 300 BC, from the Greeks.

The introduction of coinage is usefully viewed in the context of the development of centralized political authority. It is true that some believe that the earliest coinages in some places in Greece were issued by individuals or families rather than by the state. The most famous examples are the so-called Wappenmünzen (armorial-coins) of Attica. These coins may have been produced at the behest of prominent families, or by individuals deputized by the state. Just so in Republican Rome certain aristocratic families were glorified on issues of coinage, not because the families were issuing their own money, but because the state assigned members of these families to oversee coin production. There were three of these officials, the *tresviri monetales* (or *tresviri monetis faciundis*), and they had the latitude to glorify their family and friends on their coins. In the end, there is no unequivocal case in antiquity in which an individual issues coinage in his own name.

However that may be, most early coinages were issued by states. So the first coins issued by Rome had on their obverse simply the head of the goddess Roma. As the political nature of the state changed, so too did the imagery and ideals of the coinage. Whereas earlier coinages in Greece and Rome appealed to the state in general and abstract terms, when the collective qualities of the state broke down in favor of kingship, coinage reflects this change. Thus the coinage of Alexander and the Hellenistic kings shows images of the ruler, rather than symbols of the state. In Rome, with the rise of the great dynasts of the first century BC, images of individuals begin to appear on coins and these reflect the regal pretensions of the persons. Sulla first put his image on coins, followed by Caesar and Pompey. With the foundation of the Empire it became normal to put the head of the reigning emperor on the coin. After Caligula, no face but that of the emperor appears on coinage. This is not a departure from the rule about the association of coinage and state: it is characteristic of the ideology of monarchy that the king and state are equated: "l'état, c'est moi."

Monetary Policy

Since coinage was associated with the political integrity of the state, it is unsurprising that it was influenced by political events. In particular, trading and imperial powers might influence the quality and weight of surrounding coinages: states struck coins to the standard of the dominant power in their region. The history of money can for this reason be periodized according to the dominant monetary standards of the day – regimes of coinage, we might call them. These "regimes" often correspond to the dominant political power of the day. There are exceptions: in the archaic period the coins of many states were struck to the standard of Aegina, which was not at the time a great imperial power, but a great trading power.

After about 500 BC, the Athenian state struck silver in its own territory, turning it overnight into a political and commercial powerhouse. For the next 150 years Athenian coinage circulated widely in the eastern Mediterranean, and the "Attic-Euboean" standard came to be adopted by many states. In the text of one famous inscription, the "Athenian Coinage Decree," we hear that the Athenians attempted to make members of their empire cease issuing their own coinage and use Athenian coinage, and even turn in their old coinage to be re-minted (*ML* 45).

By the time the Macedonians emerged as a military and political power, the days of Athenian monetary prestige were numbered. Once Alexander gained possession of the Persian treasury he had the raw material to issue a substantial and desirable coinage. The Hellenistic kings, his successors, would follow his standard of coinage too, and thus the Macedonian standards would henceforth hold sway until they were finally replaced by Rome.

The Romans learned of coinage from the Greeks and their coin standards spread with their empire. Roman coins became widespread in the west earlier than in the east; local coinages continued to be minted in the west until the mid first century AD and the reign of the emperor Claudius. The prestige of Greek culture protected the old Greek city-states in terms of language and culture, and they were left to issue their own coinage until relatively late. By the third century AD, however, local coinage even in the east ceases.

After the collapse of the dynasty of the Severans in 231 AD, the Roman Empire was in political and military chaos for some 50 years. This chaos was reflected in the minting of money. With the state in economic distress, the quality and quantity of precious metal in the coinage was reduced until it was being produced from billon (precious metal debased with some common metal), coated with a silver wash. The severity of the problems can be reconstructed from the measures specified in the "Price-edict of Diocletian" as remedies for them. Inflation predictably ran rampant, as did the hoarding of older, more valuable pieces of money. The state in this period refused to accept its own money in payment of taxes, requiring instead payment in older, purer money, or in kind. It remained for the emperor Diocletian to put the money of the empire back on a sound footing, which would endure till the end of antiquity. He was responsible for a new standard of weights and measures and a new order of gold coinage: the *solidi*.

The original and enduring association of money with the state raises issues pertaining to its use. Only the state put money into circulation. There is no evidence that states used and planned their issues of coinage to promote the health of their economies. Rather coins were minted for the convenience of the state, in order to facilitate nuanced payments to large numbers of people. It did not stop money from subsequently circulating, or being used in further transactions among the populace, but the promotion of monetary circulation and trade and commerce was not the object, indeed does not seem to have been on the horizon, in terms of states' fiscal planning.

As mentioned above, coinage seems to have been issued in the first instance for the convenience of the state in making its own payments. Thus the extensive coinages of Athens, for example, can be explained in terms of the democratic principle of pay for office, and the state's need to compensate the many people who served the body politic in some capacity or another. Later, with the growth of mercenary and professional armies, especially in the Hellenistic and Roman worlds, money was minted in large part to pay soldiers.

Ancient states were large organizations and money offered substantial advantages in meeting their payrolls. It might be segmented into conveniently small values, so that it could be used in paying for relatively small fees; again it might be segmented in large values and a year's pay for a legionary might be carried in a small purse. At the same time, it was permanent and not susceptible to spoilage, as many kinds of payment in kind were. Thus it could be transported over long distances with minimal inconvenience.

Conclusion: The Meaning and Use of Money

Modern interpretation of ancient coinage has focused overwhelmingly on the circumstances of its production and its instrumental uses. It is easiest to speak of coinage from the perspective of production, that is, from the point of view of the state, its sponsoring agency. Yet coinage also circulated through society and it would be good to know something more of how it was understood. The difficult question of the extent of monetization bears on this problem. Of course coins circulated in ancient society, but to what extent were they regularly used in day-to-day transactions? Was barter the rule of the day? And if coinage was not normally used for transactions, what was the point of circulating it? What did people make of it? To what extent did it have a monumental significance for the ancient apprehension of their past? As we have seen, there are indications that certain aspects of coinage – in particular the portraits of rulers engraved on many of them – were understood by the ancients with reference to present politics and the historical tradition.

It is difficult to gauge the extent to which ancient societies were monetized. One clue is provided by coins of smaller denomination. One problem with using a commodity-money, as in the ancient world, is that a very small coin made of silver or gold may be worth several days' wages. A coin that represents the value of a common purchase, say a loaf of bread, may be unmanageably small, the size of a fish scale. By the fourth century BC, states begin to deal with this problem by issuing "token money" – largish bronze coins that have a low face value, and a smaller actual value – for the smaller denominations. The move to such token coinage for smaller value coins arguably reflects the growth of monetization in the economy generally.

Even so, it is unlikely that any ancient economy was as monetized as modern industrial societies; barter remained the dominant mode of exchange, particularly in the country. Coins have occasionally been recovered from environments where they seem to be treated more as jewelry than as a monetary instrument. In such situations what were the specific connotations of money?

Bibliographical Essay

For a succinct and expert introduction to numismatics, including technical aspects, see Michael H. Crawford "Numismatics," in his edited volume, *Sources for Ancient History*, Cambridge 1983, 185–233; Christopher Howgego, *Ancient History from Coins*, (Approaching the Ancient World), London 1995; in much greater length and detail, see Barclay Head, *Historia Numorum: a Manual of Greek Numismatics*, 2nd edn., Oxford 1911 (repr. Chicago 1967, abbr. *HN*). Those who can read French should look at the brief account offered by one of the greatest numismatists, Jean Babelon, in Charles Samaran, ed., *L'histoire et ses méthodes* (*Encyclopédie de la Pléiade*, 11), Paris 1961, 329–92; his general work, *Traité des monnaies grecques et romaines*, 9 vols., Paris 1901–32, is a landmark in the field; the account of the theory and history of the discipline in the first volume remains essential, and has now been translated by Elizabeth Saville, *Ancient Numismatics and Its History Including a Critical Review of the Literature*, London 2004. Among brief, illustrated introductions, Colin Kraay and Max Hirmer, *Greek Coins*, London 1966, and John P. C. Kent and Max Hirmer, *Roman Coins*, London 1978.

Among the most significant published collections of coins are the catalogues of museum collections. In English we are fortunate to have perhaps the most important of these, the collections of the British Museum, published as follows: *The British Museum: Catalogue of the Greek Coins*, 30 vols., London 1873–1927 (abbr. *BMC*); cf. the summary version of the preceding, edited by George F. Hill et al., *A Guide to the Principal Coins of the Greeks from ca. 700 BC to AD 270* (British Museum, Department of Coins and Medals), 2nd edn., London 1959: (abbr. *PC*). Herbert A. Grüber, *Coins of the Roman Republic in the British Museum*, 3 vols., London 1910, revised repr., 1970 [abbr. *BMC(RR)*]; Harold Mattingly, *Coins of the Roman Empire in the British Museum*, 6 vols., [abbr. *BMC(RE)*].

Many thematic collections of coins have also been issued, devoted to the coinages of particular places or periods. Among these I single out Colin M. Kraay, *Archaic and Classical Greek Coins* (The Library of Numismatics), London 1976; Ian Carradice, *Greek Coins*, Austin 1995 (more elementary). Coins of the Hellenistic period must as a rule be pursued according to the kingdom with which they are associated: see for example Arthur Houghton and Catherine Lorber, *Seleucid Coins, a Comprehensive Catalogue. Part I, Seleucus I–Antiochus III*, New York 2002. More general surveys of the period include Norman Davies and Colin M. Kraay, *The Hellenistic Kingdoms: Portrait Coins and History*, London 1973; Otto Morkholm, *Early Hellenistic Coinage: from the Accession of Alexander to the Peace of Apamea (336–186)*, Cambridge 1991. For Roman coins there is Michael H. Crawford's exemplary *Roman Republican Coinage*, 2 vols., Cambridge 1974 (abbr. *RRC*), and also his *Coinage and Money Under the Roman Republic*, Berkeley 1985 (more elementary); Harold Mattingly et al., *The Roman Imperial Coinage*, 10 vols., London 1923–94 (abbr. *RIC*); Robert A. G. Carson, *Coins of the Roman Empire* (The Library of Numismatics), London 1990.

For help with bibliography see Elvira E. Clain-Stefanelli, *Numismatic Bibliography*, Munich 1985; ongoing surveys of publications are provided by the series *A Survey of Numismatic Research*, which is published at five-year intervals, most recently covering the years 1985–90, Brussels 1991. The American Numismatic Society publishes an annual review of bibliography, *Numismatic Literature*, New York 1947–; for Roman numismatics, John Melville-Jones, *A Dictionary of Ancient Roman Coins*, London 1990, offers useful assistance; for some research ideas see Cornelius C. Vermeule, *A Bibliography of Applied Numismatics in the Fields of Greek and Roman Archaeology and the Fine Arts*, London 1956.

For the history of the discipline of numismatics, in addition to the first volume of Babelon's *Traité* (above), see the soon-to-be translated entry in the *Neue Pauly* 15/1, s.v. "Numismatik."

Ancient numismatics is not so well served with web-based tools as other specialist fields in ancient history. The home page of the *American Numismatic Society* (www.money.org/index.shtml) contains information on ancient coins, and much else. Useful sites include *Ancient Greek and Roman Coins* (dougsmith.ancients.info), from the collector Doug Smith, and, from Austin College, *The Virtual Catalogue of Roman Coins* (vcrc.austincollege.edu).

Love and money

On gift exchange the classic essay is by Marcel Mauss, *The Gift: the Form and Reason for Exchange in Archaic Societies*, New York 2000 (originally published as an article, 1923–4); the implications of this concept for the study of ancient society have been elaborated by many: see notably Karl Polanyi et al., eds., *Trade and Market in the Early Empires: Economies in History and Theory*, Glencoe, Ill. 1957; also his *Primitive, Archaic and Modern Economies: Essays of Karl Polanyi*, New York 1968; Moses I. Finley, *The Ancient Economy*, London 1985. On the significance of reproduction the classic essay is by Walter Benjamin, "The Work of Art in the Age of Mechanical Reproduction" (1936), reprinted in his *Illuminations*, New York 1968.

Connotations of money

Among the many essays on the association of money and excrement, see Norman O. Brown, "Filthy Lucre," in his *Life Against Death: the Psychoanalytic Meaning of History*, 2nd edn., Wesleyan 1985, 234–304; for a consideration of the relationship between class and money in the Greek context see now Lesley Kurke, *Coins, Bodies, Games, and Gold: the Politics of Meaning in Archaic Greece*, Princeton 1999; for money and the Roman aristocracy see e.g. John H. D'Arms, *Commerce and Social Standing in Ancient Rome*, Harvard 1981; Kenneth Harl, *Coinage and the Roman Economy, 300 BC to AD 700*, Baltimore 1996, 35, discusses the execution of the "damnatio memoriae" on coins. For ancient perceptions of coins see Michael H. Crawford, "Roman Imperial Coin Types and the Formation of Public Opinion," in Christopher N. L. Brooke et al., eds., *Studies in Numismatic Method Presented to Philip Grierson*, Cambridge 1983, 47–64; see further the summary of the political impact of coinage by Howgego (above), 62–87. On Trajan's coinage see H. Mattingly, "The 'restored' coins of Trajan," *Numismatic Chronicle* ser. 5, 8 (1928) 232ff. On Petrarch's attitude toward the past, see e.g. Roberto Weiss, "Petrarch the Antiquarian," in Charles Henderson, Jr., ed., *Classical, Medieval and Renaissance Studies in Honor of Berthold Louis Ullman*, Rome 1964, vol. 2, 199–209; the same, "The Study of Ancient Numismatics During the Renaissance (1313–1517)," *Numismatic Chronicle* 8, 1968, 177–87. For the role of numismatics in the quarrels of the "Battle of the Books," see Joseph Levine, *The Battle of the Books: History and Literature in the Augustan Age*, Ithaca 1991, 283–85, 337–46. The quotes regarding Ekhel in this section derive from the biographical notice published at the end of his *Doctrina*.

8

Material Culture

Graveyard Junkies

I am hooked on cemeteries. When I travel I try to acquaint myself with new ones, or revisit old favorites: Lake View in Cleveland, Woodlawn in the Bronx, Mount Auburn in Cambridge. But then, I have been fascinated with grave-yards for as long as I can remember. When I was four years old, my father preached at the Southern Baptist Church in Needles, California, an isolated desert town near the Colorado River, a little way from the bridge to Arizona. The church's parsonage backed onto the desert; my graveyard, a dusty postage-stamp marked by a tumbledown post-and-rail fence, perched on a hill nearby. No one tended it; my father buried his parishioners down in Riverview Cemetery, a dystopic green swath overlooking a dry wash at the other end of town. As a place of internment, my graveyard may have been dead, but come dark it was considerably livelier than the town's active cemetery. The place was littered with trash, what I recognize in retrospect as the detritus of midnight high school debauchery: broken beer bottles, cigarettes, and condoms. But I had suckled at the breast of television westerns like "Have Gun, Will Travel," and "The Rifleman," and for me the place fairly reeked with the narcotic fumes of the Old West; I imagined that it had served as the town's boot-hill, that its weathered, illegible headstones shaded the coffins of peach-cheeked cow-pokes, snake-eyed gunslingers, and kind-hearted saloon-dancers.

Both graveyards of Needles were set at the outskirts of town. The practice has long been common in America: most graveyards were originally set at the edges of urban centers, though as cities grow, they often come to envelop them. The Greeks and Romans also exiled their dead, burying them beyond the fortified walls of their cities. While the practice of "extramural burial" is common to many societies, it is far from universal. Medieval European cities, for example, often buried their dead in churchyards, which might be located in the hearts of their cities. A basic principle, however, is almost everywhere observed: the dead may not mix promiscuously with the living, but are quarantined to specific areas. Cemeteries are ghettos.

Although the dead may be banished to suburban cemeteries or confined within churchyard walls, traditionally at least they were not ignored. For example, no one could enter or leave Greek or Roman city without encountering them. Grave monuments lined the roads leading in and out of ancient towns, as commercial billboards and strip malls now line our highways. And crowds of them huddled just outside the city gates. Wealthy Greeks and Romans left endowments to provide for banquets in perpetuity; mausoleums were fitted out with dining benches and families or colleagues visited on significant anniversaries to feast and drink. The suburban graveyards of nineteenth-century America were typically set in more out-of-the-way places, yet they were laid out as parks; many doubled as arboretums and gardens. City-dwellers visited them on weekends to enjoy the pleasures of cultivated nature: picnics, light exercise, and the bittersweet contemplation of the common fate of mankind.

My ex-wife's grandmother had a horror of graveyards. Once I asked her why: was it because she was approaching death herself that she did not like being confronted even with the deaths of others? She disliked the question – I could have put it better, I suppose – but nevertheless told me that she had always had such feelings. My graveyard-habit seemed to her eccentric at best, and perhaps even reflected some basic character-dysfunction. I do not think of myself as morbid or perverted. I am not the weirdo; it is everybody else that is strange. Over the past century Americans have increasingly insulated themselves from death. When the elderly become too frail to care for themselves we retire them to "homes;" we send them to hospitals to die. At last we plant them in the ground and forget about them, preferring to recall them "as they were," in evergreen photographs, rather than as they are, moldering to compost in the grave. Of course if they were wealthy they may have an idyllic plot with a panoramic view; but how often do we visit? Nowadays we try to live our lives as though we will never die; we have abandoned the cemeteries to the dead. It is difficult for me not to regard the contemporary alienation from death as complicit with the more general modern alienation from the past.

Last year I drove cross-country with my son and since we were passing through Needles I decided to stop off introduce him to my childhood haunts. He was puzzled but game. I found the graveyard with no problem, though I had not visited it in 40 years. It lay somewhat closer to the town than I had recalled, was smaller and dustier; and it was now fenced off with cyclone wire seven feet high. My son was not much impressed – but I think television westerns are no longer so popular. A local explained in so many words that it was an historically significant site, that the town had put the fence up to keep out the kids, who had been going up there to drink and take drugs and god-knows-what-else, and had vandalized the tombstones. It did not surprise me that teenagers had been using the old graveyard – they had done the same 40 years before. And graveyards have always been notorious: even in antiquity they afforded shelter for weirdoes, winos, and witches; muggers hid behind gravestones in the late afternoon and into the night, waiting to ambush lonely travelers. Sex and drugs and skullduggery may be deplorable, but they represent the traditional ways that the living have always interacted with the dead. The cyclone wire cuts the cemetery off from the city; we can look at it through the wire, but we no longer live with it. Now even the junkies have been evicted from the graveyard.

We know the past only at second-hand, through the mediation of enduring objects. We live our lives among countless such survivals. Every object has a history. Some of these we notice, most we ignore. Objects continuing in use – tools, roads, buildings – are not so easily regarded in the light of their histories; their significance as heirlooms is overshadowed by their utility. It is the useless things – monuments and ruins – that insistently pose questions to us about our past. Residents do not view such survivals from the detached perspective of a tourist – like a professional archaeologist or an art historian, say. They do not peer at them through the holes in a mesh-wire fence; they live among them and use them. Monuments and ruins are integrated into the life of the community: daily interaction and shared experience provide them with their meaning.

As long as they have been walking upright people have doubtless interpreted the material world as evidence for the past. Objects, however, are mute; they cannot speak for themselves. Only those who already know are in a position to decipher their meaning. They are at the same time one of the essential touchstones that guarantee a community's knowledge of itself and its history, and the tangible evidence of the validity of the tradition and the truth of the past. Monuments had this function in ancient Greek and Roman society, and they continue to do the same work down to present times. Increasingly, however, the traditional "monumental" understanding of the past, the "collective memory," has been displaced by the antagonistic "historical" understanding of modern professional scholarship.

As generally in historicizing interpretations, modern academic interpretation of the historical significance of objects is founded on a double strategy: first, objects are isolated from informal social interaction; second, they are interpreted systematically. These methods work to segregate the ruin from the community and its informal and "anachronistic" traditions, in the name of objective and disinterested interpretation. Objects, like texts, can speak "for themselves" only after they have been rescued from the hallucinations of the present.

This approach has indisputably achieved a much more detailed and nuanced understanding of the material survivals of the past, but at the cost of severely limiting social engagement with them and creating them as the private preserve of academics. Archaeological excavation, boiled down to its essence, is the process of converting "ruins" to "sites," and the physical evidence of the transformation is the cyclone wire that fences off locals from the casual engagements and vandalisms that made the place significant to them. Professionals justify the fence as protection, yet the obsession with "conservation" and "restoration" is profoundly modern. Evanescence and damage – including damage caused by vandalism – are preeminent qualities of relics of the past, as death is a quality of life. They are the signs of the continuing and developing role of the monument within society itself, and their elimination, even in the name of "the preservation of the national heritage," assaults the community's collectively held tradition. Moderns want to "reconstruct" the past "as it was" in life, simulated in all the surrealistic clarity of an opium dream; they do not want to dwell amid the squalor and putrescence of its lingering decomposition. The site connotes a kind of immortality; the ruin, death. Ruins continue to be made, and will always be made. In the modern world we try to stem the tide either by converting them to historical sites or by bulldozing them: we annihilate them or wrap them in cellophane. Perhaps society has lost the desire, or even the ability, to commune with its past "monumentally?" A ruin that is not supported by the common memory is not really a ruin at all; only a derelict – or a site. Cyclone wire makes tourists of us all.

Disciplinary Distinctions

Curiously two academic fields, art history and archaeology, take as their object the study of material remains, things, as opposed to textual survivals, words. How do their approaches differ? Archaeologists, significantly, have felt the burden of individuation more sharply than art historians and have asserted their independence the more combatively. They have urged various criteria, often emphasizing the differences between the materials with which each field works. The distinction hinges on a general (and frequently ill-defined) dichotomy between "high" and "low" culture, for example, "art" versus "artifacts." Art historians have traditionally dealt with objects that were made precisely to communicate cultural values of some kind. They interpret objects in light of literary sources – which is arguably appropriate, since both art and literature are complicit, products of the same "hege-monic" cultural values. Archaeology, by contrast, deals with humbler objects that are made to fulfill some practical function rather than to communicate a message, and hence reflect something other than the prevailing cultural values, something perhaps even opposed to them – call it the embodied truth of labor. They deal with problems that are specific to the world of objects and it would be as much of a betrayal to subordinate the study of artifacts to the traditional concerns of literary authors as it would be to allow the cocktail chatter of the idle rich to drown out the boisterous noise of the working poor. If art historians are typically led by their paintings and sculpture to the "history of the spirit," archaeologists are inexorably channeled by their implements to the history of technology. Others have urged a methodological distinction between the two. Art historians, for example, deal with their material from a typological perspective, considering, say, all red-figure vases, or all vases of a particular shape, or all vases by a particular painter, or motifs in vase painting. Or again, they may take a transcendental, esthetic perspective. Archaeologists on the other hand are concerned with a functional and contextual analysis that allows the mute artifacts to "speak for themselves." They give their attention to the specific context of the find, they explore "assemblages."

Such comments evince a dichotomy between two opposed visions of the material remains of antiquity, one exemplary, the other historicizing. Art matters precisely because it transcends the local situation that produces it, and continues, across the ages, to speak to us. We should not "study" great art, but carry on a dialogue with it. History, by contrast, contextualizes, and in its more extreme forms denies, the transcendence of anything in favor of viewing it as a "product of its age." The dichotomy between the two fields, it seems to me, is essentially academic, and it can be best understood in light of their disciplinary histories. Archaeology and art history share common origins in the eighteenth century. In the nineteenth century both were profoundly influenced by historicism, but art history remained truer to its eighteenth-century origins and continued to focus on objects that epitomized the legacy of the past: not the objective history, but what mattered for the tradition. In this, it has more in common with philosophy (or, more recently, literary criticism) than with history. Classical archaeologists, spurred on by the pre-historians among them, rejected tradition and embraced the historical vision: what matters to them is the past "as it was" rather than its legacy.

This is a simple, sweeping discrimination between the two fields; the history of their divergence is considerably messier. For a long time it was taken for granted that the importance of the past was exemplary rather than historical. The Greeks and the Romans mattered because they thought and said much of the best of what people have ever had to think and say. No less a figure than Humboldt, the founder of the University of Berlin, could remark at the beginning of the nineteenth century that "our study of Greek history is therefore a matter quite different from other historical studies. For us the Greeks step out of the circle of history." Supported by such attitudes, art history flourished.

The modern history of classical art history and archaeology can be traced back to the same man, Johann Joachim Winckelmann (1717–68). The segregation of archaeology out of art history came when they were institutionalized as academic disciplines; before the nineteenth century, the two were not distinguished. The creation of archaeology as an autonomous field is owed not to students of classical antiquity, but to pre-historians, who by the nature of their field worked without the crutch of literary sources. Modern techniques of archaeological chronology and analysis were first developed around 1800 for the study of the Danish Iron Age by Christian Jürgensen Thomsen (1788–1865). Classical archaeologists, however, would not declare their disciplinary independence for many years afterward, in no small part because the cultural prestige, and hence economic subsidies, for the study of Greek and Roman material culture were – and are – tied to the tradition of classical literature and art. Consequently archaeological investigation in the nineteenth century was undertaken to discover new *objets d'art* and to supplement the literary sources, not with an eye to problems for which excavation was uniquely suited. The famous controversy in Germany between the historically-minded August Boeckh (1785–1867), and the philologist Gottfried Hermann (1772–1848), in the 1820s reveals much about the status of antiquities at the time: among the issues disputed by the two was the question of the role of material culture in the study of antiquity. For Hermann the value of literary texts was autonomous of other considerations. Boeckh allowed the primacy of the literary tradition, but insisted that scholars should aspire to a more general understanding of the evidence for classical antiquity; antiquities could throw light on the meaning of literary texts. Classical archaeology only comes into its own as a separate field of academic research with the inauguration of the great ongoing excavations of the second half of the nineteenth century.

Already in the age of the antiquarians, the seventeenth and eighteenth centuries, there was a perceptible tension between those who insisted on the transcendent value of the monumental remains of the past and those who grubbed and delved in barrows for utilitarian artifacts: at the time of the "Battle of the Books," for example, classicists, who tended to value texts and "high art," skirmished with the more implement-oriented Saxonists. At the time art history and archaeology had not been distinguished – the word "antiquarianism" covered both fields. Advocates of the great exemplary virtues of the past, the "ancients," railed against the nitpicking "moderns," who could not see beyond the trivialities enshrined in their curio cabinets. The usefulness of the past did not lie in detailed knowledge, which, even if true, was tiresome and pointless, but in an appreciation of what was timeless: the wisdom and artistic achievement of the ancients. The importance of a single artistic masterpiece might outweigh all of the grubby, shoddy grave goods that might ever be uncovered. Their opponents, the moderns, granted the clear and unapproachable excellence of the classical models, but insisted that these could be better understood by viewing them against a backdrop of other, comparable works.

Art history constituted itself as a recognized academic discipline in Germany by the beginning of the nineteenth century, when the department at Berlin was established. Within a few decades other departments had sprung up, including the influential program in Vienna. The discipline of art history proliferated at the end of the nineteenth century and departments are now to be found at most American colleges and universities. Different national traditions have different histories. In England, for example, the appreciation of art, like English literature, was long presumed as the common culture of all gentlemen, and hence it was studied informally. The establishment of art history as an academic field on the German model came late, well into the twentieth century.

Art history, like all academic study, was profoundly affected by the historicist revolution of the nineteenth century. For example, art historical analysis has always given special attention to the interpretation of representational conventions: iconography. It is certainly possible to treat certain common motifs, say the figure of the nursing mother, as rooted in human nature, and hence universal and natural, timeless and unhistorical. To take only the most influential modern exponent of this idea, the psychoanalyst Carl Jung (1875–1961) proposed to recognize in literature and art certain universal "archetypes." Yet it is also possible to treat representations as conventions, and decipher them with reference to comparative material: in other words, the significance of the visual can also be explained in light of historical comparisons. Such techniques became increasingly common and systematic in art history in the course of the nineteenth century.

Archaeological investigations have been carried out on ancient Greco-Roman sites for centuries. As early as the seventeenth century, wealthy individuals and learned societies such as the English Society of Dilettanti (founded 1734) sponsored excavations. The goal of such work was chiefly the recovery of objects of "high culture," monuments such as statuary and inscriptions and architecture. The epochal excavations at Pompeii, beginning from 1780, made a huge splash in Europe not least because of the dazzling works of art that were recovered and because they appeared to offer romantic Europeans the opportunity to transport themselves back to a classical past and walk in the streets of an ancient city. Excavation at Pompeii can be traced back to the Renaissance, when workmen sank wells to tunnel for lucrative statuary and paintings. Later the site was a treasure house for various nobles, and ultimately the king of Naples, who mined it for antiquities to decorate their villas. Full-scale excavations were undertaken from the end of the eighteenth century.

The exemplary, antiquarian impulse remained very much alive in the excavations of the nineteenth century. As late as the mid-nineteenth century, the first great modern excavations continued to have something of the flavor of treasure hunts. The swashbuckling businessman Heinrich Schliemann (1822–90) was spurred by an essentially Romantic desire to prove the historicity of Homer, and perhaps even "gaze on the face of Agamemnon." A wealthy amateur in the tradition of the Dilettanti, he undertook at his own expense and under his own aegis to excavate some of the most famous sites of the Bronze Age, including Troy and Mycenae.

The history of academic archaeological excavation can be traced in the history of the establishment of the various foreign schools of archaeology: the first was the German Archaeological Institute, which established a school in Rome as early as 1829; the French followed in 1875; the American Academy in Rome dates to 1893. Foreign schools came later to Greece: the French first, in 1846; the Germans in 1874; the Americans in 1881. Arguably the first rigorously academic investigation of an ancient site is the German excavation at Olympia, as late as 1875. Even this project, however, was motivated in the first place by the desire to supplement the witness of literary texts with material evidence. Well into the twentieth century classical archaeology was driven by the impulse to provide illustrations of the great, paradigmatic texts of the ancient world and so to buttress the prestige of the classical tradition. The archaeology of classical Greece continues to be dominated by the vision of the second century AD traveler Pausanias, who provided a kind of "Blue Guide" to the notable monuments of his day.

Archaeology received recognition as an academic discipline in Germany and Austria somewhat later than art history. The first professorships of archaeology there date to the middle of the nineteenth century; the first departments of archaeology are only founded from the end of the nineteenth century, and most date only to the middle of the twentieth century. Different national traditions have dealt with the fields differently. In England, for example, art history received disciplinary recognition late but departments of archaeology are not uncommon. In America, by contrast, the first professorships of archaeology date to the end of the nineteenth century, and the field has almost never been accorded departmental status: Boston University boasts that it has the only department of archaeology in the United States (founded 1982). In most American colleges and universities archaeology is no more treated as a discipline than are epigraphy and numismatics; rather it is usually regarded as a "subfield," and housed in some larger program –

typically art history, anthropology, history, or classics. The situation reflects the traditional status of archaeology as an "ancillary" discipline, literally, a "handmaiden" of history.

Nationalist motives for studying the past can be seen particularly clearly in the development of professional (as opposed to academic) archaeology. Government involvement in archaeological sites dates at least to the end of the eighteenth century, when the king of Naples exercised proprietary rights over the excavations at Pompeii. State agencies charged with the monumental past of the nation, "archaeological services" were founded in Italy and Greece in the first half of the nineteenth century: most countries now have comparable agencies charged with the preservation of the "national heritage." Laws protecting historically significant sites from development have helped to create professional (as opposed to academic) careers for archaeologists.

The development of professional archaeology, it should be noted, has its roots not only in the state support for study of the national tradition, but also in the old exemplary, antiquarian tradition. Many archaeological finds have substantial market value: the skull of a tyrannosaurus rex or the cargo of a Spanish galleon may be sufficiently valuable to attract "venture capitalists" to invest in the cost of digging them up. Commercial archaeology is at once a business and a political enterprise, with strong links to the tourist trade, private art markets, and nationalism. Even today archaeology has not entirely shrugged off its old ties to art, treasure hunting, and the aristocratic traditions of connoisseurship and property rights.

The development of the historicizing study of material culture, both archaeological and art historical, was supported by the emergence of modern museums: the earliest of these, such as the British Museum, date to the eighteenth century. Like modern archives, museums served as repositories, in which material objects were isolated from society and organized for systematic study. Of course collections of objects predate the eighteenth century: the Ashmolean Museum in Oxford was founded at the end of the seventeenth century. Significant objects have doubtless always been collected. Dedications deposited in ancient temples were at least in part viewed as conveyers of tradition, and the Greeks and Romans were aware of their significance. Herodotus' account of the history of Lydia in the first book of his history, for example, is closely indexed to objects that were or had been displayed as dedications at Delphi (cf. 1.50–2). Churches of the Middle Ages had their reliquaries, kings had their treasuries. Gentlemen of the early modern period had their "Wunderkammern" or curio cabinets. The idiosyncratic disarray of such collections was replicated in the displays of the earliest museums: some splendid surviving examples include the Pitt-Rivers in Oxford, or in America the Fairbanks Museum of St. Johnsbury, Vermont.

The modern museum, however, is (or will become) different in its relationship to the state, in its systematic organization of objects and its alliance with other, broader institutions of knowledge.

An "art historical" bias continues to loom large even in the academic study of archaeology through the middle of the twentieth century. Reaction to it within classical archaeology – pre-historians had long since necessarily sloughed off such influence – has become more pronounced since the 1960s. Increasingly archaeologists have criticized art history for its aesthetic absolutism and reliance on literary texts, and called on each other to "let archaeology be archaeology" and "focus on archaeological issues" rather than problems deriving from literary texts; classical archaeologists have modeled their methods and goals on those developed by pre-historians. This reorientation has arguably been the most important development in classical archaeology of the last half-century, and it is manifested in practical terms by the rise of survey archaeology, which has made it possible to shift the focus of archaeology from the urban centers and great shrines that have dominated the field from the nineteenth century to the countryside: instead of excavating, investigators "walk the field," collecting what comes to view. The technique allows the survey of large areas, and provides a picture of regional land use. A world unknown from the literary sources has been opened up. Furthermore, survey archaeology, unlike excavation, is "non-invasive:" it neither destroys nor closes off what it investigates. Whether or not such techniques result in an understanding that has any relationship to the community's informal "collective memory" of the past is another question.

In certain respects, the interests of art historians and archaeologists have lately been converging. This is in part due to the concession of some art historians that high art is not the only thing worth looking at; popular "visual culture" also is revealing – not so much of the great exemplary intellectual truths, but of historically specific popular mentalities. Some archaeologists in the meantime have come to think that investigations of the utilitarian truths of tools is not a sufficient goal for archaeology; it is also desirable to come to grips with the social and cultural meanings of objects and assemblages of objects (this has been a particular focus of the so-called "processual" and "post-processual" archaeology). Thus art history has moved toward archaeology by concentrating on the commonplace, and archaeology has moved toward art history by focusing on the symbolic.

Material Culture

Only certain materials are likely to have survived the ages since antiquity. The combination of air and water is deadly to many materials. Greece and Italy have temperate climates that are not kind to most organic materials: here finds are typically limited to objects made of fired ceramic, stone, bone, glass, and metal. A desert climate, like that of Egypt above the high water mark of the annual river-deluges, on the other hand, is extraordinarily favorable to materials that would not elsewhere survive. Objects made of perishable materials, such as wood, fabric, leather, or papyrus, are seldom found outside the desert settlements of the ancient Near East and North Africa.

People everywhere make use of a vast variety of objects in their day-to-day lives. Objects of all kinds have been recovered from the ruins of the ancient world, from tools to toys to toilet-seats, weapons to wheels to weaving-weights, monuments to mirrors to musical instruments. Other things, which cannot be regarded as "artifacts," have also been collected and studied: pollen, fruit-pits, seeds, and bones. For the classical archaeologist, however, by far the most important survival is pottery. Ceramic was the plastic of the ancient world: it was used everywhere for a vast array of purposes, and is well nigh indestructible, no matter the environment. The modern study of ancient material culture is built on a foundation of potsherds. Archaeological chronology is based on stylistic analysis of pottery. Analysis of fabric and style permits in many cases identification of their place of manufacture; hence they can be use to elucidate ancient trade patterns. Consideration of pot capacities determines prevailing standards of measurement. Painted pots provide evidence for aspects of ancient life that would otherwise be poorly, or not at all, attested. Artistic conventions of depiction provide datable stylistic comparisons for other forms of art, such as sculpture or metalwork – and occasionally vice-versa. Furthermore, when pottery is found associated with other objects, for example in the foundation trenches of buildings or in funerary assemblages, it provides dates for them as well.

Some of the objects made by the ancients were always intended to bear witness to future generations: monuments such as statues and buildings were fabricated with the ambition that they should be seen and admired in the future, and should so convey some sense of the past. As Thucydides has Perikles remark in the Funeral Oration,

> We need no Homer to sing our praises, or another who will delight with verse for the moment, though the truth will harm their interpretation of the deeds; we have forced every land and sea to give access to our daring, and everywhere we have founded imperishable monuments of our successes and failures. (2.41.1)

Such "monuments" were made to serve as historical sources of a kind, and should be regarded with all the more suspicion and skepticism for that reason. Many other objects, by contrast, were made without the expectation that they would serve such purposes. Tools such as shovels and hoes, for example, are made to work, not to signify. Of course they can be interpreted as sources for the past, and it is one of archaeology's boasts that it manages to take such things, which were made without the strong ideological prefix of monuments, and wring from them a sense that was never intended, and which perhaps for that reason is somewhat truer than the meaning of monuments.

There is a strong antipathy between meaning and utility. It can be difficult to see the meaning of an object so long as it is in use: what does a hammer "mean?" Formal analysis of the history of the tool might yield surprising results: the head, for example, was in some cases modeled on a fist, the "claw" on outstretched fingers. Tools, it is imagined, are made to be functional, not communicative; they are practical, not ideological, and in designing them appearance is subordinated to efficiency. When such things, however, become superannuated, we may become more sensitive to formal aspects of their design: no objects, for example, speak more eloquently about Victorian aspirations and values than their machines.

Any object under the right circumstances may become an heirloom: my wife's grandfather was a plumber, and we have inherited his tool chest; she is surprisingly sentimental about his pipe-wrenches. Other objects are made to serve as messengers from the present to future generations: the practice may be universal. The ancient Greeks and Romans erected monuments, and understood them as evidence for the past. They did not, however, interpret such objects as do modern scholars, contextually, or systematically; rather they understood them "monumentally," that is, in terms of their relationship to the present.

One of the most impressive and thoughtful ancient students of material evidence was the historian Thucydides. Nevertheless, his approach was not that of a modern historian or archaeologist. For example, at the beginning of his history Thucydides surveys the early history of Greece (1.2–19). This, the so-called "Archaeology," corresponds to something more like the modern notion of "ancient history" than to the modern cognate word "archaeology." At one point, however, he notes that a people of Asia Minor, the Carians, in earliest times settled the islands of the Aegean (he does not specify an absolute date, but makes them contemporaries of Minos, the mythical ruler of Crete). "The evidence for this is as follows. . . . " he says:

During the present war, when Delos was purified by the Athenians (i.e. 426 BC; cf. Thuc. 3.104), and when the graves were removed, so many as there were of those who had died on the island, more than half appeared to be Carian, and they were recognizable both by the weapons buried with them, and by the way in which they are yet now buried. (1.8)

The argument is impressive, but note that Thucydides does not identify the graves as Carian on the basis of comparative historical evidence. Rather his arguments hinge on the similarities of these graves to those of Carians of his own day. How old were these graves? What does Thucydides (or any Greek, or for that matter, Carian) know of the Carians of that day? How does he know that such graves are not typical of (say) Cretans of the Bronze Age? I am not saying that he is wrong – we do not know – only that his argument is not that of a modern archaeologist. To make such an argument is beyond him, as it would be beyond a modern scholar, if transported back to Thucydides' day. Modern dating systems and systematic collections of artifacts are the cumulative accomplishment of centuries of scholarship. No individual could generate a persuasive modern archaeological interpretation without the support of an institution of knowledge.

I could multiply examples from other Greek and Roman authors, but the point would be the same: for Greeks and Romans the material remains of the past were firmly embedded in the present circumstances; they understood their heirlooms on a case-by-case basis. The ancients were not unique in this approach to material culture. It would be accurate to say that this is the common and universal presumption of traditional societies: the past exemplifies present values and traditions. For instance, in Italy scholars of the Middle Ages possessed artifacts from the ancient world; they lived in a landscape dominated by the ruins of the antiquity. Pilgrims to Rome wrote guidebooks to the ruins and marvels from at least the ninth century on, in which remarkable anecdotes and histories of the remains were recounted. Nevertheless, they did not attempt to understand, say, the Pantheon by looking in a comparative way at other round and domed buildings from the ancient world (had they done so they might have been impressed by its oddity). Instead they understood it in terms of the received tradition about it: they dealt with it as an isolated object.

Chronology of Material Culture

Modern archaeology begins with the chronological studies of the Danish pre-historian Thomsen; the techniques used to establish a "material chronology" distill what is distinctive in the methods of the field. Modern art history and archaeology are both products of the nineteenth-century historicist revolution: in terms of methodology this means that they interpret contextually, with due attention to the unities of time and space, however these may be defined. Before archaeologists could cut themselves loose from the literary tradition it had to be possible to work in a comparative way with implements that were produced or discovered in the same place and at roughly the same time. For art historians, if the artistic heritage was not to be seen as simply transcendental, eternal, and universal, it had to be possible to group objects in some meaningful way and establish fields of comparison. This move to contextual analysis was at odds with the "great ideas and art" approach of traditional exemplarity.

Determination of geographical "regions" has always been controversial, and will always be controversial (above, chapter 2). Where do the precise boundaries of Greek material culture lie? Where should the end of Roman material culture be drawn? The answer depends on the question. If one is interested in tools, for example, it may make sense to draw the region very wide, perhaps taking in most of the Mediterranean and Near East; if one is interested in an iconographic convention or a pottery style it may make sense to draw the unit very small.

The crucial development, however, was the establishment of a general chronology of material evidence. Division of this chronology into meaningful units of analysis, "periods," typically remains open to discussion, and depends again on the type of analysis being done (above, chapter 3). The "material chronology" of the ancient world has been determined by the cumulative work done by generations of scholars from roughly the seventeenth century on; it is from this time that the possibility of the work became thinkable. The most important work on archaeological chronology, however, has been done since the second half of the nineteenth century.

The first step in the determination of absolute dates is the establishment of a relative chronology. In excavation, as a matter of principle, more recent remains are found higher, and older objects lie beneath them. We may characterize this as "the dirty laundry principle:" as one tosses dirty clothes into a laundry basket (or the back of the closet), the first objects tossed will be buried by layers of more recent laundry. Thus, by careful attention to the layers of deposit on a site ("stratigraphy" in the jargon of the field), the relative dates of objects found can be determined. By the same principle, it can be generally assumed that objects found together, for example, in graves, are roughly contemporary. Attention to disturbances is required: for example, if someone at some time dug a hole in the middle of your site, discarding the dirt nearby, the stratigraphy of the dirt from their excavation will be reversed. The best sequences obviously come from deposits that have been continuously filled (like my laundry basket): rubbish heaps, for example, or wells. Using such stratigraphic sequences, relative chronologies can be worked out for virtually any kind of object.

By looking at stratigraphy, certain patterns may become apparent, whether of tool design or iconography of painting. These patterns form the basis of a "stylistic" chronology. Statistical analysis of the frequency of the discovery of a particular type or style of object ("seriation") allows a general reconstruction of the chronology of the use of that object: styles as a rule come gradually into common use, which then tapers off. Using stylistic analysis of this sort, archaeologists can persuasively associate objects found without stratigraphy or provenience with a general relative chronology.

Of course, this is only a relative chronology. How do archaeologists move from this sequence of objects to a firm date? How can they say, for example, that a particular vase likely dates to c.550 BC? Various scientific dating techniques have been used. The most famous of these is "carbon-dating," which was developed by physicists in the 1940s. All organic materials contain amounts of Carbon-14, which on death decays at a measurable rate: the element has a half-life of 5,730 years; that is, every 5,730 years half of the carbon remaining in the object vanishes. Radiocarbon dates carry with them a substantial range of error: the technique is very useful for dealing with the vast expanses of time encompassed by, say, the Paleolithic period, but is less useful for dealing with the very detailed history of the first century BC.

A more accurate scientific dating-technique, and one with more limited opportunities for application, is "dendrochronology." The method was developed at the beginning of the twentieth century by archaeologists studying the American Southwest. Trees grow at different rates, depending on the weather; a chronology can be generated by measuring and counting the tree-rings in ancient trees and timber. Newly discovered bits of wood can then be dated with reference to the pattern. The method has produced notable results, particularly for the study of the Aegean Bronze Age.

For historians of classical Greece and Rome such scientific techniques are at this time mere curiosities. Absolute archaeological chronology of the historical period rests, ironically, on literary chronology. Archaeologists look for events dated in the literary record that can be perceived in excavation. From the fifth century BC on examples are so numerous that I will here restrict myself to examples from the Greek archaic period – which are frequently problematic. For example, we may know that a particular town was founded in a particular year. The Sicilian city of Gela, for example, was supposedly founded by Greeks in 688 BC (if we can trust that Thucydides has accurate information: 6.4–5). Consequently Greek remains discovered on the site of Gela should be later than that date. We may know that certain cities were destroyed at certain dates. The city of Athens, for example, was sacked by the Persian general Mardonius in 480 (Herodotus 9.13). This destruction left a thick layer of ash and debris on the city, which German archaeologists have christened the "Perserschutt" ("Persian rubble"). Objects found above this layer should date after 480; what lies below it should be earlier. If we know the date of the construction of a building, such as the Siphnian Treasury in Delphi (c.525 BC if Herodotus is right, and we cannot evaluate his sources of information: 3.57–8), we can be confident that coins and potsherds found in the foundation trenches are earlier. Objects found in a datable grave, such as the mound erected over the bodies of those who fell at the battle of Marathon in 490 (e.g. Pausanias 1.32.4), presumably date for the most part to approximately the time of the burial.

In considering the relationship between relative and absolute dates, we might picture a line with a set of pegs in it, the line corresponding to the relative sequence, the pegs to the absolute dates. The thicker the cluster of pegs in a segment of the time-line, the more reliable the absolute dates assigned to the relative chronology for that period. Absolute dates for the Greek Bronze Age, for example, are based on the rough estimates of carbon dating and dendrochronology, and on the occasional contact with Egypt (the chronology of which is known in detail from the third millennium). Iron age dates are determined from evidence of comparable quality and quantity. Chronology from the eighth century is somewhat better known, based on the literary accounts of uncertain accuracy, such as Thucydides' account of the foundation dates of the Sicilian Colonies (Thuc. 6.4–5). From 480 on, archaeological dates are very reliable indeed.

Most archaeological dates are based on pottery. Pots are the most common material survival of the ancient world, and hence the relative and stylistic chronology of their design and painting is most thoroughly known. Potsherds are frequently used to date other objects: for example, a datable potsherd found in the foundation of a building provides a "boundary" after which (a *terminus post quem*) the building was constructed.

The chronology of art history is based on comparable reasoning. I take the example of sculpture. For various reasons many of the surviving sculptures have appeared "without provenience:" the root cause is doubtless the prestige (and consequent monetary value) of ancient art. Since antiquity sites have been plundered for their statuary: Romans, for example, acquired Greek art both by force and by purchase. Many of the statues studied by art historians were so famous in antiquity that they were themselves mentioned by ancient authors; such statues were frequently reproduced. Other sculpture has been preserved in connection with datable objects: as decoration on buildings, for example. The chronology of ancient statuary can thus be determined on the basis of literary testimonia and the archaeological context of architectural sculpture. The stylistic trends manifested in this chronology can then be used to provide approximate dates for otherwise undatable statues and fragments.

Conclusion: Excavation and Evacuation

European excavations of classical sites began in the eighteenth century, funded by the various learned societies that sprang up in these years. Certainly Europeans had traveled to the Mediterranean before this time, and had observed art and buildings with curiosity and awe. In the Middle Ages pilgrims to Rome wrote guidebooks for the edification of subsequent pilgrims. From the Renaissance on travelers and businessmen and diplomats made a point of visiting classical sites, and kept accounts of their observations. One of the earliest and most important of these is the account of the businessman Cyriacus of Ancona (1391–1452), who traveled in Turkey in the fifteenth century. Others followed, including James Stuart (1713–88) and Nicholas Revett (1720–1804), who cooperated to make sketches of the sculptures of the Parthenon (published in a book entitled *The Antiquities of Athens*, 1825–30), before many of them were stripped and taken to England by Thomas Bruce, Lord Elgin ("Elgin" with a "hard" G; 1766–1841) (they now are displayed in the British Museum).

Such casual voyages and depredations, however, gave way to more thorough investigations in the eighteenth century. For example, when English travelers of the seventeenth and eighteenth centuries came to Eleusis, they found a small modern village built in and among the substantial ruins of the ancient shrine of Demeter. One of the most notable of these remains was a marble caryatid from the monumental gateway to the sanctuary, variously identified as Demeter or Persephone. The villagers were accustomed to wreath it with flowers, or to heap up manure around it, because they associated it with the continued fertility of their fields. Loss of the statue would mean the loss of the harvest, and it was "believed that the arm of any person who offered to touch it with violence, would drop off." In 1802 a young English gentleman named Edward Clarke, impressed by the beauty of the statue and its degrading circumstances, bribed a Turkish official and had it carried it away. The local people protested to no avail. Clarke had the statue shipped to England where he donated it to the Fitzwilliam Museum in Cambridge (where it may still be seen). A couple of years later another English visitor, Edward Dodwell passed through the village. "In my first journey to Greece," he says, "this protecting deity was in its full glory, situated in the centre of a threshing-floor, amongst the ruins of her temple. The villagers were impressed with a persuasion that their rich harvests were the effect of her bounty, and since her removal, their abundance, as they assured me, has disappeared."

Informal archaeological excavations like those at Eleusis were pursued sporadically in the first part of the nineteenth century. The English Society of the Dilettanti sent an expedition of exploration to the Mediterranean that in 1812 stopped at Eleusis and cleared some areas of the site. The French carried out some limited excavations at the site in 1860. Finally in 1882 the Greek Archaeological Society began a regular, annual exploration of the site that has continued to this day. Archaeology destroys as it discovers, and at Eleusis, as often in Greece and elsewhere, the excavation of the site meant the destruction of the village. Houses were dismantled to lay bare the ruins below. At present much of the ancient sanctuary has been exposed. The villagers no longer live among the ruins; the houses of the living begin at the wall that separates them from the past.

In this case we can see the gradual evolution of the contrast between a traditional and an "historical" attitude. When Europeans first arrived, their investigations were fired by their own exemplary notions about classical antiquity. The original conflict between the local Greeks and the English tourists was not so much between a traditional and a modern point of view as between two competing traditional points of view. Sites were ransacked for art to be brought back to Europe; there was no particular desire to replace the traditional ruin with a site. The situation changes in the course of the nineteenth century, when the area becomes a permanent site, segregated from the local community.

The story of the development of the site at Eleusis finds parallels throughout the Mediterranean world. The inauguration of an archaeological site means the end of habitation. For example, at Delphi, the existing village was simply moved down the road and the entire site was devoted to archaeology. Likewise in Athens, where most of the ancient city lies beneath the most venerable part of the modern city, the Plaka district, the excavation and preservation of the Agora has required the purchase of increasingly expensive land, and the expulsion of businesses and residents. Contrast the more traditional arrangement of the Athenian "Street of the Tripods," where ancient monuments still stand amid – and even built into – residences. The same is the case of Rome, and is typically true of most cities with long histories. In such cases excavation would require the removal of the population of historic districts: archaeological investigation would paradoxically mean the destruction of tradition, if tradition means the living engagement of the population with its past.

Bibliographical Essay

On archaeology generally, including techniques, useful resources include Graeme Barker, ed., *Companion Encyclopedia of Archaeology*, 2 vols., London 1999; Tim Murray, ed., *Encyclopedia of Archaeology*, 2 + 3 vols., Santa Barbara 1999–2001; Brian Fagan, ed., *The Oxford Companion to Archaeology*, Oxford 1996; Kevin Greene, *Archaeology, an Introduction: the History, Principles and Methods of Modern Archaeology* (*Batsford Studies in Archaeology*), 4th edn., London 2002; Colin Renfrew and Paul Bahn, *Archaeology: Theories Methods and Practice*, 3rd edn., London 2000. For art history there is now Michael Kelly, ed., *The Encyclopedia of Aesthetics*, 4 vols., Oxford 1998; see briefly Laurie Adams, *The Methodologies of Art: an Introduction*, New York 1996.

On the history of archaeology, see Glyn Daniel, *A Hundred and Fifty Years of Archaeology*, 2nd edn., London 1975; Bruce Trigger, *A History of Archaeological Thought*, Cambridge 1989; Brian M. Fagan, *A Brief History of Archaeology: Classical Times to the Twenty-First Century*, New Jersey 2005. For the history of classical archaeology see as usual the hopefully soon-to-be-translated *Neue Pauly 13* s.v. "Archaeologische Methode;" Alain Schnapp's wide-ranging and lavishly illustrated book, *The Discovery of the Past*, New York 1997; Ian Morris, "Archaeologies of Greece," in his edited volume, *Classical Greece: Ancient Histories and Modern Archaeologies* (*New Directions in Archaeology*), Cambridge 1994; Nancy Thomson de Grummond, *An Encyclopedia of the History of Classical Archaeology*, Westport 1995; for more popular histories of classical archaeology see Paul McKendrick, *The Greek Stones Speak: the Story of Archaeology in Greek Lands*, New York 1981; and the same, *The Mute Stones Speak: the Story of Archaeology in Italy*, New York 1983. On the history of art history, the standard work is Udo Kultermann, *History of Art History*, New York 1993; for more specialized discussion and bibliography see Elizabeth Mansfield, ed., *Art History and Its Institutions: Foundations of a Discipline*, New York 2002.

For the traditional archaeology of buildings and monuments there are many introductory textbooks. Reliable starting points include: for Greece, William R. Biers, *The Archaeology of Greece*, 2nd edn., Ithaca 1996; for Rome, Nancy H. Ramage and Andrew Ramage, *Roman Art*, 4th edn., New York 2004; for orientation on the various classical sites, see R. Stillwell, ed., *The Princeton Encyclopedia of Classical Sites*, Princeton 1976 (now available on-line via the Perseus Project). Michael Grant, *The Visible Past: Greek and Roman History from Archaeology*, New York 1990, provides a review of some of the most famous archaeological discoveries of the past half-century, intended for undergraduates. For a sampling of work based on "survey archaeology" see Mark Bowden, ed., *Unravelling the Landscape: an Inquisitive Approach to Archaeology*, Charleston 1999; A. M. Snodgrass, *An Archaeology of Greece: the Present State and Future Scope of a Discipline*, Berkeley 1987, esp. 93–131. An exemplary application of survey techniques in Greece is owed to the "Argolid Exploration Project:" see Michael H. Jameson et al., *A Greek Countryside: the Southern Argolid from Prehistory to the Present Day*, Stanford 1995; for other applications in Greece, see the overview by Susan Alcock, John Cherry, and Jack Davis, "Intensive Survey, Agricultural Practice and the Classical Landscape of Greece," in Ian Morris, ed. (above), 137–70; for the Hellenistic world, Alcock in the same volume, 171–90; for Roman history, Kevin Greene, *The Archaeology of the Roman Economy*, London 1986, especially chapter 5.

Many up-to-date handbooks of the history of classical art and archaeology are available. The three volumes published in the *Oxford History of Art* series are uniformly good, recent, and historically oriented, though topical and selective: Robin Osborne, *Archaic and Classical Greek Art*, Oxford 1998; Mary Beard and John Henderson, *Classical Art from Greece to Rome*, Oxford 2001; and Jas Elsner, *Imperial Rome and Christian Triumph*, Oxford 1998. For more encyclopedic coverage it is necessary to turn to the older textbooks and handbooks: see e.g. the still useful *Enciclopedia dell' Arte Antica Classica e Orientale*, Rome 1958–66; C. M. Robertson,

A History of Greek Art, 2 vols., Cambridge 1975; Martin Henig, ed., *A Handbook of Roman Art: a Survey of the Visual Arts of the Roman World*, Oxford 1983. John Boardman et al., eds., *Lexicon Iconographicum Mythologiae Classicae*, Zurich 1981–, a collection of representations of myths, deserves a special mention. Jerome Pollitt has provided collections of ancient sources pertaining to ancient art: *The Art of Ancient Greece: Sources and Documents*, Cambridge 1990; and *The Art of Rome, c. 753 BC–AD 337*, Cambridge 1983.

The range of Greek and Roman artifacts is vast, and orientation, even for professionals, can be difficult. If one wants to see a collection of Roman slave collars where does one go? Medical instruments? Ancient dice? The only attempts to provide encyclopedic coverage date to the nineteenth century, but they nevertheless remain useful as a point of entry: Charles Daremberg and Edmond Saglio, *Dictionaire des antiquités grècques et romaines*, Paris 1877–1919, or in English William Smith, ed., *A Dictionary of Greek and Roman Antiquities*, 2 vols., New York 1854–7. As a rule those looking for discussions of certain kinds of artifacts will do well to look for books on a related and more general subject and check their bibliography: so for slave collars one might start by looking at recent books on Roman slavery. Certain books can be held up as models in their demonstration of the value of material evidence and art for even the most traditional problems of ancient history. For Greece see Claud Bérard et al., *A City of Images: Iconography and Society in Ancient Greece*, Princeton 1989; Paul Zanker, *The Power of Images in the Age of Augustus*, Ann Arbor 1998.

Archaeology and art history are well served with web-based resources. For archaeology in general see ArchNet (archnet.asu.edu); Kevin Green's *Archaeology: an Introduction* (above) includes a supplementary website (www.staff.ncl.ac.uk./kevin.greene/wintro). Duke University hosts a dictionary of art historians (www.lib.duke.edu/lilly/artlibry/dah). In England the *Reading Classics Gateway* (www.rdg.ac.uk/AcaDepts/lk/Link/) includes a good collection of on-line classical art and archaeology resources.

Graveyard junkies

On the social place of ruins, cf. David Loewenthal, *The Past is a Foreign Country*, Cambridge 1985; John Brinckerhoff Jackson, *The Necessity for Ruins, and other Topics*, Amherst, Mass. 1980. For graveyards, see generally Glennys Howarth and Oliver Leaman, eds., *Encyclopedia of Death and Dying*, New York 2001; Edward L. Bell, *Vestiges of Mortality and Remembrance: a Bibliography on the Historical Archaeology of Cemeteries*, Metuchen 1994; for Roman burial see Jocelyn M. C. Toynbee, *Death and Burial in the Roman World*, Baltimore 1996; on American cemeteries see David C. Sloane et al., *The Last Great Necessity: Cemeteries in American History*, Baltimore 1991, and various writings by John Brinckerhoff Jackson. So much has now been written on the history of the museum that its study is frequently now characterized as if it were a discipline, museology: see e.g. Tony Bennett, *The Birth of the Museum: History, Theory, Politics*, New York 1995, and more recently his *Pasts Beyond Memory: Evolution, Museums, Colonialism*, New York 2004.

Disciplinary distinctions

For the central role of tools in archaeological research and utility in archaeological interpretation see Gordon Childe, *History* (Past and Present 6), London 1947. I owe the quote from Humboldt to Ian Morris: see Marianne Cowan, ed. and trans., *Humanist Without Portfolio: an Anthology of the Writings of Wilhelm von Humboldt*, Detroit 1963, 79. For the influence of historicism on art historians see Catherine Soussloff, "Historicism in Art History," in Michael Kelly, ed., *The Encyclopedia of Aesthetics*, vol. 2, Oxford 1998, 407–12. On Winckelmann see e.g. Alex Potts, *Flesh and the Ideal: Winckelmann and the Origins of Art History*, New Haven 1994. An accessible statement of Jung's notions about universal symbolism can be found in his *Man and His Symbols* (1964, and often reprinted). Of the vast bibliography on Pompeii, start with Christopher Parslow, *Rediscovering Antiquity: Karl Weber and the Excavation of Herculaneum, Pompeii, and Stabiae*, Cambridge 1995; Alison E. Cooley, *Pompeii*, London 2003; for a splendid example of the Romantic fantasies the excavations prompted, see Wilhelm Jensen's 1903 novel, *Gradiva*, with Freud's discussion of it ("Delusion and Dream in Gradiva," 1907). On Schliemann there is the controversial recent biography by David A. Traill, *Schliemann of Troy: Treasure and Deceit*, New York 1996. For Herodotus' use of dedications as sources for his historical tales, see Charles W. Hedrick, Jr., "The Prehistory of Greek Chronography," in V. Gorman and E. Robinson, eds., *Oikistes: Studies in Constitutions, Colonies and Military Power in the Ancient World, Offered in Honor of A. J. Graham* (*Mnemosyne* supp. 233), Brill, 13–32, especially 22–3. For the growing concern of archaeologists with symbolic and cultural aspects of the past see Anthony Snodgrass, "Archaeology," in Michael H. Crawford, ed., *Sources for Ancient History*, Cambridge 1983, 137–84. The key figure in "processual archaeology" is Lewis Binford; some archaeologists particularly associated with "post-processualism" include Ian Hodder, Michael Shanks, and Christopher Tilley.

Material culture

On Thucydides' use of material evidence see Charles W. Hedrick, Jr., "The Meaning of Material Culture: Herodotus, Thucydides and their Sources," in R. Rosen and J. Farrell, eds., *Nomodeiktes: Greek Studies in Honor of Martin Ostwald*, Ann Arbor 1993, 17–38, and "Thucydides and the Beginnings of Greek Archaeology," in D. Small, ed., *Methods in the Mediterranean: Historical and Archaeological Views on Texts and Archaeology* (*Mnemosyne* sup. 135), Leiden 1995, 45–88.

Chronology of material culture

For the dating of pottery, William Biers, *Art, Artefacts and Chronology in Classical Archaeology*, London 1992; for scientific techniques, M. J. Aitken, *Science-Based Dating in Archaeology* (*Longman Archaeology Series*), London 1990.

Conclusion

For Eleusis see the sources collected in George Mylonas, *Eleusis and the Eleusinian Mysteries*, Princeton 1961, 9–12; James G. Frazer, *The Golden Bough: a Study in Myth and Religion*, 3rd edn., London 1911–15 (and often reprinted), vol. 3, 64–5.

Index

Coverage of subjects here is selective, guided by my notions of what a general audience might reasonably and usefully expect to find; I have aimed for a more complete listing of proper names. Famous Greek names and words are provided in their familiar forms: for example Thucydides (not Thoukudides); others are more faithfully transcribed: for example *ekdosis*. Renowned Romans are listed according to the popular spellings of their names: so Caesar (not Julius Caesar, Caius) and Cicero (not Tullius Cicero, Marcus), and Caligula, Roman emperor (not Caesar Augustus Germanicus, Caius). Others appear according to family name (gentilicial): for example, Aemilius Paullus, Lucius. I have tried to give the names of modern scholars as they referred to themselves, using initials or full names: so Richard Bentley but A. E. Housman. With a couple of exceptions, topics and words from the bibliographic appendices are not indexed here.